Barbara Bush   Library Friends
Building a better library   *one book at a time.*

Donated by

Mrs. Barbara Bush

You Can Do It!

Presented to

_____

_____

By

_____

_____

Date

_____

You Can Do It!

Lives of great men all remind us
We can make our lives sublime
And, departing, leave behind us
Footprints on the sands of time.

—Henry Wadsworth Longfellow

Published in Nashville, Tennessee, by Thomas Nelson, Inc., and distributed in Canada by Lawson Falle, Ltd., Cambridge, Ontario.

Library of Congress Catalog Card Number 92-60702
ISBN 0-8407-4333-5

Printed in the United States of America
1 2 3 4 5 6 — 95 94 93 92

CONTENTS

INTRODUCTION

Commonly it is thought that achievement is greatly dependent upon not what you know but who you know, or, as another wag said, "The real test is who knows me." Fortunately, at an early age I was given a better plan. Because of my father's academic and theological standing (and my mother's good cooking), our home was constantly filled with outstanding guests. It was the age when children were to be seen and not heard, but my father insisted that we were to be seen—that we were to sit quietly, listen to the conversations, and learn. It was also a time when men gathered in the living room for open, frank discussions, and debating each other was a form of flattery. After the guests left, there were discussions around the dinner table in which we were quizzed on what we had learned and what we thought. Such rearing taught me the value of mentoring—that personal development is enhanced by letting people of achievement impact your life.

Reality set in when at Furman University I was offered a position that would pay me $30 a week, which, in 1950, was an extremely large income for a student assistant. Another position would provide me with $50 a month. My parents had extreme financial limitations so earning personal income was a factor. Yet remembering the value of mentoring, I enthusiastically took the $50 a month position because it would allow me to work with a most respected leader. It seemed far better to miss a meal than to miss the opportunity to learn by example and to emulate his strengths.

Education is in turmoil, but it is encouraging to know that so many from every walk of life are addressing the problem. However, we may be overlooking the most obvious way for young people to grow and benefit—by setting admirable examples before them and even, without apology, again believing in heroes. This book, edited by Bob Budler, provides such an opportunity. Very carefully, Bob has chosen the people you meet in these pages, most of whom it has been my privilege to know personally and admire deeply. The story each tells is very brief, but the two or three minutes it will take to read each one can be life-changing.

Not only does it seem natural that I should write the introduction because I believe that biographies can have an impact, but also because it is my privilege to serve as CEO of IGA. We are America's oldest food system with the same mission, and in the last years the fastest-growing element of the supermarket industry. If you try to number the reasons for our accomplishments, there is one that would rise above all the others, and that is that we believe in the people in the communities who are being served by our 4,000 supermarkets located in the United States and Canada, Australia, Japan, and Papua, New Guinea. We want today's young people to have this book as a positive force in helping them expand their vision. We believe in the philosophy of the late John R. Mott that the only way we'll live beyond our own lifetime is through the investment we place in youth.

IGA worldwide is a community of givers, and we have found that we receive by our giving. That's why under our advertising umbrella of "Hometown Proud" we are dedicating this book to Special Olympians. They have been a gift to us, and as we have underwritten this book of insights to inspire those who have no excuse, we now dedicate it to those who might have every excuse but have rejected an easy way out.

We thank each person who has contributed and are glad that you now have an opportunity to read this book and pass it on. We at IGA are proud to present this collage.

Thomas S. Haggai
Chairman & CEO
IGA, Inc.

SPECIAL OLYMPICS

We would like to thank all the contributors to this excellent book for sharing their individual experiences and philosophies with the youth of America. These messages challenge our young people to strive to reach their full potential. Likewise, Special Olympics International is motivating and challenging millions of young people and adults with mental retardation to reach their full potential through sports training and competition.

Our appreciation goes, also, to IGA, Inc. and its chairman and CEO, Tom Haggai, for underwriting this project and dedicating the book to Special Olympics. Throughout the United States, Canada, Australia, Japan and Papua New Guinea, IGA has been a committed and stalwart friend of Special Olympics, and this support has made a significant difference in the lives of people with mental retardation.

Special Olympics believes that, through sports training and competition, people once called "retarded" or "handicapped"—and with futures termed "hopeless"—are now able to benefit in all areas of their lives: physically, mentally, socially and spiritually. Instead of a future doomed to hopelessness, their lives are now rich with promise as they gain self-esteem and self-confidence through sports training and competition. As another benefit, families are strengthened and the community-at-large enriched as an environment of equality, respect, and acceptance is developed.

The 1991 International Summer Special Olympics Games, held in Minneapolis, involved 6,200 athletes from more than 100 countries—athletes who trained as long and as hard as any other athlete preparing for major competition. In their training and in their competition, these Special Olympics athletes overcame physical, social, and psychological barriers that would be discouraging even to athletes training for the 1992 Olympic Games in Barcelona.

In the United States, Special Olympics programs take place in 25,000 communities within the framework of chapters in all 50 states, the District of Columbia, and the three territories. Around the world, from Asia to Latin America, from Europe to Africa, there are now accredited Special Olympics programs in over 100 countries, and developing programs in an additional 20 other nations.

More than 500,000 volunteers enable Special Olympics to offer sports training and competition 365 days a year around the globe—and to do it with an energy, dedication and commitment which lights a candle of hope for the estimated 300 million people with mental retardation who live in our world today. It was the energy, dedication and commitment of 35,000 volunteers during the 1991 International Summer Games in Minneapolis which made those Games a resounding success.

It is our privilege to welcome the men and women who have shared their experiences and philosophies in this book into the Special Olympics "World of Winners"—a world where all men and all women, regardless of their ability, have the opportunity to reach their fullest potential.

Eunice Kennedy Shriver
Founder & Honorary Chairman

Sargent Shriver
Chairman

GUEST AUTHORS

ACKNOWLEDGEMENTS

Hundreds of people have contributed to this book, but, it would not have been published without the initial acceptance of the book's concept and on-going support from Tom Haggai and Paul Fullmer.

Special thanks are due the guest authors who, in the midst of the clamor of life, made time to share their experiences and thoughts that our youth might draw upon them to enrich their daily lives.

My daughter, Mary Freund, logged long after-work hours to put the book on computer disk. Her four children, Kristy, Sarah, Lisa, and Jason (ages 10 to 17) proved a good sounding board and their inquisitiveness, as they sought clarification of some materials, made their grandfather do a better editing job.

Mary Helen Batten, executive secretary to Tom Haggai, along with her counterparts in organizations throughout the country, got their bosses to meet our deadlines despite their busy schedules.

IGA's Ron Burkhart, Cathy Bert and Jeff David, Sally Cole and David Phelps, of Special Olympics International, and Bill Fox, of Thomas Nelson Publishers, assisted with the project throughout the year it took to compile and edit the book.

Mary Ellen Dunne, of the Bensenville Community Public Library staff, saved the author countless hours in research time with her vast knowledge of information sources.

My life's companion, Rita, who has been the "wind beneath my wings" for 51 years, helped with the project until sidelined by illness. She continues to be a daily inspiration as she demonstrates the greatest test of courage—to struggle without losing heart.

—Bob Budler

You Can Do It!

Bob Budler

THOMAS NELSON PUBLISHERS
NASHVILLE

RICHARD F. "DICK" ABEL
President
Fellowship of Christian Athletes

Dick Abel was elected the fifth president of the Fellowship of Christian Athletes in 1988. He is responsible for fulfilling the purpose of FCA:

> *To present to athletes and coaches, and all whom they influence, the challenge and adventure of receiving Jesus Christ as Savior and Lord, serving Him in their relationships and in the fellowship of the church.*

The Fellowship of Christian Athletes is the oldest and largest athletic outreach to athletes and coaches in America with 50,000 official members and almost 4,500 official Huddle groups on junior high, senior high and college campuses across America. Dick's experience with FCA spans more than 20 years as a volunteer from the grass roots Huddle program to serving on the Board of Trustees.

Abel was born in Akron, Ohio, where he graduated from St. Ignatius High School. He earned his Business Administration degree at the University of Detroit and was commissioned in the Air Force. During his military career, he was a pilot, leader of an aerial demonstration team, assistant football coach at the Air Force Academy, and a public affairs officer for the U.S. Pacific Command. Later he was special assistant for the Chairman of the Joint Chiefs of Staff. He concluded his military career on the personal staff of the Secretary of the Air Force.

Dick retired from the Air Force in 1985 and accepted the position as director of legislative and public affairs for the United States Olympic Committee. His accomplishments include the Air Force Distinguished Service Medal and membership on the advisory counsel of the American Academy of Achievement.

Dick and his wife, Ann, have four children who are or have been involved with FCA. The Abels make their home in Kansas City, Missouri.

The Truth Shall Set You Free

Prison is not a place. Prison is the absence of freedom.

This paradox is so evident when we see "prisoners" who are "free" and when we see "free" people who are "imprisoned."

Nearly 20 years ago I came face-to-face with several prisoners—the prisoners of war in Vietnam—as the first American they had seen after being held captive over eight years, some who had been in solitary confinement for four years!

Yet, as I watched them line up on the flightline at the Hanoi airport, I saw the quick winks and the dancing smiles invade their placid faces and I could see that inside there was a freedom that eight years of captivity could not destroy. Later, I stood in awe as I heard their leader speak for the group in a message to the free world: "Thank you for the privilege of serving: God bless America!" This, from a group of men who were captives, not prisoners, expressing their freedom to serve.

How did they do it? So many cited their faith. Larry Guarino, four years in a 6 x 9-foot cell with a cement slab for a bed and no window, admitted: "If it wasn't for Jesus Christ, I couldn't have made it. He told me, 'Larry, you'll make it'." He expressed his freedom to live.

Robbie Risner used a wood dowel to painstakingly wear a hole through an 8-inch concrete wall—then shared Jesus Christ with the man in the next cell, sharing the freedom of eternity (the man later died). And the group singing of "Amazing Grace," which the guards could not silence, a freedom to share their faith.

Since then, I've learned that we can be imprisoned anywhere, even where there are no guards, no bars—where we are captives of anger, hate, depression, loneliness, economics, peer pressure, and, yes, even captive to the fear of death. Traveling the country, I see this kind of imprisonment even in the young people. What keeps them captive is drug abuse, sexual promiscuity, even suicides. How does a country turn such a lost generation around? We, as a country, turn around and face God and fight for the freedom to live, the freedom to share, the freedom to serve and, yes, even the freedom to die.

Then, you press on toward the goal of knowing the Truth—for the Truth shall set you free.

Dick Abel

19

RONALD W. ALLEN
Chairman & CEO
Delta Air Lines, Inc.

A native of Atlanta, Mr. Allen joined Delta in 1963 as a part time analyst during his senior year in college. For the past 28 years he has served in several positions at the Atlanta-based airline, including senior vice president for personnel and administration. He served as president and chief operating officer from 1983 to 1987 when he was named chairman of the board and chief executive officer.

Allen is a 1964 graduate of the Georgia Institute of Technology where he received his Bachelor of Industrial Engineering degree. He currently serves on the boards of directors of The Coca-Cola Company, National Service Industries, Inc., The C&S/Sovran Corporation, and the Atlanta Chamber of Commerce. He is a member of the board of trustees of Presbyterian College.

He has served as a member of the Georgia Institute of Technology's national advisory board, the board of trustees of Christian City Home for Children, the Metropolitan Atlanta Red Cross, and the United Way of Atlanta.

Delta's growth from the first aerial crop dusting company to the third largest scheduled airline in the U.S. has been characterized by hard work, persistence, and a dedication to customers. "We Love to Fly and It Shows" is the true spirit of the 68,000 member Delta family operating more than 470 aircraft to 158 communities in the U.S. and 57 foreign cities.

Each Day Brings Opportunities

Each day comes to me with both hands full of opportunities...

Those are the words of a woman born in Alabama in 1880, who lost her sight when she was 19 months old, yet inspired thousands of people throughout the world. Her name was Helen Keller. On March 3, 1887, three months before she was seven years old, this exceptional student met an exceptional teacher, Anne Mansfield Sullivan. Their accomplishments are an important lesson in what can happen if we learn to work as a team.

Ludwig Van Beethoven, born in Bonn, Germany, in 1770, grew up in a musical family. It was not until after 1819, when he was completely deaf, that Beethoven composed some of his greatest works, among them the Ninth Symphony.

It was an inventor who said, "Genius is one percent inspiration and ninety-nine percent perspiration." That same inventor, Thomas Alva Edison, is credited with more than 1,000 patents, among them the electric light bulb and the phonograph. Edison's contribution of a small transmitter made the telephone, Alexander Graham Bell's invention, of practical use. Despite a hearing impairment, Edison's genius touches the lives of millions each day.

Franklin Delano Roosevelt contracted polio in the early 1920s, and served as the 32nd President during two of the most challenging decades in U.S. history. FDR is the only U.S. President to have been elected to a fourth term in office.

Two masters of modern music excel at composition and as pianists and entertainers, as well. Yet, neither Georgia-born Ray Charles, nor Stevie Wonder, can see the notes they so easily maneuver, nor the many gold records they have been awarded.

These talented, dedicated individuals share two common characteristics. They have all faced major obstacles, yet have made significant contributions to the quality of life in the world around them. Each of them has accomplished more than most of us could ever dream of accomplishing in one lifetime. Helen Keller summed it up well: *"Each day comes to each of us with both hands full of opportunities."*

Ronald W. Allen

STEVE ALLEN
Author/Actor/Composer
Comedian/Musician/Scholar

Andy Williams once said, "Steve Allen does so many things, he's the only man I know who's listed on every one of the Yellow Pages." It is, in fact, difficult to believe there is only one Steve Allen. Not only is he the only TV comedian from the Golden Age of Comedy of the 1950s still appearing frequently on TV, but he has:

Created and hosted the Tonight Show.

Authored 36 published books.

Starred on Broadway in The Pink Elephant.

Starred in motion pictures, most notably Universal's The Benny Goodman Story.

Written over 4,000 songs, including This Could Be the Start of Something Big, Picnic, Impossible, Gravy Waltz, and South Rampart Street Parade.

Written the score for several musicals, including the Broadway production of Sophie and the CBS-TV version of Alice in Wonderland.

Made some 40 record albums.

Written the stirring Irish drama, The Wake, which won an L.A. drama critics nomination as best play of 1977.

Starred in the critically-acclaimed NBC series The Steve Allen Comedy Hour.

Created, written and hosted the Emmy award-winning PBS-TV series Meeting of Minds.

Been inducted into the TV Academy's Hall of Fame.

Allen is married to actress-comedienne Jayne Meadows.

Most Important Skills

I am pleased to have the opportunity to contribute to this collection of suggestions directed to young Americans. Earlier in the present century I might have spoken of traditional virtues, of the importance of concentration on work assignments or something of the sort. But now, I find it more important to make a few suggestions about the importance of reading and writing.

You can do nothing more important than to learn to read and write well. Without these basic skills you have an almost insurmountable handicap in your journey through life and in the workplace.

Literate manpower has become one of management's top priorities. Management has learned that the creative talents of many valued employees are shackled by their inability to communicate effectively. In this high-tech age, simply learning to cope with industrial jargon is vital to most business operations. If you are deficient in reading and writing skills, promotions will not come your way. Instead, you'll join the ever-growing number of others who are stagnated in menial jobs at the bottom of the employment ladder.

I suggest you make use of all the writing resources available to you. You might start by dusting off your grammar and English textbooks from your school days. Become familiar with your local library, which will offer you a bevy of books, as well as videotapes and on-site programs to improve your ability to read and write. Once you've honed these skills a whole new world will open up to you.

Literacy makes no promises of wealth or fame; in fact, it makes no promises save one—learn to read and write well and you'll at least have a chance to realize your dreams and ambitions.

WALLY "FAMOUS" AMOS
Entrepreneur/Author

Wally "Famous" Amos has been described as Horatio Alger in a Panama hat and as a walking advertisement for "everything great about America." He's a parable for free enterprise, a hymn to guts, and a promise that opportunity still lives in this nation.

He grew up in Tallahassee, Florida and New York City. After a stint in the Air Force and a career with the William Morris Agency working with such acts as Simon and Garfunkel, the Temptations and Dionne Warwick, he accepted the entrepreneurial challenge "to find a niche and fill it." He borrowed $25,000 and formed the Famous Amos Chocolate Chip Cookie Corporation, which turned out to be an exemplary entrepreneurial effort. His story has been well documented but his fame is not grounded in his unique cookie mix—but rather in quality, substance and a strong positive mental attitude he describes as "the power in you."

In 1979, Wally became national spokesman for the Literacy Volunteers of America, which combats the problem of adult illiteracy. He has travelled throughout the United States speaking to millions of people on behalf of the literacy group; sponsoring workshops; preparing public service announcements; and organizing state programs. He is also TV teacher/host of 50 episodes of state-of-the-art programs for adult basic learners that air on PBS stations. In Hawaii, where he lives, he is on the board of Hawaii Literacy, the Governor's Council, and the Aloha United Way board. In 1990, the Caring Institute presented him its Caring Award which recognizes contributions of those whose deeds help sustain society.

Amos has been the recipient of many other awards. Dr. Amos received an honorary doctorate in education from Johnson & Wales University. He has been inducted into the Babson College Academy of Distinguished Entrepreneurs, and is the recipient of the Horatio Alger Award and President's Award for Entrepreneurial Excellence. His battered Panama hat and colorful trade-mark shirt are in the Smithsonian Institution's Business Americana Collection.

The Power in You

I believe there is something only you can accomplish—an idea with your name on it. It's up to you to grab it and do it or it will never get done.

Nothing in life is worth working on more than you. Begin with a positive attitude. Attitude is not the result of success. Success is the result of attitude.

The biggest obstacle that will come between you and your goals is the lack of total commitment. Commitment is never "I'll try." It is always "I will."

Bring enthusiasm to everything you do. Enthusiasm is to your life what electricity is to a light bulb. Nothing happens until you flip the switch.

Everything starts inside of you. You create everything in your world whether you do it consciously or unconsciously. Life is an inside job. You have the power in you to accomplish all your goals and make your dreams come true. You can do it!

Wally is also an author. He wrote his autobiography, The Face That Launched a Thousand Chips, *in 1983. In 1988, he collaborated with his son, Gregory, a free-lance writer, on* The Power in You, *an inspirational book sharing his philosophy and life experiences.*

WALTER H. ANNENBERG
Publisher/Diplomat/Philanthropist

Walter Annenberg has enjoyed a challenging career as an editor and publisher, broadcaster, diplomat and philanthropist.

Born in Milwaukee, he was graduated from The Peddie School, Hightstown, New Jersey (his classmates voted him most likely to succeed), and attended the University of Pennsylvania's Wharton School. He entered the family publishing business in Philadelphia at age 32.

While serving as editor and publisher of the Philadelphia Inquirer, Annenberg saw the need for a publication for teenage girls and established Seventeen Magazine. In 1953, he established TV Guide and turned it into the largest circulation magazine in the United States.

Expanding into radio and television, he pioneered a number of broadcasting concepts, including educational programming via television. He earned the prestigious Alfred I. DuPont Award and the Ralph Lowell Medal for "outstanding contributions to public television." In 1981, Annenberg announced he would give $150 million over the next 15 years to the Corporation for Public Broadcasting.

Annenberg's performance as U.S. Ambassador to the Court of St. James lifted him to the ranks of respected statesman. He earned the rare distinction among U.S. ambassadors to Britain of being knighted.

His philanthropic donations total over $1 billion, e.g., $21 million to the University of Pennsylvania in 1989, $50 million to the United Negro College Fund.

In 1986, he received the Medal of Freedom from President Reagan. The same year, he was elected to the Wharton School Hall of Fame by votes of the school's students, and received the Linus Pauling Medal for Humanitarianism.

Prepare Yourself

You must be prepared to discipline yourself and to strive to develop affirmative characteristics. Our character is what distinguishes us from others. It is what we really are, not what others think we are. Reputation is what you are supposed to be; character is what you are. Countless successful people, who began with little, disciplined themselves and won life's battle—you can do it, too!

You must prepare yourself for occasional shocks in life because harassment is just around the corner. Success breeds envy. The higher you climb, the bigger target you become.

You must prepare yourself to strive for inspiration from the ashes of adversity. Trouble and difficulty are a real and necessary part of our existence. Without them there are many lessons in life we'd never learn. Poet Robert Hamilton put it well:

> *I walked a mile with Sorrow*
> *And ne'er a word said she*
> *But, oh, the things I learned from her*
> *When Sorrow walked with me.*

MARY KAY ASH
Chairman Emeritus
Mary Kay Cosmetics

Mary Kay Ash started her dream company in 1963 with $5,000 and plenty of determination and perseverance. Under her direction, the company has grown from a small direct-sales company into the largest direct-selling skin care company in the world.

A unique combination of enthusiastic people, quality products, innovative marketing concepts and an ambitious set of goals has turned Mary Kay Cosmetics, Inc., into an American business success story.

Today, more than 200,000 independent beauty consultants sell the company's products in the United States, Canada, Argentina, Australia, Mexico, Germany and 16 other countries.

The Mary Kay success story began after she retired from a long and prosperous career in direct sales. She began thinking about her own dream company, one based on the golden rule and one which would give women unlimited opportunities for success.

Mary Kay is a much sought-after speaker and has received numerous awards and honors. Her latest laurels include the Outstanding Business Leader Award from Northwood Institute, the Circle of Honor Award from The Direct Selling Education Foundation and the First Annual National Sales Hall of Fame Award presented by the Sales and Marketing Executives of New York. She is also the recipient of the prestigious Horatio Alger Award.

Mary Kay is also active in helping find a cure for breast cancer through funding educational and research programs through the Susan G. Komen Foundation and the American Cancer Society.

Confidence Keys Success

If you were to ask me, "What is a common denominator among women?" I would have to say it is a lack of faith in their own God-given abilities. Did you ever hear a man say, "If I can," "I hope," or "Maybe"? That seems to be a female disease. Most men have enough sense to bluff their way through and pretend confidence, even if they don't feel it.

At Mary Kay Cosmetics, we try to instill confidence in women by "praising them to success" one small achievement at a time, urging them on to greater success.

From early childhood my mother instilled confidence in me by constantly repeating, "You can do anything in this world you want to do, if you want to do it badly enough—and you are willing to pay the price!" You can do it!!!

Mary Kay Ash

CATHLEEN BLACK
President & CEO
American Newspaper
Publishers Association

Prior to becoming head of ANPA, the major newspaper organization in the U.S. and Canada that represents 1,400 newspapers, Cathleen Black was publisher of USA TODAY, executive vice president / marketing of Gannett, USA TODAY's parent company, and a member of the Gannett board of directors.

Prior to joining USA TODAY, Black was publisher of New York magazine. At the time of her appointment in '79, she was the first woman ever to be publisher of a weekly consumer magazine.

A graduate of Trinity College, she completed her term as a member of its board of trustees and has been named to chair the school's newly formed board of regents.

Recently, she was appointed by President Bush to the board of directors of the Points of Light Foundation. In addition, she is active on the boards of the Advertising Council, United Way of America and the board of visitors for the School of Foreign Service at Georgetown University.

She has received numerous honors. In 1990, Ladies Home Journal named her as one of "The Fifty Most Powerful Women in America." The Sara Lee Corporation awarded her their 1989 Frontrunner Award for business excellence. Manhattan College's De LaSalle Medal, the Matrix Award, the Catalyst Award and NOW Legal Defense and Education Fund Award also acknowledged her achievements. She holds honorary degrees from Simmons College, Trinity College, Ithaca College and Capitol College.

Black resides in Washington, D.C. with her husband, Tom Harvey, and their young son, Duffy.

Stretch to Your Limit

You can do it! You certainly can. In fact, the advertising slogan for the Nike shoe campaign may be most appropriate. What it says is, "DO IT NOW!"

When I think about what's important to succeed, I think that the message is singular. We can almost do anything we want to do, if we have courage, self-confidence and a can-do spirit.

Surely one of life's greatest mistakes is not stretching to one's own limit. It has helped me in my career to not let self-imposed boundaries deter me from surging forward.

You can do it, too—good luck.

Cathleen Black

EDDY BOAS
President
Direct Marketing Division
IMS International

Eddy Boas was born in Holland in 1940 at the outbreak of World War II and spent nearly three years in a German concentration camp with his father, mother and brother. As far as is known, they were the only family that went into a concentration camp and survived as a family.

On returning to Holland they decided to migrate to Australia. In 1948, when Eddy was eight years old, his father passed away. His mother supported the family by taking a job as a cleaning lady. Eddy left school at age 15 to work in a Sydney radio station while attending night school. After six years in radio, he became an office equipment salesman with Olivetti and continued to study at night.

He joined IMS in 1975. He worked his way through the ranks and was transferred to the United States in 1989 as president of the Direct Marketing Division of IMS International, a subsidiary of Dun & Bradstreet, which includes responsibilities in Europe, Australia and the United States.

His interests have always been in sports. He has participated competitively in modern Pentathlon (running, swimming, fencing, pistol shooting and horse racing), as well as soccer. He is a qualified soccer referee and for four years was president of the local Junior Soccer Club.

He has two sons in their early '20s. The youngest, Marc, is in the Australian regular army while the elder son, Philip, has chosen a career in advertising.

How to Survive

From a young child, survival in a tough world has been part of my life.

It started by surviving World War II and continued until today where survival in a tough business world is paramount to one's success.

To be successful, whether in sports or business, one has to be a team player and have a positive attitude.

To be a winner in life, a positive mental attitude is essential. "Everything is possible—you just have to make the effort."

To survive in today's business world you have to be one step ahead of your competitors. Do not be afraid to ask. My mother, who is 80 and is a real survivor, early on in life gave me a saying which I still use today— "Don't be afraid to ask because No you have got and Yes is a maybe." This is so true because many of us think in a negative way while in actual fact the results can be quite positive.

Young people today should not be afraid to ask questions of their peers. Unfortunately, in a negative world where we are continuously told that business is bad and jobs are difficult to get, our young people feel that there is nothing to strive for in life. This is totally wrong, since a positive attitude and a will to win will give you more opportunities in life.

Our leaders, in whichever country, need to set examples for our young people, as well as our handicapped people. Far too often they make excuses for what has gone wrong with this world, instead of being true leaders and showing a positive attitude.

Look upon business as you look upon sports. It's a team effort. No manager is capable of running a business by him/herself. They need a team effort to be successful. The same as the best quarterback can't win a game by himself. It doesn't matter how far he can throw, he needs to have protection and receivers who can catch the ball.

To survive today, think of how well off you are. Look around and you'll always find someone worse off than yourself. Think about the handicapped people, who have made a success of themselves, and compare their accomplishments with yours.

Be proud of yourself for what you have achieved in life and you will survive to go on to better things.

Eddy Boas

PAT BOONE
Author/Entertainer

Pat Boone has enjoyed eminent success as an entertainer and author for more than 35 years, but he's most proud of his accomplishments as a father and Christian.

He married his high school sweetheart, Shirley Foley (daughter of country music legend Red Foley). They were married his first year in college. In 1958, he graduated Magna Cum Laude from Columbia University majoring in speech and English. By this time, the Boones had four daughters.

While at Columbia, in 1956, he signed a million dollar contract with 20th Century Fox and subsequently starred in 15 films. The same year, ABC signed him for the Pat Boone Chevy Showroom, making him the youngest performer with his own network show.

As a recording artist, Pat set an all-time record by staying on the charts for more than 200 consecutive weeks. He's sold more than 45 million records.

On cable, he's a co-host on the Shop Television Network and, with Shirley, on the Nashville Network as "RV" travelers. They took part in Gospel America Tour '88 and completed a sold-out concert tour in Hong Kong and Japan. His Pat Boone Radio Show continues successfully on 300 stations worldwide.

His first book, Twixt Twelve and Twenty, *a guide for teenagers, sold more than 800,000 copies, with all royalties going to the Northeastern Institute of Christian Education. In addition to the 15 books he's written, including his most recent* Miracle of Prayer, *he's co-authored two books with Shirley,* The Honeymoon is Over *and* Together: 25 Years With The Boone Family.

Pat has been national chairman and host of the Easter Seal Society telethon for ten years and he authored The Human Touch, *the Easter Seal story. He's an astute businessman and a partner in many diverse projects, but perhaps the most exciting aspect of his life centers around his grandchildren, now a combination of 14 boys and girls.*

The Miracle of Prayer

Prayer has been the greatest source of help in my life. Everything I've ever achieved has come as a result of including prayer in whatever I do. It led me to write a book, *The Miracle of Prayer,* to share with others my strong belief in the power of prayer.

Space limitations here prevent my going into great detail, but I assure you the most important prayer you'll ever pray is that which provides the basis for everything else: turning to Jesus Christ and receiving Him as your Saviour. That's where prayer must begin.

I believe it is quite possible to achieve success in any field by employing the right approach to prayer. This has been documented over and over again. Throughout this book some of America's most successful people acknowledge it as well.

Prayer is simply conversation with God. Talk to Him like you would to your own father, your best friend, even your boss. He's all of these to you.

God does want us to be contented and successful. Take your problems to Him, who listens and answers. "Therefore I say to you, whatever things you ask when you pray, believe that you receive them, and you will be given them." (Mark 11:24) Be patient. Keep asking and you'll find that's a written guarantee you can count on.

I also suggest you read Proverbs, a 31-chapter gold mine of human and practical wisdom. It's a fantastic "how-to" book for practical living in this world.

One final word—the greatest doers in human history are all gone. They stand as evidence that human victories, no matter how exciting or encompassing, are relatively short-lived, temporary. There must be more to life. And there is!

Jesus is the only person who got out of this world alive. Make Him your partner, talk to Him through prayer, and you'll be a success—it's guaranteed!

FRANK BORMAN
Commander/Apollo 8 Mission
Business Leader

A hero of the American space odyssey, Frank Borman led the first team of American astronauts to circle the moon, extending man's horizons into space. He is internationally known as Commander of the 1968 Apollo 8 Mission. A romance with airplanes that began when he was 15 years old took him to the Air Force, then to NASA, and to leadership in the aviation industry.

A career Air Force officer, his assignments included service as a fighter pilot, an operational pilot and instructor, an experimental test pilot, and an assistant professor of thermodynamics and fluid mechanics at West Point. When selected by NASA, he was instructor at the Aerospace Research Pilot School at Edwards AFB, California.

A native of Gary, Indiana, he was raised in Tucson, Arizona. He earned a Bachelor of Science degree from the U.S. Military Academy, West Point, in 1950, and a Master of Science degree in aeronautical engineering from the California Institute of Technology in 1957. He completed the Harvard Business School's Advanced Management Program in 1970.

During his tenure as chief executive officer of Eastern Airlines, the industry went through the enormous change caused by deregulation. The company enjoyed the four most profitable years in its history under his leadership.

Recipient of many honors, he received the first Congressional Space Medal of Honor from the President of the United States. He is a member of the International Aerospace Hall of Fame and the holder of the Harmon International Aviation Trophy, in addition to many honorary degrees, special honors and service decorations.

Today he is chairman, CEO and president of Patlex Corporation and resides in Las Cruces, New Mexico, with his wife, Susan. They have two sons and four grandchildren.

You Have to Pay the Price

After a reasonably successful high school football career, I entered the U.S. Military Academy at West Point. One of the first voluntary actions I took was to go out for football. Of course, I had not been recruited and at the time weighed all of 145 pounds, but the thrill of playing football for Army was one of the reasons I applied for West Point. The other being I wanted an opportunity to become a military pilot.

I didn't last long in the screening exercises, but rather than quit I opted for the next best thing and became a student football manager. I have always thought that act was one of the more fortuitous events in my life.

Though the student manager's job was hardly glamorous and the position was held in low esteem, it placed me in direct contact with Colonel Earl "Red" Blaik. This austere man epitomized leadership. In my four years at West Point he produced post-war teams that were among the best ever in college football. And he did this without the enormous pool of talent that was available at the academy during the war years.

His theme for life and success was the title of a book he authored, *You Have to Pay the Price*. By that, he meant that you have to be prepared if you are to succeed in life and that preparation often involves sacrifice, dedication and enormous effort. This rule applies the same if you are preparing for football, science, medicine or any other career. Throughout my military and civilian career, subsequent to my graduation in 1950, Colonel Blaik kept in touch, even though I was only a manager on the Army teams. He offered personal encouragement at all times, advice when it was needed, and congratulations when I was successful. This encouragement had an enormous impact on my thinking long after my association with the football team was gone.

Even more important was the indelible stamp that he placed on me and so many of the cadets he coached. The essence of his message was, "You can do it," you can succeed, you can achieve, but you must be prepared, "You Have to Pay the Price."

ADAM J. BOZZUTO
Chairman & President
Bozzuto's Incorporated

Adam Bozzuto was born in Waterbury, Connecticut. Today, he resides in Middlebury and is head of one of the largest and most successful food distributorships in the Northeast. He's known for his philanthropy, which is part of his lifelong philosophy to give something back in appreciation for success.

A self-made man, he learned much about life in the "school of hard knocks." During the depression, to help his family make ends meet, he worked in grocery stores doing all sorts of menial tasks. Intrigued by the many facets that go into a retail food operation, he often worked extra hours without pay to learn about the business.

The toughness of the times helped him discipline himself to spend less than he earned. By 1945, at age 29, he had built his own nest egg which he used to found Bozzuto's, in Waterbury, Connecticut. It was the first step toward his goal to become a leader in the food industry.

Well on the way to achieving his goals, he suffered a devastating setback in 1955, when a violent flood swept through Waterbury and wiped out his business in its wake.

From the adversity came a valuable lesson—the importance of the strength of relationships developed in running a business. He was amazed by the support he received, beyond his family, from friends, employees, loyal customers and business acquaintances, who helped him resurrect his business from its watery grave.

Success has not deterred his interest in other people. Today he provides strong support to schools, churches, charitable organizations and the Special Olympics in Connecticut. He still believes happiness is a result of what we give our fellowman—not what we take.

Guidelines for a Happy Life

There are many formulas for success. I think the most important aspect of life is to be happy by enjoying your family, friends and work. Happiness is not always easy to find because we look for it outside ourselves, when, in reality, it comes from within.

I'd like to share with you some suggestions to help you enjoy a sound, secure and happy life:

1. Live a simple life. Be temperate in your habits and avoid selfishness.

2. Spend less than you earn. Avoid extravagance and keep out of debt. It may be difficult, but it pays big dividends.

3. Think constructively. Train yourself to think clear, useful thoughts. Avoid unwholesome ideas.

4. Try to see the other person's point of view. Resist the tendency to want things your own way.

5. Develop good friends and business associates. This support network will be there for you in times of need.

6. Rule your moods, don't let them rule you. Remember, a lifetime of unhappiness can be caused by a moment of emotional instability.

7. Next, give generously. There is no greater joy in life than to bring happiness to others.

8. Be interested in other people.

9. Work with righteous, honest motives. No one who does wrong is ever really happy.

10. Live one day at a time. Concentrate on the task at hand and avoid attempting too much at one time.

11. Develop some means of diversion and relaxation.

12. Finally, and most important, keep close to God. It will do more to bring you happiness than any other single endeavor. And God, in turn, will help keep you close to all other attributes of happiness.

Adam J. Bozzuto

ROBERT J. BROWN
Chairman
B&C Associates, Inc.

Robert Brown was born in High Point, North Carolina, the great grand-son of a slave who dug ground to make way for railroad tracks to weave their way through the state.

In 1960, against the advice of many who knew him, he left his job with the Federal Bureau of Narcotics in New York and returned home to High Point to start his own public relations firm.

Clients did not rush to his door. Despite lack of business, each day he would don a suit and tie, pick up his briefcase and head for the office—a room not much bigger than a closet on the second floor of an abandoned theatre. He made calls, wrote letters, and searched newspapers and telephone books for prospective clients.

Finally, as he describes on the next page, a lucky break came his way—and he leveraged it into a successful career.

In 1968, Robert Brown was appointed Special Assistant to President Nixon. His duties included oversight responsibility for community relations, civil rights, emergency preparedness, small towns and day care. He started and developed the U.S. Minority Enterprise Program and initiated the U.S. Government Black College program.

Today his public relations / crisis management firm, B&C Associates, is one of the largest and most respected black-owned firms in the nation. B&C's clients include Dow Jones and Fortune 500 companies such as Woolworth Corp., SC Johnson Wax, Nabisco Brands and Sara Lee Corporation, as well as a number of small businesses.

Brown has been honored by numerous colleges, universities, and organizations. He holds eight honorary doctorate degrees and six national achievement awards. He was honored in 1990 as a recipient of the Horatio Alger Association of Distinguished Americans Award.

A major part of his life has always revolved around giving. He and his wife, Sallie, have put many needy children through school, and he is

Never Give Up

One day in 1960, I was sitting in the office of my newly-founded company wondering if I'd made the biggest mistake of my life. I had left a good job in New York to start this public relations company and clients were few and far between.

My office consisted of a desk, a chair, a telephone and a file cabinet. I had hidden my car behind the pool room because I was three months behind on payments. As I struggled to figure out what my next move was going to be, the telephone rang.

Sitting there, looking at the phone as it chimed away, I wondered if I should pick up the receiver. On the other end could be any number of people I owed money to: the used car dealer saying he was coming for the car, or the phone company calling to inform me they were on the way to take out the phone.

Then my grandmother's words sounded in my ear: "Have faith in God, work hard, and make sacrifices, and you can achieve anything. Nothing can stop you, son."

I did answer that call, and it resulted in my company's first major corporate client: F.W. Woolworth. After that, one thing led to another and I started to have some measure of success.

To the young people today who are trying to achieve something, I can give no better advice than my grandmother's words.

No matter what kind of adversity you face, be it no shoes, no food, or intangible injuries such as discrimination, remember that faith, hard work and sacrifice will be the key to success.

Never give up.

Know that God will work wonders through your faith.

Robert J. Brown

---

president of the International Concern Foundation, which channels support from the private sector to disadvantaged groups around the globe.

JOHN H. BRYAN
Chairman & CEO
Sara Lee Corporation

John Bryan is a native of Mississippi. He is a graduate of Rhodes College, Memphis, where he received a Bachelor of Arts degree in economics and business administration. He began his business career in 1960 with the family owned and operated Bryan Foods in West Point, Mississippi. In 1968, Bryan Foods was sold to Sara Lee Corporation of Chicago.

In 1974, Mr. Bryan became executive vice president and a director of Sara Lee Corporation. That same year he was elected president, and the next year was named chief executive officer. He was elected chairman of the board of Sara Lee Corporation in 1976.

Mr. Bryan is a member of the board of directors of Amoco Corporation and First Chicago Corporation and its subsidiary, the First National Bank of Chicago. He is the past chairman and a member of the board of directors of Grocery Manufacturers of America, Inc., a member of the Business Council and the Business Roundtable, a trustee of the Committee for Economic Development, and national chairman of the Business Committee for the Arts. Mr. Bryan is also a member of the board of the National Women's Economic Alliance and serves on the National Corporations Committee of the United Negro College Fund.

Active in a variety of organizations in the Chicago area, Mr. Bryan is vice president of the board of trustees and treasurer of the Art Institute of Chicago, is a member of Chicago United, a director of the United Way / Crusade of Mercy, a trustee and vice chairman of Rush Presbyterian St. Luke's Medical Center, a trustee of the University of Chicago, and chairman of the Business Advisory Council of the Chicago Urban League.

Mr. Bryan's awards include the French Legion of Honor, Holland's Order of Orange Nassau conferred by Queen Beatrix, the National Humanitarian Award of the National Conference of Christians and Jews, and the William H. Albers Award given by the Food Marketing Institute.

Focus on Your Objectives

The 1990s mark a great milestone in our history, for they mark the last decade in this millennium. There is something awesome about the closing of a 1,000 year cycle—a time that has seen the Dark Ages, the Renaissance, revolution, and now the age of technology. The year 2000 will be an exciting call to action, as well as a catalyst for change on all fronts. With these changes come enormous opportunities, more specifically, opportunities for leadership.

If you aspire to capture these opportunities—to take up leadership roles—I should like to offer, from my experience, three prerequisites that I believe are the most important for leadership tomorrow or at any time.

The first is integrity. You must guard your honor with all you have. Leadership is based on respect and trust. A reputation for ethical behavior is the cornerstone of successful leadership in business, as in life.

Second is that effective leaders are truly concerned about other people—for leadership demands a genuine respect for those you lead. We cannot accomplish very much alone. I watch a lot of people getting selected for leadership positions. Those selected are most often chosen because their peers want them to be their leaders. Showing respect for your peers, and for those you lead, is just as important as showing respect for those who lead you.

The third point is that leaders must perform. He or she must become identified with accomplishment—whether it's the general in battle, or the coach on Saturday afternoon, or the company president striving to meet financial objectives, or the college president aspiring to make his or her institution the very best.

A lot of factors do affect accomplishment. But of those you can control, the most important is this: It is being intensely focused on the proper performance measures of whatever is your assigned task. Tragically, most people scatter their efforts—and even worse many never understand their objectives. Today, this focus on your objectives is usually called vision. It is surely among the critical factors for success.

John H. Bryon —

43

BARBARA BUSH
38th First Lady

Barbara Bush, wife of President George Bush, has lived a life that reflects her husband's varied career in business and public service, her involvement as the mother of five children, and her own energy and commitment to a wide variety of community projects.

Barbara Pierce Bush was born on June 8, 1925, grew up in Rye, New York, and married George Bush on January 6, 1945. They have five children, four daughters-in-law, and 12 grandchildren. By virtue of George Bush's service as a member of Congress, U.S. Representative to the United Nations, chairman of the Republican National Committee, chief of the United States Liaison Office in the People's Republic of China, director of the Central Intelligence Agency, and the vice president of the United States, the Bushes have lived in 17 cities and 29 homes since their marriage.

Mrs. Bush has chosen the promotion of literacy and the importance of reading as her special areas of focus. She is a sponsor of Laubach Literacy Volunteers, a world-wide program committed to eradicating illiteracy. She is honorary chairman of the National Advisory Council of Literacy Volunteers of America, Inc., a national volunteer tutorial organization. She is honorary chairperson for the National Committee on Literacy and Education of the United Way. She serves as honorary chairman of the Reading is Fundamental Advisory Council.

Mrs. Bush is honorary chairperson of the Barbara Bush Foundation for Family Literacy, an organization whose mission is to establish literacy as a value in every family in America, to support the development of family literacy programs, and to break the intergenerational cycle of illiteracy.

Reflecting her own years as an active volunteer, she encourages volunteerism and the giving by people of their time and energies for the betterment of others and their communities. She also has taken a particular interest in the problem of learning disabilities and has encouraged many national

Three Special Choices

(From Commencement Address, Wellesley College, June 1, 1990)

I hope that many of you will consider making three very special choices in your life. The first is to believe in something larger than yourself, to get involved in some of the big ideas of your time. I chose literacy because I honestly believe that if more people could read, write and comprehend, we would be that much closer to solving so many of the problems plaguing our society.

Early on I made another decision which I hope you will make as well. Whether you are talking about education, career or service, you are talking about life—and life must have joy. It's supposed to be fun! One of the reasons I made the most important decision of my life—to marry George Bush—is because he made me laugh. It's true, sometimes we've laughed through tears, but that shared laughter has been one of our strongest bonds.

The third choice that must not be missed is to cherish your human connections: your relationships with friends and family. For several years, you've had impressed upon you the importance to your career of dedication and hard work. This is true, but as important as your obligations as a doctor, lawyer or business leader will be, you are a human being first and those human connections—with spouses, with children, with friends—are the most important investments you will ever make.

At the end of your life, you will never regret not having passed one more test, not winning one more verdict or not closing one more deal. You will regret time not spent with a husband, a friend, a child or a parent.

Barbara Bush

---

organizations that seek to bring about greater public awareness and effective treatment for the problem.

Since becoming First Lady, Mrs. Bush has received honorary degrees from Bennett College, Smith College, Morehouse School of Medicine, St. Louis University, and the University of Pennsylvania.

Mrs. Bush is an exercise enthusiast and also enjoys reading, gardening, the family dog, Millie, and being with her family.

ROBERT L. CALLAHAN
President
Ingersoll Engineers

Bob Callahan heads an international manufacturing consulting firm. Since 1957, he has been striving to help manufacturers become competitive with offshore producers.

He started his career working as a machine operator in several factories. Bob served his apprenticeship in a die shop. Then he gained experience in industrial and manufacturing engineering in the automotive and business machine industries. Beginning as a trainee, Bob spent 16 years with the consulting firm of Booz Allen & Hamilton, after which he moved to his present firm. Along the way, he has helped numerous organizations, including a number of Fortune 500 companies.

Over the last 15 years, his favorite tools for communicating opinions about what's right and wrong with American industry today are his White Papers. These brief, hard-hitting, and frequently controversial essays describe what must be done in manufacturing and how these changes fit into today's manufacturing environment. These White Papers have become popular throughout the manufacturing community.

Dare to Be Different

You can do it, but to do it, you've got to be different. What does this mean? I think it means to become an individual rather than a member of a herd. Let me try to illustrate.

When I was much younger, the most important thing in my life was the acceptance of my friends. I badly needed to be liked. I wanted to be included in what they did. Acceptance by my peers dominated my thinking.

While I never had a chance to join a fraternity, those that have seem to me to be similarly motivated. They need to be accepted. They need brothers. They have to be part of an exclusive group, know the secret handshake.

Those that do it (accomplish something) somehow make the break from their herd—they become individuals. They find they no longer need to be with people who think the same, have a common enemy, are of the same race, ethnic or social group. How do they become individuals? I'm not sure I know. In my case, as best I can remember, I unconsciously weaned myself, over time, away from the herd.

As it occurred, I became interested in things different from my former herd members. I slowly became an individual able to take aim at non-herd objectives like my career, my family, my community, even my golf game. In this way, I suppose I became selfish, which seems to me to be a near synonym for individualism.

It's an evolving internal motivation to be different rather than the same, to rise above the rest, to do more than the next guy, to be better than he is, to make a mark on the world, state, city, or organization, or to be wealthy or respected. And I suppose others use their individualism to seek power, influence or political office.

Yet, I observe not all young people are herd members. How I envy those few who, as early as high school age, seem to want to excel at something on their own. You can do it, but, you can't do it in a herd. You've got to start becoming an individual. Not a loner, though. Only a select few loners accomplish much; Einstein, after all, was an exception. Rather, an individual accomplishes it by working effectively with other individuals—if that's what it takes to get his or her job done.

So, I am a former herd member turned individual. Along the way, I've done everything I found I wanted to do. I did it by being me, whoever that is—I guess it's not important that I know. All I do know is that I did it. And believe me, if I did a little bit of it, anyone can.

Bob Callahan

JOHN CALLAWAY
Broadcast Journalist/Executive

John Douglas Callaway has been a news person since he started selling his dad's weekly newspaper on the streets of New Martinsville, West Virginia, at the age of six. He later went on to become the editor of his high school newspaper and wrote for the college paper at Ohio Wesleyan University until he left school with 71 cents in his pocket and hitchhiked to Chicago in February, 1956.

He intended to make some money, pay off some bills, and return to college. Instead, he ended up living at the Chicago YMCA in a nine-dollar-a-week room and working as a police reporter for the famed City News Bureau of Chicago (his first take-home pay was $34 a week).

After nine months at City News, John became one of the first street reporters for WBBM Radio-TV, the CBS outlet in Chicago. For the next 17 years, he worked as a documentary-maker, street reporter, talk-show host and news director for CBS in Chicago and New York. He helped develop the all-news radio stations nationally for CBS Radio.

For the past 17 years, John Callaway has worked as an executive and broadcast journalist-program host for WTTW, Chicago's Public Television Station. His John Callaway Interviews series was broadcast nationally on PBS. He has hosted the Emmy Award-winning Chicago Tonight with John Callaway nightly news analysis program on WTTW since 1984.

In addition to his public broadcasting duties, John was the founding director of the William Benton Fellowships in Broadcast Journalism program at the University of Chicago in 1983.

John is married to the Chicago actress, Patrice Fletcher. He is the father of Ann Hampton Callaway, one of New York's leading cabaret singers and Liz Callaway, one of Broadway's leading musical theatre performers.

My Prayer for You

Here are my hopes and prayers for each of you:

That you will try to do what you really feel in your heart you need to do. That you will go with your instincts and take healthy chances. That you will try to take the right bite out of life. That you will not try to go it alone. That if you are hurt, lonely and overwhelmed you will seek out those who can help you, or at least talk with you about your troubles. That you will read with a passion and write if you can.

I pray that if you are lucky enough to be blessed with faith that you will try to keep it and honor it and if, by chance, you lose it, that it will someday return.

I hope that you will try to sing your own music, but that you don't listen to yourself sing (that is, don't take yourself too seriously). I hope that you will just do what you do best and let it burst forth gloriously.

I pray that you will do your homework and then do some more homework and then some more. I hope that when you find yourself debating another person that you will take care to acknowledge your opponent's argument and be prepared to make his or her case better than they can. Then your own interests and arguments will come easily.

I pray that you will not be afraid of defeat and that you will know the wisdom of confession. I pray that you will be blessed with delicious intimacy and rich family life and that you will find a life partner whose passions and vision mesh with your own.

I hope you will have the grace and good humor to hold competing truths in your mind, to embrace paradox. I pray that when you experience or encounter tragedy that you can learn and grow from it and that when you experience or encounter the thrilling beauty of life that you will carry it in your heart and mind for all your days.

John W. Caldwell

CURTIS L. CARLSON
Chairman
Carlson Companies, Inc.

Curt Carlson started in business all by himself in downtown Minneapolis in 1938. With $50 in borrowed capital, he began his entrepreneurial effort by founding the Gold Bond Stamp Co. (trading stamps).

Today, Carlson heads an empire of hotels, resorts, the largest travel agency in North America, restaurants and incentive companies spanning the globe employing more than 70,000 employees.

His Carlson Companies is ranked by Forbes magazine as one of the ten to 15 largest privately-held corporations in the U.S., with annual systemwide revenues of $8.1 billion, and plans to reach $9.2 billion in 1992.

One Step at a Time

I have been in business now for over 50 years and have found that if a person is to be successful in life, no matter what one does, he or she must have good self-esteem.

Your opinion of others may vary, but one thing that should never falter is your own self-esteem and confidence that you can do the job. A person should have complete faith in doing the task coupled with the courage to back it up. Forget what others may think or say and leap over the fears and timidity of those who lurk on the sidelines with negative thoughts. They will only impede your progress.

A successful person will make his or her own decisions, set definite goals which are realistically attainable, then shore up that confidence with the ability to reach those objectives and then "go for it!"

I have always tried to work toward goals, whether they be newspaper subscription prizes I sought to achieve while carrying a newspaper route, or when I was a soap salesman for Procter & Gamble and was seeking one of their bonuses. I was brought up to decide on what it was I wanted and then to work until I had it.

I always wanted to be in business for myself and that makes me an entrepreneur—a category of the human race I have always been most proud being a member. Entrepreneurs are risk-takers and can only exist in the American free enterprise system. They are idealists and provide the spark and create the jobs which make the United States a fantastic place to live, play and to be in business for yourself.

To be in business for myself also meant I had to succeed by myself. I will let others decide whether or not I am successful, but, in the beginning, I remember I set a goal to earn $100 a week. I did not, at the time, set a deadline to reach my goal. Instead, I simply wrote "$100 a week" on a slip of paper and put it in my wallet and began to work toward my goal.

When I finally did attain the $100 a week goal, I threw away the paper and replaced it with one which read "$200 a week." I kept that up for much of my business life, using the paper as a measure of my progress.

What is the lesson here? It is that success is something you must work at slowly—one step at a time.

Curt Carlson

NANCY LIEBERMAN-CLINE
Women's Basketball Great

Nancy Lieberman-Cline may be the best female basketball player ever. A standout in women's amateur and professional hoops, Nancy made history in 1986 by becoming the first woman to play in a men's professional league, signing with the Springfield Fame in the United States Basketball League. That triumph was followed by another first when she joined the 1987-88 Globetrotters-Washington Generals World Tour.

From her introduction to the sport on the playgrounds of her native Brooklyn, at age 7, she led the American team to the gold medal in the 1975 Pan-American Games. A year later, she was the only high school member of the silver medal Olympic team.

Nancy attended Old Dominion University, leading the women's varsity basketball team to a national championship in 1978-80. After graduation she turned pro, joining the Women's Basketball League, which eventually folded. Then, in 1984, she won ABC's Women's Supersports competition and then joined the short-lived Dallas Diamonds. She became a role model for female athletes everywhere, leading her team to the WABA title in 1984, after winning the MVP award in the league's All-Star game.

Beyond the basketball court, she was the first female named to President Reagan's Sports Drug Awareness Program and has been a driving force in such charities as the Special Olympics, Just Say No Foundation and the Juvenile Diabetes Foundation. She also conducts free clinics for youngsters combining the teaching of basketball basics and motivational messages to encourage youth to be the best they can be. In 1986, Nancy was named one of the nation's Top 10 Women by Glamour Magazine.

As a respected authority, she has been an analyst / commentator for NBC, ESPN and Sports Channel America. Her credits include the NCAA Women's Final Four in 1986 and 1989, as well as the 1988 Olympics in Seoul, Korea.

Nancy is currently vice president of ProMotion Events, Inc., a sports

Product of Environment

I really believe that people are a product of their environment. I'm a product of the schoolyards in Harlem, where I played basketball, and my home in Far Rockaway, New York.

When I was 12, my parents got divorced. My brother clung to his studies, for me basketball helped me through the difficult time. I always wanted to play because it made me happy. I grew up like any "little boy" in New York.

My biggest dream was to play in Madison Square Garden. I had my heroes like kids today have Michael Jordan and Magic Johnson. Mine were Walt Frazier and Willis Reed. These guys were the New York Knicks! I wanted to play as good as they did and where they did. I knew that I wanted to be the greatest woman basketball player ever!

I started playing basketball when I was 10. If I wanted to play in games with the boys, I had to be at least as good as them. But that wasn't enough. I started playing with them, and by imitating the way my heroes played, I found I could beat some of them. It came down to respect. I learned not to be afraid to take the A train to Harlem for even more basketball games. It might have scared my mother, but not me. Don't ever let fear beat you.

My attitude of never being afraid and always trying my hardest to beat the best led me through my youth in New York. As I went on to play in college, the Olympics, professional women's and men's basketball leagues, my attitude was always to beat and be the best. I suggest you never stop working, wanting or dreaming—which has remained my motto.

Young people today have a lot of distractions. Don't let bad grades in school, alcohol, drugs, gangs or bad influence keep you from being the best at whatever you choose to do. For me it was basketball. If it's sports for you, terrific! If you want to be the best pianist or musician, great! If you want to be a doctor, go after it! As I did, you CAN make the best of your own situation.

You may be a product of your environment, but that doesn't mean that you can't do something now or later to change or make it better.

Nancy Lieberman-Cline

---

marketing firm based in Omaha, Nebraska. She resides in Dallas with her husband, Tim Cline, a teammate when she played for the Washington Generals team.

MARVA COLLINS
Founder
Westside Preparatory School

Marva Collins, an inner-city elementary teacher, founded the Westside Preparatory School in 1975. Her methodology, stressing adherence to the phonics system of reading and emphasis on memorization and interdisciplinary learning, enabled her to transform supposedly "unteachable" ghetto children into accomplished readers and overall students.

Mrs. Collins' achievements have earned her recognition from such institutions as the National Education Association, the American Academy of Achievement and the National Urban League.

Her devotion to students and family was the focus of "The Marva Collins Story," a Hallmark Hall of Fame CBS television special starring Cecily Tyson as Mrs. Collins and Morgan Freeman as her husband.

Mrs. Collins continues to teach while presiding over a staff of instructors she has retrained to use her teaching methods. In 1985, with a grant from Prince, the rock star, she founded Westside Prep's National Teacher Training Institute, which seeks to train 1,200 teachers throughout the United States.

Her plans for the future include running a high school and day-care center. Another objective is an adult-education facility because of her belief that many parents need the same education as her students receive.

Her honors include educator-of-the-year awards from Phi Delta Kappa and the Chicago Urban League, a United Negro College Fund Award, the Jefferson Award of the American Institute for Public Service, and designation as Legendary Woman of the World by the City of Birmingham, Alabama.

Howard University, Amherst College, Dartmouth College, and the University of Notre Dame have awarded her honorary doctorate degrees.

You Must Have Goals

"You can do it, all you need to do is remove the 't' from can't and you have can," said four-year old Talmadge to a five-year old, who was a bit ambivalent about attacking the reading of Tolstoy's selection, The Plum Bit.

I have always believed it impossible to put a band-aid on a hemorrhage, and so the very first thing I attempt to do with our students is to teach them self-reliance, self-determination, and the innate belief that "I can't simply means that one refuses to try." Every student at Westside Preparatory School, therefore, is first given an indoctrination as to what the ingredients of a West Side Prepian are.

Each student is taught to believe that life is filled with road markings, and it is our choice as to what marking we choose on this road. For example, we tell them that one road may have the markings, "fun," "play," "drugs," "hard work," "sticktoitiveness," "determination," etc., and it is left up to the individual player in life as to which marking they choose. In other words, the very first lesson our students learn is that there are no free rides in this world and that he or she who rides the back of the tiger usually ends up inside the tiger's mouth.

Therefore, it is not unusual to hear a four-year old say to a hesitant classmate, "You had better finish that work because in this school if you do not work, you do not eat." Ah! There's the rub. Now learning is easy because they have learned the most important rule of all: no pains, no gains, or, the grasp of man or woman is equal to reach.

Thousands of visitors from all over the world come to our Spartan, non-government, non-corporate-funded school to see what they call a miracle. I call it common sense. Ralph Waldo Emerson said, "Man is astounded by common sense," and that is actually what we do here. I expect the very, very best from our students and they always meet that requirement. I expect the very same from our students that I would from the sons and daughters of Harvard and Yale graduates, and I get it.

Visitors are amazed when three and four-year-olds are mastering division, multiplication, and can use vocabulary words that most elite graduate students have never heard of. Not only can the young children use these words, they can also spell and write them. They can supply synonyms, antonyms, and homonyms for the words, too. They can read such great classics as Boadicea, Suetonious, Father Hidalgo, Mary Queen of Scots, Rachel Carson, Dr. Martin Luther King, Jr., Leontyne Price, and other great works.

While many contemporary, heavily funded government aided schools declare our children illiterates and impossible to teach, I develop the attitude that the good teacher makes the "poor" student "good" and the "good" student "superior". I believe that like Pygmalion, I, the teacher,

(Continued on page 260)

LODWRICK M. COOK
Chairman & CEO
ARCO

Lodwrick (Lod) Monroe Cook was born in Castor, La., and was raised in Grand Cane, La. He received BS degrees in mathematics and petroleum engineering at Louisiana State University in 1950 and 1955, the latter coming after a tour of duty in the U.S. Army. Later, while working, he finished an evening MBA program at Southern Methodist University.

His ARCO career began in 1956 as an engineer trainee. He went on to hold various management and executive positions before becoming President in 1985. He became Chairman of the Board and Chief Executive Officer in 1986. Mr. Cook is also Chairman of the Board of Directors of ARCO Chemical Company.

His interests outside the company focus on education, youth and minority programs. He has had a long association with Junior Achievement and serves on the National JA Board of Directors, of which he is a past chairman. His other national volunteer work includes serving as director of the Points of Light Foundation, trustee of the Aspen Institute for Humanistic Studies, and director of the LSU Foundation.

Mr. Cook's California community involvements include serving as chairman of United Way's Alexis de Tocqueville Society, member of the Board of Governors and Executive Committee of the Music Center of Los Angeles County, director of the America-China Society, trustee of the San Diego National Sports Training Foundation, and chairman of the Ronald Reagan Presidential Foundation.

His business interests include serving as director of the Business Roundtable, Business Council, World Affairs Council, Citizens Democracy Corporation and American Petroleum Institute. He is a member of the Board of Directors of H.F. Ahmanson & Company and Lockheed Corporation.

Mr. Cook is married to Carole Diane Cook and has five grown children and three granddaughters.

56

Set Your Sights High

I grew up in a very small town—Grand Cane, Louisiana. It's a wonderful experience for a youth, except for one thing: It's hard to imagine being part of the larger world in any important way. Important things always seem to happen someplace else—in big cities or exotic places around the world.

But, looking back, after many years away from Grand Cane, I can tell you that achievement has nothing to do with where you've come from and everything to do with who and what you become, how you develop your character and talent. Your success ultimately depends on yourself, not your circumstances.

My high school graduating class had only five students, yet it was clear to me that being a good student and a school leader really depended on good work habits and a desire to make a contribution, not class size or elegant buildings. Colleges and employers everywhere seek people with a history of personal commitment, not privilege.

They're also looking for young men and women who have a sense of curiosity about the world. Who could benefit from your help? What activities capture your heart and mind? Science, business, communications, social service? And what institutions or companies are involved in what you like to do?

Careful self-evaluation will lead you to appropriate avenues for your talents and ambitions. The journey will involve no more than the qualities we have discussed—initiative, discipline, curiosity, creativity, diligence and vision.

By doing your best, striving to grow and serve to the extent of your ability, you can travel light years from the humblest beginning. So set your sights high: the world is full of opportunities for service and anxious to make use of your talents.

DENTON A. COOLEY, M.D.
Famous Cardiac Surgeon

One of the world's most successful and celebrated cardiac surgeons, Dr. Cooley is surgeon-in-chief of the Texas Heart Institute. He graduated with highest honors from the University of Texas in 1941 and Johns Hopkins University School of Medicine in 1944. Between 1946 and 1948, he was a captain in the Medical Corps and chief-of-surgery at the 124th Station Hospital in Linz, Austria. After completing surgical training at Johns Hopkins in 1940, he spent a year with Lord Russell Brock in London, where he participated in the first intracardiac operations in England.

Dr. Cooley has been described as the world's most productive cardiac surgeon, as well as one of the most skilled technicians in his field. Even more important, he is an innovator in the field of cardiovascular surgery, constantly revising and improving existing procedures as well as developing new surgical techniques to correct previously inoperable conditions.

In 1969, he became the first surgeon to implant an artificial heart in man. By 1989, Dr. Cooley and his team had performed over 75,000 open heart operations. He has contributed to the development of techniques for repair and replacement of diseased heart valves and is widely known for operations to correct congenital heart anomalies in infants and children.

One of Dr. Cooley's most significant contributions to the field of cardiac surgery and cardiology was founding the Texas Heart Institute in Houston. Within 27 years, since the founding in 1965, the Institute has become a world-renowned leader in research, education and patient care in the field of cardiovascular diseases.

Dr. Cooley is a member or honorary member of over 50 professional societies around the world and a dozen fraternities and clubs. He is the author or coauthor of more than 1,000 scientific articles and several texts. Among his 45 honors are the Medal of Freedom, the nation's highest civilian award, and the Rene Leriche Prize, the highest honor of the International Surgical Society.

Take ACTion

Getting what you want from life is not always easy, but it can be done. You can do it through ACTion, that is,

A chievement
C ourage, and
T enacity.

Achievement begins by setting goals. Setting goals sounds simple, yet most of us never take the time to write down our goals. Most of us, in fact, never even identify goals, or if we do, they are of the New Year's resolution type that we never really plan to achieve.

To establish goals and to set a reasonable time frame for achieving them, you must first assess your resources. Ask yourself what is realistic. Then, take action and evaluate your results. Study success. Ask yourself questions. Who is achieving the goals I want to achieve? What are they doing? Guide yourself down the same path as others who are achieving what you would like to achieve.

Once your goals are set, you need the courage to achieve them, even the courage to fail. As infants, we have this type of courage. Take, for example, a ten-month-old infant who is learning to walk. Falls, injuries and failures occur at a shattering rate, a rate that later in life would discourage almost anyone from learning a new activity. The same can be said for many other activities—learning to ride a bicycle, to roller-skate, and to play competitive sports.

You should always maintain this youthful courage. Do not, in your maturity, become inflexible. The on-set of inflexibility is insidious, almost never recognized by the victim. It occurs when one stops questioning and evaluating—when one takes the ideas and convictions thus far accumulated and settles them in concrete, protecting them from change or modification. A person afflicted by this deadening phase of inflexibility finds new ideas uncomfortable, even a little frightening. He has arranged his mind, his attitudes, his life so that there is no room for expansion—expansion may be risky. He feels safe. But he has stopped growing.

To continue to grow, to overcome the falls, the failures, the obstacles to success, you need tenacity. You need to be able to pursue your goals, even beyond what you perceive are your capabilities. In my opinion, success is earned in the vast majority of instances. Hard work, determination, and self-discipline are the keys to success. A few achieve success through "luck," but I believe that the harder one works, the "luckier" he becomes. Perseverance toward goals usually provides the rewards of success.

You can choose not to *stumble* through life. Just remember to ACT.

Denton A. Cooley

HELEN K. COPLEY
Chairman & CEO
The Copley Press, Inc.

Helen Copley is one of the foremost women executives in America. Besides heading Copley Newspapers, which publishes 11 dailies, 46 weeklies, and one bi-weekly newspaper, she is also publisher of the San Diego Union-Tribune.

Mrs. Copley succeeded to these positions in 1973, upon the death, at age 57, of her husband, James S. Copley. Her courage in overcoming personal hardships, outstanding effort in reorganizing the corporation, her impeccable integrity and humanitarianism earned her the prestigious Horatio Alger Award in 1990.

Born Helen Kinney in Cedar Rapids, Iowa, she graduated from Benjamin Franklin High School there and later attended Hunter College in New York City. She has received honorary degrees from Coe College, Pepperdine University and the University of San Diego.

Mrs. Copley was the first woman elected to the board of directors of the California Chamber of Commerce (1974-1977). She is active in numerous civic, charitable and cultural organizations, as well as patriotic and professional groups. In 1990, she received the Boys and Girls Club of San Diego Golden Achievement Award for meritorious and unselfish service to San Diego and its youth. She is the first woman recipient of this award in the 28 years of its existence.

Mrs. Copley is a trustee of the Howard Hughes Medical Institute and trustee emeritus of Scripps Clinic and Research Foundation in LaJolla, California.

She was appointed to the National Commission on the Observance of International Woman's Year by President Ford in 1975, and was appointed by California Governor Jerry Brown to the Commission on Government Reform in 1976.

Among the scores of awards she's received is the Golden Plate Award from

A Worthy Vocation

I spent a memorable New Year's Eve in West Berlin at the time when the wall had just been torn open between East and West Germany. Everywhere there were toasts to freedom. I was struck by their depth of meaning and feeling.

As a newspaper publisher I feel a deep responsibility toward the development and preservation of freedom for all. Newspapers are a key part of the communication explosion which is now spreading the seeds of freedom in the soil of Eastern Europe.

There is still a question about how the new-found freedom will thrive. It may depend upon how many young Horatio Algers spring forth in the nations where free enterprise has been extinct. In my mind, there is no question that a free press is essential for democratic success at home and abroad.

I urge you to keep informed through our free press. Beyond the electronic media, become an in-depth reader of newspapers, periodicals and books. Take advantage of one of America's most precious resources— your local library. There you can travel the world, share the accomplishments of successful people you can emulate as role models, and you can explore every subject on earth.

I also encourage you to consider journalism as a vocation, and the newspaper field in particular, for your life's work. Not only will it be a self-satisfying experience, it will also enable you to participate in preserving freedom for everyone.

Helen K. Copley

the American Academy of Achievement as one of forty eminent "exemplars of excellence" from the nation's many fields of endeavor.

Mrs. Copley and her son, David, reside in LaJolla, California.

MICHAEL W. COPPS
Chairman & CEO
The Copps Corporation

Michael W. Copps took over as chairman and CEO of The Copps Corporation in 1980. He joined the company in 1970 and climbed the executive ladder while gaining experience in various company functions. He served as real estate and site researcher, personnel director, warehouse superintendent, vice president / warehousing and transportation, and executive vice president / wholesale operations before assuming his present position.

The Copps Corporation is a wholesale and retail food distribution business headquartered in Stevens Point, Wisconsin. The firm distributes grocery products to independent and corporately-owned IGA stores in a 150-mile radius around Stevens Point.

In the early 1980s Copps pulled out of the general merchandise business to concentrate solely on the food business. In six short years, the company built ten new super centers, added significantly to its independent business and doubled sales. They also doubled the size of their distribution facility and are prepared to double business again in the early '90s.

Copps has a bachelors degree and law degree from the University of Wisconsin. He is married with two children, Clint, 16, and Carolyn, 12. His affiliations include serving as a board member of the Independent Grocer's Alliance, Goodwill Industries, and Pacelli Foundation. A Special Olympics ambassador, he is also fund drive chairman for the United Way of Portage County. In 1988, he was named Citizen of the Year by the Stevens Point Chamber of Commerce.

Use Your Ability to Reason

What I want to urge you to consider is exactly the same thing I stress to my own children. The most important gift you have is the ability to reason. You should never act nor should you ever subordinate your thoughts to another person unless it is consistent with your reasoned judgement.

Failure to reason allows bigots and those people preaching prejudices to flourish in various societies. Individuals like Adolph Hitler, James Jones, Saddam Hussein, and countless others, rely on the fact that their following is totally involved emotionally and thus capable of being led without any appeal to reason.

This same sense of reason should apply to your actions in your daily life and chosen profession. First and foremost, you have to listen to yourself over all others, including those whom you consider your superiors. This is the only way you can be accountable and responsible for your actions. You eventually have to say that it is because of the choices I have made that I am where I am and not the choices or forces of someone else. Remember: there is a correlation between your control of your life and your mental well-being.

Other helpful thoughts:

1) The world will definitely let you have what you want. It's an amazing fact, but only five percent of all people in the United States read more than one book a year. That means there is an incredible avenue ahead of you to travel on. A modest amount of discipline will have you surging ahead of the masses. Think of this, there is a proven direct correlation between a large vocabulary and success in any given field. Can you imagine the gift you'll give yourself if you just add a word a day to your vocabulary? It also enhances greatly your power to reason that we talked about above.

2) The strongest language known to mankind is actually unspoken. It's a smile. You'll find that most people who succeed are not power mongers. In fact, they're quite gentle. They intuitively, or by the use of their reason, realize the power and sanctity of a smile. It's appeal is that it shows you as a kind and considerate person. It shows that you respect the dignity of all people, including those below you as well as those above you. If you smile, you're approachable, and its effect is to lay out a red carpet for you to walk on the rest of your life.

3) Do the job that you're doing now to the best of your ability. At various stages in life we all get caught up in some type of job or activity that we don't appreciate. The best advice I can think of is to do the job uncommonly well so that it becomes the stepping stone to the job you do want. A complainer might have a legitimate reason to complain, but if it's

(Continued on page 260)

BOB COSTAS
NBC Broadcaster

Bob Costas began his professional career at WSYR-TV/Radio while studying at Syracuse University in 1973, where he majored in journalism. At age 22 he landed a job at KMOX Radio in St. Louis, Missouri, one of America's most prominent radio stations. He broadcast a wide variety of live, play-by-play, and studio programs for KMOX from 1974 through 1981. One of his primary assignments was play-by-play for the ABA's's Spirits of St. Louis team. He did regional NFL and NBA telecasts for CBS (1976-79) and was the radio voice of the University of Missouri basketball games (1976-81) and the NBA Chicago Bulls (1980).

In 1980 he began his career at NBC Sports, initially as football and basketball play-by-play man. From 1983 through 1989, Costas teamed with analyst Tony Kubek on NBC's baseball "Game of the Week" telecasts, forming one of baseball's most popular broadcasting teams. He has hosted the network's popular "NFL Live" since 1984. Costas has been involved in the coverage of four league championship series and four World Series for NBC. He has hosted Super Bowls XX and XXIII, and was one of the hosts for the 1988 Summer Olympiad XXIV in Seoul, Korea.

Bob won the Emmy Award as Outstanding Sports Broadcaster in 1987 and 1988. He has also been named by his peers as the National Sportscaster of the Year in 1985, 1987, and 1988. When he first won this award in 1985 he was 33—the youngest announcer to be so honored. In 1991, the American Sportscasters Association presented him its Sportscaster of the Year Award.

Beginning in 1988, Bob diversified beyond sports broadcasting. He served as a substitute for Bryant Gumbel on NBC's "Today Show," and now hosts his own late-night program, "Later—With Bob Costas." Bob also hosts a weekly syndicated radio sports talk show, "Costas Coast-to-Coast."

Costas is a native of Queens, New York, who grew up on Long Island. He fell in love with sports as a child while following the New York Yankees'

What Is Success?

One definition of success is to do something you care about as well as you are able to do it.

Too often we view success in terms of the most obvious achievements. The larger salary, the promotion to a more prominent position. Finances and professional standing are valid considerations, of course—up to a point—but, ideally they should be an outgrowth of a job well done, in a field which provides personal satisfaction.

The work I do is very visible work, more likely to draw reactions of approval (or occasionally disapproval) on a larger scale. My wife, on the other hand, taught elementary school for many years. She wasn't just a competent teacher, she was extraordinary. She gave her heart to it. It was an extension of her personality. Hardly a week goes by now without her hearing from a student she taught in kindergarten or third grade. A young person now in high school or college remembers her fondly and appreciates the contribution she made to their life. On her terms, my wife is every bit as successful as I have been on my terms.

My sister is a woman in her 30s. What does she do? She's a clown. That's right, a professional clown. She entertains at children's hospitals, birthday parties, whatever. She dresses up like Emmet Kelly and carries a bag of tricks. Her files bulge with letters of appreciation from the parents of children whose lives she has brightened. Could she make more money and enjoy more prestige of a certain kind doing something else? Sure. Could she be as successful, though? What do you think? What she does is a legitimate way of blending her profession with her heart. There is a warmth and childlike quality about her, in or out of makeup. She has found a way to make who she is a part of her work. She is one of the most successful people I know.

Everyone's circumstances, talents, ambitions, relationships, and obstacles faced are different. My only advice would be to think of success in personal terms and not be constrained by narrow prevailing notions of success which may limit you. Identify a legitimate set of goals that have meaning for you, then pursue them with determination and integrity.

Mickey Mantle. Bob resides in St. Louis, Missouri, with his wife, Randy, and their children, son Keith and daughter Taylor

JOHN DAVID
Executive Chairman
Davids Holdings Pty. Limited

Joe David, father of John David, opened his first grocery store on May 17, 1927, one year after J. Frank Grimes founded the IGA system. John David joined the business on his return from California, in 1955, after receiving his master's degree in food service from the University of California.

Today, Davids Holdings has approximately 15 percent of the grocery business in Australia (chain and wholesale) with 62 warehouses (including Cash & Carrys) throughout the Eastern seaboard of Australia. The company also has strategic shareholding in other wholesalers, including Composite Buyers Ltd., Victoria Foodland Associated Limited, Western Australia, and Independent Holdings Limited, South Australia.

John David is a director of Australian Airlines, immediate past chairman of the Australia Retailer's Association, foundation chairman of the Australian Supermarkets Institute, a director of the Food Marketing Institute (USA), and a director of the Independent Grocers Alliance.

His favorite sport is sailing.

My Dad's Rules

My father, Joe David, was a man of little education. He was the second son of seven children of Lebanese migrants. Joe began his working life as a boy in the coal mines at age 14. He left the mines to work as an itinerant salesman with one of his uncles.

In 1927, he came to Sydney, Australia, and opened a small grocery store at Woolloomooloo. He married and had 12 children. At the time of his death, he headed the largest wholesale grocery operation in Australia and had extensive farming interests in the northern territory.

Joe has been an exciting role model. He was a humble and religious man, who at no time forced his beliefs on his children. He brought up his family and ran his business along very simple lines:

> He was firm, some say hard, but always fair.
>
> He did not discriminate between men and women, or between races or religion, even during an era when such was the norm.
>
> He was scrupulous in his honesty in all matters.
>
> He did not ask anyone to do anything which he had not, or would not, do himself.
>
> He did not praise his children for being good, or doing good, because he expected that from us.
>
> He did, however, criticize if he thought you did not behave correctly.
>
> He did praise his children for achievement at school and university because he believed in the education which he had missed.

Our father encouraged us in our various pursuits—be it in business, religious life, farming, and home life.

We, his children, have all attempted to pass on to our children his rules, and I am happy to say the results are looking good. He would not be disappointed in any of his 12 grandchildren, and we know they will carry on the tradition he began.

Joe David is my best example of You Can Do It!

John J David

WILLIAM E. C. DEARDEN
Chairman of the Board (Retired)
Hershey Foods Corporation

Bill Dearden is a rarity. He's a man who was helped in adversity by his hero, Milton S. Hershey, and then went on to emulate his role model so well that he became head of the empire his late benefactor had built. The odds of that happening are staggering.

When his mother died, Bill's father, an out-of-work Philadelphia factory worker, got him into the Milton Hershey School. It was a wholesome setting for boys who had lost one or both parents and needed financial support.

After graduating from Hershey, where students still live in 85 houses with house parents and must do chores as well as study, Dearden attended Albright College, earning his BS degree in economics. He took graduate work at Harvard and Temple Universities. He served in the U.S. Navy in World War II and the Korean War.

Feeling the need to repay the debt he felt he owed the school for what it had done for him, he left a lucrative corporate career to return to serve the school as assistant business manager. It soon became evident that he was a leader and he joined the Hershey Foods Corporation staff. He proved an outstanding planner and sales executive as he scaled the corporate ladder to the top. Under his leadership, the company moved from being a chocolate and confectionery business to become a major, diversified, international food and food related company.

Dearden's many directorships, awards, honorary degrees and other recognitions (too numerous to mention) reflect perhaps the most important lesson he learned from Milton Hershey—to share with others. He is especially happy when he reads the annual reports of the company's continuing success, knowing the school where he got his start still owns 42 percent of the company stock, while maintaining voting control.

Have a Role Model

Write down on paper what you want to be, what will be required to accomplish your plan/dream, the significant milestones you must successfully pass along the way to be on schedule. Why put it on paper? Because that's the only way you will seriously consider the matter and evaluate the alternatives. You should carry it in your wallet and read it every day to remind you where you want to go.

Once established, you must then pursue your plan/dream with a dedication and single-mindedness that will carry you over the rough spots. You must have the courage to stay with it. This means you must be willing to make the sacrifices and put forth the work to make your plan a reality. It won't be easy, but the rewards of success are second to none.

In all of this it pays to have a role model—a hero—someone whose life and deeds are such an inspiration to you that you want to emulate his/her life. Mine was Milton S. Hershey, the man who developed the Hershey bar and made the name Hershey synonymous with chocolate throughout the United States.

A poor farm boy from a broken home, he only had a fourth grade education, received in eight different schools because his family moved so often. At age 13, he was apprenticed to a candy maker in Lancaster, Pennsylvania, and that is where he found his life's work/dream.

At age 19, he completed his apprenticeship and started his own business in Philadelphia in 1876—our centennial year. During the next ten years he failed miserably in the candy business. He returned to Lancaster in 1886 with only the clothes on his back and was ridiculed as a failure.

Despite the criticism, he was determined to be a successful candy maker and borrowed money to start a fourth time in a loft in Lancaster. To make a long story short, this time he was a huge success—so much that in 1900 he sold his caramel business for $1 million. While in the caramel business, he had been experimenting with chocolate and, at age 46, he broke ground in 1903 in a cornfield that is now Hershey, Pa., for his chocolate factory, investing his $1 million in the new venture.

After a slow start, the business grew and with the profits he built a beautiful community for his employees and visitors. He and his wife founded a school for orphan boys because they could have no children of their own. At the school's dedication in 1909, he said if the school graduated 100 children it would be a good thing. However, his business grew so fast that in 1918 he turned over stock of Hershey Chocolate Company valued at $60 million to a trust for the perpetuation of the school. Today Milton Hershey School has an enrollment of 1,200 boys and

(Continued on page 261)

ARTHUR J. DECIO
Chairman & CEO
Skyline Corporation

Art Decio, of Elkhart, Indiana, heads a leading U.S. producer of manufactured housing and recreational vehicles with 31 operating companies in 14 states from coast to coast.

He has received presidential appointments to three national commissions and has served on the boards of more than 30 civic, religious, business, educational and financial institutions, including the Federal Reserve Bank of Chicago. Decio currently is a trustee and fellow of the University of Notre Dame, a vice chairman of the National Salvation Army Advisory Board, and a director of Special Olympics International, Washington, D.C.; Banc One Indiana Corporation, Indianapolis; NIPSCO Industries, Inc., Hammond, Indiana; and Schwarz Paper Co., Chicago.

His community involvement is extensive. He is president of the Elkhart General Hospital Foundation and the Elkhart Park Foundation, Inc., serves on the advisory boards of Indiana University and Goshen College, and is a member of the Finance Council of the Diocese of Fort Wayne-South Bend.

Born in Elkhart, he attended Marmion Military Academy and DePaul University, Chicago, and holds honorary degrees from the University of Notre Dame and Indiana State University.

Among his many awards are the 1987 Alexis de Tocqueville Award from the United Way of America, Alexandria, Virginia, for outstanding voluntary service to community and country; the Salvation Army's William Booth Award and its Others Award; and the 1984 Career Achievement Award of the National Italian-American Foundation, Washington, D.C.

In 1989, he was the recipient of the Rev. Howard J. Kenna C.S.C. Award from Notre Dame and its founding religious community, and the Rev. John J. Cavanaugh C.S.C. Award for distinguished public service from the Notre Dame Alumni Association. In 1991, he was the first recipient of the Indiana CAUSE Award, presented by the Indiana Association of

Take Advantage of Today

All of us have a choice. We can waste our time reliving yesterday or daydreaming about tomorrow. Or, we can delight in God's great gift— today.

As long as we live, today never will be repeated. It is as unique and fragile as a snowflake. It is 24 hours, 1,440 minutes, 86,400 seconds packed with opportunities.

Our obligation is to take advantage of every second, to make full use of our talents, to never do less than our best.

By being true to ourselves. Each of us is different. Each has been blessed with a special set of interests and attributes. So we must try to understand ourselves and how we fit into the world around us. We must look into our own hearts to learn who we are and what we can be.

By setting goals. Letting life just happen is a formula for failure. We need to decide what we want for ourselves and for all who will be affected by our lives. Then we must outline a plan of action that will bring our goals to reality.

By accepting responsibility. It's easy to blame our problems on our parents or school or society. But blaming others does not solve problems. It only keeps us from seeing the truth. We cannot change others. We can change ourselves.

By increasing our knowledge. The changing world of the 1990s has little room for the uneducated and unskilled. For every person in every walk of life, learning is a lifelong necessity.

By being sensitive to others. All of us were called to help those who are incapable of helping themselves. By listening to others, by sharing our time, energy and resources, we enrich not only them but ourselves.

By strengthening our faith. By giving us today, God opened the door to love and friendship, challenge and adventure, beauty and laughter, to all the treasures of human existence. We cannot return the favor. But we can offer thanks as we work to build a world that lives up to the expectations of all of God's people.

Art Decio

Rehabilitation Facilities. The award was created to recognize an Indiana resident who has made a positive difference for persons with disabilities. Art and his wife, Patricia, have five children.

DR. ARTHUR DeKRUYTER
Founding Pastor
Christ Church of Oak Brook

Arthur DeKruyter was born in Grand Rapids, Michigan, where he was raised by Christian parents who belonged to the Christian Reformed Church.

His religious education began at Calvin College and Calvin Theological Seminary in his home town, where he received his Th.B. Later, Princeton Theological Seminar granted him a Th.M. and Westminster College in New Wilmington, Pennsylvania, conferred a D.D. degree.

Right out of Princeton, he accepted a call to Western Springs Christian Reformed Church in suburban Chicago, where he pastored for over 13 years. In 1965, he was called to found a new church in Oak Brook, Illinois. The parish started with five families. Today, Christ Church of Oak Brook has more than 5,500 members with about 2,300 families. His "Pulpit of Christ Church" has reached television viewers since 1980.

Since 1972, Dr. DeKruyter has been a member of the board of trustees of Fuller Theological Seminary, Pasadena, California. During that period the seminary has become the largest inter-denominational seminary in the world with over 3,000 students. Because of his reputation and interest in preaching, a Preaching Chair has been endowed and named in his honor at Fuller. In 1989 he was appointed Eastern Europe representative of Fuller Seminary with the assignment of the establishment of an ecumenical seminary in the U.S.S.R. He has made several fact-finding trips to the Soviet Union in this capacity. The seminary officially opened in Leningrad in 1990.

Under his leadership, Christ Church of Oak Brook has become known for its creative leadership in the development of mega-church ministries. Each fall ministers come from the entire Midwest to learn about church growth. Dr. DeKruyter has a special interest in young ministers and makes himself available to a growing number of clergy who seek his advice and counsel.

Principles for Productive Living

The experiences of life are never the same. Every day something new happens. Some people welcome change, and other people become very afraid. Some people see trouble and anticipate problems. I encourage you to see life as a constant flow of opportunities. For me there have been five very simple rules for seizing opportunities and making the most of them.

The first one of these rules is: Be Willing to Learn. Early in life I discovered that the people I wanted to associate with were the people who were better than I. In a sport, I discovered that when I played with my superiors I played better. In my profession I have always gone to listen to others who were doing it better than I.

When I discovered that I had some potential abilities, I decided to find someone who could help me by example as well as by precept. I traveled distances to relate to these people. I listened to them, I watched them, I imitated them, and then I found my own identity. The most exciting thing is to learn how to do things in a new and better way.

A second thing to learn is: Never Feel Sorry for Yourself. Feelings of bitterness because one feels very sorry for oneself is one of the worst things that can ever happen. Promise yourself that you will never feel sorry for yourself no matter what the circumstances are. Always look to find something for which to be grateful and thankful. That has kept me out of many troubles, and it has kept a very positive attitude in my mind.

A third thing that I had to learn was: I Am Never Alone. Remember that you are never alone. God is always present with you through his son, Jesus Christ. Talk to him. Listen for his guidance. Take time to study the Bible. Learn to be productive in life, to practice inner peace, and to have great hope for the future. Never start the day without talking to God, asking for his presence, his wisdom, and his guidance. Never go to sleep at night without thanking him for being your friend, for being near to you and giving you wisdom, for forgiving your sins and picking you up when you fail, and for keeping you humble in times of success. One day at a time lived in the presence of God will make all things possible.

A fourth thing that is very important is: Keep Your Sense of Humor. We must be able to laugh not only at others but at ourselves. People who insist on doing everything exactly right and are super-sensitive to the criticisms of others lose the joy of living. They often punish themselves for mistakes. They remember for a long, long time the things that others did that hurt them and the things that failed. Learn to be forgiving and put failures behind you. I continue to learn all the time and discover that by trying again and again things can be accomplished that I thought were impossible. Never give up when you know that what you are working on

(Continued on page 261)

MIKE DITKA
Chicago Bears Coach

Mike Ditka holds the unique distinction of being a Super Bowl champion as a player, assistant coach and head coach.

His career in the National Football League began in 1961 when the Chicago Bears selected him in the first round out of the University of Pittsburgh, where he was an All-American end. He made an instant impact by earning NFL Rookie of the Year honors.

Mike played five more seasons with the Bears, earning a Pro Bowl trip each year. He was known for his intensity. After dislocating his left shoulder, he played the 1964 season in a harness and virtually one-handed caught 75 passes, then an NFL record for tight ends and still an all-time Bears mark.

After two years with the Philadelphia Eagles, he joined the Dallas Cowboys. He played four seasons with Dallas, where he caught a touch-down pass in their 24-3 win over the Dolphins in Super Bowl VI.

As a coach, in nine seasons as a Dallas assistant, Ditka helped the Cowboys win three NFC titles and a Super Bowl. His eight years in Chicago have included three trips to the NFC title game, five division crowns, and a Super Bowl victory.

The final accolade to his outstanding playing career was bestowed upon him in 1988 when he became the first tight end inducted into the Pro Football Hall of Fame.

Ditka is a highly sought after motivational speaker and is actively involved in numerous charitable endeavors including Misericordia, Fellowship of Christian Athletes, Sports Teams Organized for Prevention of Drug Abuse and Say No to Drugs. He has established the Mike Ditka Endowed Scholarship at the University of Pittsburgh.

An avid golfer, he plays in various charity events. He was part of CBS-TV's playoff coverage and played himself in an episode of the popular television series, "L.A. Law."

Conceive, Believe, Achieve

I remember telling the Bears football team back in the fall of 1984, "What your mind can conceive, and your heart will believe, you can achieve."

This is not just an idealistic statement, but rather the motivational factor by which all of us should live. Does it work? The Bears team, which won the Super Bowl in 1985, is evidence that it does.

The human will is a great and powerful force. It enables us to do far more than we feel we are capable of doing.

I truly believe we must set in our mind the goals we want to achieve, then we must find the methods and apply the work ethics that will help us reach these goals.

In order to achieve anything in life, we must make a commitment and have a deep conviction that we will relentlessly pursue our goals. We must exercise great discipline and sacrifice in order to find success. We must be sure that the goals and rewards we seek in life are worth the price we will have to pay. Success does not come easy.

Every single person is a creation of God and has a God-given talent. We must find that talent and then maximize it to the best of our ability. In other words we must be the best we can be.

You can do it, just as I can do it. We can do it and the team can do it.

GRACE E. EASLEY
Poet

Grace E. Easley was born on January 24, 1928, in McComb, Mississippi. Her father worked on the Illinois Central Railroad, and her mother took care of Grace until she died with pneumonia at a very early age.

After that Grace was sent to St. Mary of the Pines, a Catholic boarding school for girls, which was run by the School Sisters of Notre Dame, at Chatawa, Mississippi, near McComb. Her father faithfully visited her every Sunday, always telling her colorful stories of the railroad, to which he devoted his life.

On one occasion, one of Grace's teachers scolded her for spending too much time on her poems, and not enough on her books, to which Grace replied, "I could sooner stop breathing, than I could stop writing." That has remained true until this day.

Grace is a lover of nature, animals and of all things beautiful. Her poems reflect her feelings and have been widely published.

Lesson

They said "you'll never make it,"
And they thought that they were right,
But I kept on plodding onward,
Because I hoped I might.
They shook their heads in wonder,
That I lacked the sense to quit,
But I held my chin up higher,
And I didn't mind a bit.

They said "you'll never make it,"
As the problems multiplied,
But I had to make an effort,
And to know at least I tried.
So I dug my heels in deeper,
Though sometimes my spirits lagged,
And I shouldered what was lightest,
And the rest I sort of dragged.

And I found to my amazement,
At the ending of the day,
That what they said I couldn't,
I had managed anyway.
It only took three little words,
"Lord help me," and I rid
Myself of doubt, and all they said
I'd never do—I did.

Grace E. Easley

JOHN J. EDL
President
Noble Production & Recording, Inc.

John Edl is a successful small businessman who epitomizes what being an entrepreneur is all about. He founded his company with only $400 capital. During the firm's early years, he performed all of the company's research, administrative, development, sales, advertising, promotion and service functions himself. A hands-on technician, he enhanced his knowledge of electronics and business by studying technical manuals, attending seminars, and taking courses offered by companies in his field of interest.

Starting in a one-room home-based studio he developed Noble into a corporate entity which today occupies a 10,000-square-foot facility which houses a full-service photo laboratory, and a state-of-the-art audio-visual communication center which includes a slide imaging resource and full-service bureau.

His current client roster reflects his success with leading companies like Ace Hardware, Shell Oil Company, Boise-Cascade, Lady Remington, Universal Oil Products, ENESCO, McDonald's Corporation, and the Illinois Department of Transportation now among his clientele.

Upon returning from service in the U.S. Air Force following the Korean War, John worked for various companies honing his management, production and service skills. This experience convinced him that he could make it on his own. The rest is history.

Long active in community affairs, Edl served 22 years on the Board of Fire and Police Commissioners in Bensenville, Illinois, where he has lived for 41 years. For 16 of those years he chaired the board which was recognized for its innovation in the development of testing and training programs used throughout Illinois. He created the Fire and Police Commission Manual and other courses still being used at the University of Illinois.

Like most entrepreneurs, John had a special asset—his wife, Elaine, who encouraged him from the start. They functioned as a two-person staff for

78

Entrepreneurial Challenge

Being a successful entrepreneur is one of the most rewarding experiences one can have in life. Aside from the financial rewards, nothing can match the satisfaction and pride that comes from knowing you succeeded on your own.

I think the primary reason that people limit themselves is fear. It's a real demotivator. My success came because I could not afford to fail—so I did not tolerate it. This doesn't mean that I didn't have setbacks and make mistakes, everyone does. I learned from them and kept moving toward my goal.

What keeps a person moving forward? Desire. To be a success on your own you must have a burning, all-consuming desire to realize your dream. You've got to want to reach your goal with such intensity that you are willing to make the sacrifices, and put in the long hours and hard work necessary to achieve your objective.

Lack of education is another bugaboo for many would-be entrepreneurs. In reality, uneducated people pioneered many of the innovative and sophisticated techniques used by today's most progressive companies. Circumstances may preclude your going to college, but don't let the lack of a diploma stop you. Creativity isn't taught in school, it comes from inside you—just let it out. Go for it.

Timing can throw a monkey wrench into your plans. All sorts of great products and ideas have failed because they reached the marketplace at the wrong time. I speak from experience because I was a pioneer in interactive video and got nowhere. While it was a great educational endeavor for me, I was too far in the forefront with a technology that wasn't accepted until years later.

Finally, let me note that the long-standing entrepreneurial challenge to "find a niche and fill it" still applies today. In our gadget oriented world the most over-worked phrase is state-of-the-art. It pertains only to equipment and has nothing to do with skill and experience. It's a fact that 80% of the people who own VCR's, which represent state-of-the-art, can't program the equipment. I found my niche in adapting ever-changing equipment and technology to the needs of the marketplace.

If I could make it as an entrepreneur so can you—if you have the desire to be the best you can be.

John F. Edl

---

several years as she became a *"Jill-of-all-trades,"* handling various company functions until more staff could be hired.

The Edls are good role models for would-be entrepreneurs who are willing to work hard, take risks, and make sacrifices to achieve their goals.

CHRIS EVERT
Professional Tennis Champion

Chris Evert, master of the baseline, was the world's No. 1 ranked seven times during her 16-year professional tennis career that included 18 Grand Slam titles (three Wimbledons, seven French Opens, two Australian Opens and six U.S. Open Championships), before she retired in 1989 at age 34.

Chris won 1,309 matches, holds 157 singles titles, and won at least one Grand Slam singles title for 13 consecutive years, each a record for either men or women in professional tennis history.

In 1985, the Women's Sports Foundation named her "Greatest Women Athlete in the Last 25 Years."

Chris is in her unprecedented ninth term as president of the Women's Tennis Association. She oversees the overall operation of the player's organization and helps coordinate the activities of more than 1,500 players.

In 1990, she was among nine Women of the Year selected by Glamour Magazine in honor of her outstanding commitment to social causes. Chris serves as spokesperson for Clean Start, the public/private funded program to help drug addicted pregnant women and their babies. She organized and hosted the Chris Evert/Phar-Mor Celebrity Tennis Classic which raised nearly $1 million to benefit the program. It is administered through Chris Evert Charities, Inc. and the Governor of Florida. Chris also raised $350,000 to build a drug treatment center in Delray Beach, Florida.

A board member of the President's Council on Physical Fitness and Sports, she was presented the Flo Hyman Award by President George Bush in 1990 in recognition of her contributions to sports.

Chris is married to Andy Mill, the former Olympian and No. 1 American skier for seven years. The Mills welcomed their first child, Alexander, October 12, 1991.

Have a Passion in Life

My dad, Jimmy Evert, a teaching tennis pro, thought tennis provided a wholesome atmosphere to raise his five children. In between teaching us how to hit ground strokes and two-handed backhands, he sprinkled in some fatherly advice that has helped me on and off the court.

"Never lose your temper" was a cardinal rule. I've seen some big matches lost and meaningful relationships broken because a person became upset. Learn to control your temper by realizing that it's not the situation that angers you—it's your reaction to the situation. I remembered that even on center court at Wimbledon.

Sports provide a natural high. Drugs cannot match the feeling one gets in winning a hard-fought match. Tennis, in particular, is most exhilarating because you're on your own—no one can make the shots for you.

Sports and other special interests offer you ways to avoid drugs and crime. I believe everyone should have a passion in life, especially kids. Mine was tennis. You should have a reason to wake up each morning—some activity that makes you stretch to your own limit.

Doing something worthwhile, working hard and doing it well breeds confidence. When you're confident any reasonable goal is within your reach—go for it!

Chris Evert

BOB FELLER
Baseball Hall of Famer

Robert William Feller was born on November 3, 1918, in Van Meter, Iowa. He played baseball throughout his grade school and high school years. In his spare time, Bob played catch with his father, which helped to develop a pitching arm capable of throwing a baseball at over 100 miles per hour.

Bob played four years of American Legion baseball, as well as amateur and semi-professional ball, before signing with the Cleveland Indians at age 16. In his first start, he struck out 15 St. Louis Browns. Later the same year, he fanned 17 Philadelphia Athletics, setting a new American League record. In 1938, he established a new major league record by striking out 18 Detroit Tigers.

Two days after the Japanese attack on Pearl Harbor, he enlisted in the United States Navy. He served three years aboard the USS Alabama, earning eight Battle Stars. After his discharge, Bob returned to the Indians and soon established an American League record of 348 strikeouts in a single season, pitched three no-hit games and 12 one-hitters.

The first pitcher in major league history to win 20 or more games before age 21, he played in nine All-Star games, two World Series, and was elected into baseball's Hall of Fame in 1962. In 1969, he was selected "Greatest Living Right-Hand Pitcher" as part of Professional Baseball's Centennial Celebration.

He has authored three books, Strikeout Story, How to Pitch *and* Now Pitching. *Feller and his wife, Anne, live in Gates Mills, Ohio. Bob heads the Cleveland Indians Speakers Bureau, takes part in various baseball promotion events, and is involved in numerous corporate activities.*

Disposition Is Important

There are a lot of things that go into the makeup of a baseball player. One seldom-noted attribute is disposition.

Physical assets, such as the ability to hit a ball hard, to throw with speed and accuracy, and to run fast, are all necessary. But, without proper disposition, the athlete blessed with natural ability will not make the grade in the major leagues.

The disposition of a pitcher can often be most accurately measured by watching how he pitches when he is behind and is apparently pitching for a losing cause. Baseball scouts will not make up their minds on a young pitcher in the minor leagues until they see how he pitches when he's getting beat.

Disposition means a person is industrious. In baseball they call industriousness "hustle." It's a word players hear every minute, every hour of the day in spring training—and through the season. Some otherwise worthy players never make it to the big leagues because they have the wrong disposition.

The late Lou Fonseca, one-time American League batting champion and an excellent batting instructor, often used Ty Cobb as an example to young players he spoke to in clinics. Most people don't realize that Cobb was not a great natural hitter. He studied opposing pitchers and players. He studied himself and made adjustments in his batting stance, even developed his famous "hands-apart" grip on the bat. His concentration on a winning performance was so steady, so relentless, that it made a great difference in this great player.

I suggest all young people develop a good disposition toward everything they do. With the proper attitude and "hustle" you can be a success. It is only with the proper disposition that you will gather the strength to meet the stresses and crucial moments that come to all human beings.

Bob Feller

GERALD R. FORD
38th U.S. President

President Ford was born in Omaha, Nebraska, and raised in Grand Rapids, Michigan. He worked his way through the University of Michigan by serving nurses and interns in the university hospital and washing dishes at his fraternity, DKE. He earned his varsity M on three Michigan football teams, including the 1932 and 1933 national champions.

After earning his Bachelor of Arts degree from Michigan, he went on to Yale to earn a degree in law. While there, he served as assistant football coach and freshman boxing coach.

In 1942, after a brief stint in the law profession, he entered the U.S. Navy, serving almost four years during World War II, and participated in 3rd and 5th Fleet operations aboard the aircraft carrier USS Monterey for two years in the Pacific theater. He was discharged in 1946 as a Lt. Commander.

In 1948, he married Elizabeth Bloomer. They are the parents of four children and are the grandparents of five granddaughters.

President Ford was elected to the U.S. House of Representatives in 1948 and re-elected every two years through 1972, serving 25 years in the House. He was elected Chairman of the Republican Conference in 1963 and chosen Minority Leader in 1965.

In November, 1963, President Lyndon Johnson appointed him a member of the Presidential Commission investigating the assassination of President John F. Kennedy. He subsequently authored (with John R. Stiles) Portrait of the Assassin *(1965).*

President Ford was nominated vice president to succeed Spiro T. Agnew, who resigned. He succeeded to the presidency following the resignation of Richard M. Nixon, serving from August 9, 1974, to January 20, 1977.

Since leaving the White House, President Ford has lectured at 178 colleges and universities. His autobiography, A Time To Heal, *was published in*

Be True to Yourself

I can't stress enough how important this period of time is in your life. By forming good morals and learning the meaning of right and wrong now, you are forming a pattern that will follow you throughout life.

I encourage you to set goals and strive for excellence in all you do. The experience, knowledge, and discipline you acquire during your youth will be of immeasurable benefit in your adult life and how you affect this nation and its people.

I have had the privilege of working closely with Mrs. Ford raising funds for the Betty Ford Center for Alcohol and Drug Abuse. I have seen first-hand how alcohol and drugs can affect one's life. It is so easy to slip into dependency; therefore, I ask you not to give into peer pressure. It's okay to say NO! Celebrate your life by being true to yourself.

Warmest, best wishes for success and happiness now and in the future.

Gerald R. Ford

1979. The Gerald R. Ford Library, in Ann Arbor, Michigan, and the Gerald R. Ford Museum, in Grand Rapids, Michigan, were dedicated in 1981. President Ford has always been very active in various charitable events and is the recipient of numerous awards and honors from many civic organizations. Numerous public and private colleges and universities have bestowed honorary doctor of law degrees on the former president.

PAUL FULLMER
President
Selz, Seabolt & Associates

His first "real" present was a typewriter. Paul Fullmer's parents were right on target with the gift because he never wavered from a writing career.

Like most youngsters, he loved sports. But, Fullmer soon realized that he wasn't going to be a great athlete (bad eyes and no speed were just two of the reasons!). So, sports reporting in high school was a natural outlet for Paul and the new typewriter.

He started covering the sports teams of his high school (Immaculate Conception in Elmhurst, IL) for the school paper, and soon began writing, too, for the local weekly paper. By his senior year he also was covering the conference for the dailies and the Catholic weekly in Chicago.

Notre Dame was next and he had his eye on a sportswriting career until he interviewed with Thomas Stritch (nephew of the former Cardinal in the Chicago Archdiocese and head of the Notre Dame Journalism Department), who quickly informed Fullmer, "We don't turn out sportswriters here. If you plan to be successful here, you'll learn to be a good all-around journalist." He did that, but he also served as sports and associate editor of the Scholastic, Notre Dame's weekly news magazine.

After graduation in 1955, he worked for two years as a reporter and columnist at the Aurora, IL Beacon-News, before joining the Chicago-based public relations firm, Selz, Seabolt & Associates, Inc.

Fullmer has worked for the same firm for more than 30 years, and was elected president in 1979. Selz, Seabolt was a founding member of Pinnacle Worldwide, an international consortium of independent public relations firms, and Fullmer was elected to a two-year term as Pinnacle president in 1990. He also is the former president of the Chicago Chapter of the Public Relations Society of America.

Active in civic and charitable organizations, Fullmer has served as chairman of the Junior Board of the National Conference of Christians and Jews in Chicago, president of the Notre Dame Club of Chicago,

"Fast Track"

Young people spend a lot of time talking about the "fast track." How long should I stay in this position? Should I jump to another company? What about the big move cross-country to a new and exciting challenge?

In short, they focus on the positive side of mobility and quick advancement. Seldom do they examine the downside of the equation.

This is even more critical today in a more sluggish economy. In this era of corporate restructuring, leveraged buyouts, downsizing and mergers, senior management may well be looking for a real sense of old-fashioned LOYALTY.

Many fast track young professionals have been caught in the "last in, first out" crunch. What had been the fast track quickly became the last track. They don't have friends or even more importantly, mentors, to help position them in the new structure.

As one of the rare breed who has spent nearly his entire professional life with one organization, I strongly believe that the majority of young people can build their own version of the fast track without job hopping.

My advice to young people has always been to identify with an organization that provides an opportunity to learn—to grow professionally. Do not accept a position or a promotion unless you can learn a great deal from your boss. It's important, therefore, for you to find out during the interview how much time your future boss will have to work with you. If the response is, "As soon as you get up to speed, you can run your own ballgame," that job isn't for you. All you'll do is run in place and repeat the same mistakes.

If the boss indicates you'll work as a team and outlines challenges that are interesting, you're onto something good. That's when you begin to build your own "fast track" within the organization. Work to free your boss of details so he/she can concentrate on the bigger picture.

There are very few superstars in this world. And, there are even fewer shortcuts. There's no substitute for common sense, a smile, hard work, persistence and loyalty. To me that is the "fast track"—to business success and personal satisfaction.

Paul Fullmer

treasurer of its Scholarship Foundation for 20 years, board chairman of St. Mary's Academy in Nauvoo, IL, and founding member and chairman of Amate House (a young adult volunteer organization in Chicago). He is married to the former Sandra Clifford, an amateur golf champion. They have two children, Monica and David.

GEORGE GALLUP, JR.
Chairman
The George H. Gallup
International Institute

Besides serving as co-chairman of The Gallup Organization, Inc., George Gallup, Jr. is presently chairman of The George H. Gallup International Institute and executive director of the Princeton Religion Research Center.

He was born in Evanston, Illinois, on April 9, 1930. In addition to his BA degree (Department of Religion / Princeton University), he also holds six honorary degrees.

This percentage specialist inherited a passion for facts and figures from his late father, who pioneered opinion polling. His professional activities cover the fields of health / drug and alcohol abuse, survey research, education, children and youth, religion and public affairs.

Gallup is chairman of the board of the Quill and Scroll Honorary Journalism Society, an honor society for high school journalists. He also serves on a score of other boards in the professional areas in which he works.

He loves the theatre and has performed in more than 40 theatrical productions over the last 30 years, mostly Gilbert and Sullivan. His favorite sport is soccer, which he played and coached until age 45. Presently, he is an eager but unskilled tennis player.

Gallup has written numerous articles on survey research, religion, health, urban problems and many other topics. His ten books include Varieties of Prayer *(1991) and* The People's Religion *(1989).*

Anyone Can Be a Success

The best way for me to respond is to share our discoveries from a national Gallup Poll on the topic of "success." The survey was based on a sample of 1,000 persons listed in Marquis' *Who's Who in America*, and reported in a book called *The Great American Success Story,* published by Dow Jones Irwin in 1986.

One of the lessons of this book (which I wrote with my brother, Alec, and William Proctor) is that anyone can be a success. Although many people automatically assign themselves to the status of an also-ran, the results of our study show that most of us have the potential to be high achievers. For example, common sense, which high achievers consider the most important personal characteristic for success, is something upon which we all draw.

Also, successful people place a lot of importance on old-fashioned virtues and list hard work, the desire to excel, goal setting, and caring about others, as essential to achieve success.

One of the happiest surprises for me was that the achievers we interviewed are not overly aggressive or insensitive people who are only out for "number one." In our society, we tend to admire the wheeler-dealer who scores by aggressive but not necessarily admirable behavior. In contrast, our survey respondents prove that personal success often involves a great social consciousness as well. They care about others, they volunteer their time to aid the needy, and the large majority give money to charity.

George Gallup, Jr.

LEONARD A. GENTINE
Chairman
Sargento Incorporated

Leonard A. Gentine is a man who has achieved success in the true spirit of American entrepreneurship. At one time he was running a funeral parlor, a mink ranch, and a mail-order cheese business, all at the same time—and all were doing well!

He was born and raised in Milwaukee, the only child of a French immigrant father and Wisconsin farm girl mother. His father insisted that he learn a trade so his formal education ended with high school and he went to work in a Milwaukee factory. He became interested in the mortuary business while moonlighting as a $4-a-day hearse driver for a local funeral home. Leonard applied for a mortuary apprenticeship and completed a two-year course at the Wisconsin Institute of Mortuary Science, while continuing to work nights at the Falk Corporation.

With limited resources, he and his wife, Dolores, went into the funeral business in Plymouth. Gentine commuted 60 miles to work each day to work the night shift on his factory job until the funeral home was solvent.

His entrepreneurial spirit led him into taking a short course in genetics and becoming interested in mink ranching. Before long he was operating a 10-acre farm with 250 head of mink.

Capitalizing on the popularity of Wisconsin cheeses, he launched a deli and mail order cheese business from a carriage house behind his funeral home in Plymouth. Four years later, he founded the Sargento Cheese Company in 1953.

The packaged cheese product caught on. Sales soared. More product innovations followed and today Sargento ranks as the second largest-selling brand of natural cheese in America's supermarkets.

Opportunities Await You

People often say that there just aren't as many opportunities today as there were 50 years ago. I don't agree.

I think young men and women are better prepared, better fed, and better educated than my generation. And while career opportunities have changed, the important thing is that the opportunities are there. It's up to you to explore them and to find your place—your niche—in the business world.

You may have to take a few risks along the way, but the risks are worth taking. The road to success is lined with a few failures, but look on those as experiences, not failures.

It has been said that there's no substitute for experience and I can vouch for that. My career path took a very winding route which is another way of saying that I had more than my share of different jobs. And that's the lesson learned. Look on every job experience as a positive forward step in your career path.

I don't care if you're bagging groceries or delivering pizza during your summer break, take the approach that this is going to be your permanent job—your career job. Keep in mind that the mere fact that you'll be dealing with different kinds of people, in different environments, in different situations, is going to help you. It's going to give you better insight on how people react in different situations and it will prepare you for the decisions you'll be called upon to make later in life.

Don't be afraid to change directions in your career. Just because you're a graduate engineer, for example, doesn't mean you shouldn't take a sales job. I'm not advocating job-hopping, but I am suggesting that you not close the door to any opportunity.

Don't expect to find the perfect job, because it probably doesn't exist. And don't be afraid to take risks as long as you have confidence in your abilities. You can do it!

Leonard A. Genthner

CONGRESSMAN FRED GRANDY
U.S. Representative
Sixth District, Iowa

Fred Grandy, elected in 1986, is in his third term of serving the Sixth Congressional District of Iowa. His district is the second largest producer of corn and soybeans in the nation.

Grandy, a Republican, became the ninth Iowan ever to become a member of the prominent House Committee on Ways and Means when he was appointed in January, 1991. The committee, responsible for all federal revenues, has jurisdiction over issues ranging from taxes, the budget, and trade to social security, medicare, and health care. In 1989, he became the first Iowan ever appointed to the House Ethics Committee.

After only four years in Congress, Grandy is recognized as a leader of domestic issues. As a former member of the House Agriculture Committee, he was a major contributor to the 1990 Farm Bill (the five-year blueprint for U.S. agricultural policy) and authored major groundwater legislation which was incorporated into the bill.

While Grandy has been active for Iowa's concerns, he has also introduced important legislation to improve health care and education. He has received awards for his continued support of American business and his voting efforts to reduce the federal budget.

Grandy was born in Sioux City in 1948. He received his bachelor's degree in English literature with high honors from Harvard in 1970. His public service began as a legislative aide and speech writer for U.S. Rep. Wiley Mayne (R-Iowa), who represented Grandy's home district.

Following his tenure with Rep. Mayne, Grandy pursued his long-time ambition in the theatre. He appeared in several successful off-Broadway plays and two films. In 1975, Grandy began his role as "Gopher" on the television hit series, The Love Boat.

Grandy is married to novelist Catherine Mann.

Something Greater than Self

When I attended the 25th reunion of my high school class, I was astounded so many people in their early 40s were growing old, getting fat and becoming bald. And the men didn't look much better.

I thought if they look this way to me how must I look to them? This was such a terrifying revelation that my first impulse is to advise all young people: If any of you are thinking of growing up, reconsider.

Then I paused and reflected upon the sight of my classmates at mid-life and I was comforted. Because everything I witnessed confirmed the teachings around which I molded my life. I refer to the wisdom of Lennon—John, not Vladimir—who said life is what happens when we are making other plans. My friends and companions in the class of 1966 did not meet my expectations or their own. Thank goodness.

There was the kid from Nevada, Iowa, who had planned to be a doctor and discovered halfway through medical school that he couldn't stand to be around things that were sick. So what became of him? He is now one of the premier elephant trainers in the United States and currently in charge of large animals at the National Zoo in Washington, D.C. More important, he loves what he's doing. So does the guy who most of us believed would be the first among us to make the FBI's Ten Most Wanted list. He was a disappointment, too. In the 25 years he's been loose in the world, he has gone from cab driver to cardio-vascular surgeon.

Then there was the round-faced kid from Sioux City. He planned on being a big shot lawyer until he took the law school entrance exam—and got a score that wouldn't have gotten him into a good bowling league. He bounced around in show business for 15 years before deciding to try his hand at politics and public service.

As someone whose life has been a mysterious combination of careful planning and complete accident, I can say that certain things will probably be revealed to you when you least expect it. William Butler Yates called it "heaven blazing into the mind," James Joyce referred to it as an epiphany, Luke Skywalker knew it as The Force. I can only describe it as a moment when that which has been confusing becomes clear, and that decision which was opaque becomes obvious.

Let me illustrate with an example from my own life. In early 1986, when I was exploring my candidacy for Congress, I found myself in a high school gym in Paullina filled with angry farm families who were not enthusiastic about listening to a Hollywood actor discuss the crisis in agriculture. I was despondent, even before confronting this hostile audience, because political pundits in Washington were giving me only a 30 percent chance of winning.

I plunged into my speech, took a few questions from the crowd, then feeling utterly defeated, headed for my car. I was approached by an 18-

(Continued on page 262)

HORACE GRANT
Basketball Player
Chicago Bulls

Horace Grant played a key role for the Chicago Bulls as the team won its first NBA championship in 1990-91.

The former Clemson University star was the Bulls second first-round draft pick in 1987. During his four years with the Bulls he improved his regular season record each year and had an impressive showing in the playoffs as the Chicago team topped the L.A. Lakers for the title.

He played in all 17 playoff games, shooting .583 from the field (91-156) and .733 from the foul line (44-60) while pulling down 138 rebounds. In the five-game series against the Lakers, he shot .627 (32-51) and hit nine of 12 foul shots. He had 39 rebounds and scored 73 points, a 14.6 average per game.

Off-court, Horace is a dedicated family man and Christian. A few questions provide an insight into him as a person.

What are you most proud of in your life? My wife, Donna, and son, Horace, Jr.

What is the last book you read? Joshua.

What three words describe you best? Loving, understanding and considerate.

What would you do if you had more time in your day / life? Spend time with the homeless in our country and tell them that God loves them.

What is your secret ambition? To someday live to see world peace.

Faith Makes Champions

Winning the NBA Championship as a member of the Chicago Bulls is my biggest thrill in sports. But I know only too well that yesterday's championship means little today.

I have much to be grateful for, a lot to still learn, but I do know the most important asset a person can have—faith in God. It gives one faith in self and others. It's like a dynamo—faith makes champions!

In the midst of celebrating our victory, the Bulls took time to say a prayer of thanksgiving. Prayer was a part of our team throughout the season. We don't pray for any special favors because God doesn't take sides. We just pray the prayer Jesus taught His disciples. We figure that what happens on the court will be right. We pray "as though everything depends on God and then go out and play as though everything depends on us as a team." That's what happened in the crucial series with the Detroit Pistons—our faith helped us keep focused and we swept the two-time defending NBA champions.

I give God complete credit for the wonderful life I have. I believe prayer is the key to successful living and I want my children to grow up with that knowledge.

Horace Grant

JAMES P. GRANT
Executive Director
UNICEF

James P. Grant has been UNICEF's executive director and an under-secretary of the United Nations since 1980.

Born in China in 1922, he received a B.A. from Berkeley in 1943 and a Doctorate in Jurisprudence from Harvard in 1951. His long career in the field of development began with service in China in 1946-47 for the United Nations Relief and Rehabilitation Administration.

In the 1950s and 1960s, he held a succession of high-level positions with the U.S. Agency for International Development and the State Department, and served as president of the Overseas Development Council from its establishment in 1969 through the beginning of his tenure at UNICEF.

He has received numerous honorary degrees from American and foreign universities, as well as awards for his work for Third World development and the world's children.

He says his biggest satisfaction (aside from the births of his three sons) was helping to bring the world together for children at the World Summit for Children, which took place on September 30, 1990. It was the largest gathering of world leaders ever to assemble and discuss any issue, and they committed themselves to providing all children, everywhere, with a better life.

Never Stop Asking Why

Most healthy children, at around age two or three, go through a period sometimes referred to as "the whys," when they constantly bombard their parents with questions about why things are the way they are. No answer seems to satisfy children in this stage of innocent inquisitiveness, often to the exasperation of adults.

A few months later the "why" phase is over. I suspect that, all too often, it is because children soon learn through bitter experience that grownups get uncomfortable or even angry when asked too many questions—especially hard-to-answer questions about why the world is as it is.

My colleagues and I at UNICEF have never gotten over "the whys."

We look at the world in which one out of every five people—over a billion human beings—lives in dire poverty and we ask "why?" We ask why it is that every day 40,000 children die of largely preventable causes. We ask why more than 100 million children are denied primary education and more than 30 million live on the streets. We ask about military budgets, about environmental destruction, about bias against women and girls, about foreign aid that doesn't aid people.

I would like to invite young people to join us in asking these and other critical questions as we approach the 21st century, for you will be inheriting the planet—whatever shape it may be in—from the adults of the last decade of the 20th century. The problems we face may be complex and immense, but their solution starts with each one of us asking "why?" Young people make the best activists because of their energy, enthusiasm, and ability to imagine better ways of doing things.

I urge you to continue asking the hard questions and challenging the adult world to provide sensible answers. It's your right—and our responsibility.

James P. Grant

LT. GEN. HOWARD D. GRAVES
Superintendent
U.S. Military Academy

On July 22, 1991, Lieutenant General Howard Dwayne Graves became the 54th superintendent of the U.S. Military Academy, West Point, N.Y.

Born in Roaring Springs, Texas, General Graves grew up in the Texas panhandle, in and around Amarillo. He graduated from the U.S. Military Academy in 1961 with a Bachelor of Science degree and a commission as a second lieutenant in the Corps of Engineers. After graduation, he attended Oxford University in England for three years as a Rhodes Scholar, where he earned Bachelor of Arts, Master of Arts and Master of Letters degrees.

General Graves has broad experience as a commander of military units and installations. In Washington, at the national command level, he has held several key joint service assignments. Those include military assistant to the Secretary of Defense; vice director of the Joint Staff; and assistant to the chairman of the Joint Chiefs of Staff. In the latter assignment, he served as the principal military representative in critical international negotiations.

In addition to his academic work at Oxford University, he served as an instructor, assistant professor and associate professor at West Point. As commandant of the Army War College, he was responsible for the final level of professional military education for senior officers of the Army, including many who held key command and staff positions in Operation Desert Storm.

Among General Graves' military awards are the Defense and Army Distinguished Service Medals, the Defense Superior Service Medal, the Legion of Merit with Oak Leaf Cluster, and three Bronze Star Medals. He is also a master parachutist.

General Graves and his wife, the former Gracie P. Newman, have two children. Gigi (Mrs. Eric Kail) is a graduate of Georgia State University. Greg, a graduate of the Military Academy's Class of 1988, is an Army first lieutenant currently stationed at Fort Carson, Colorado.

Try and Don't Quit

On June 14, 1911, Dwight D. Eisenhower climbed the long hill from the little railway station at West Point to the administration building where his initiation process began. This is how he described it:

> My main impression of that first day was one of bewilderment and calculated chaos. By the end of the day we were all harassed and, at times, resentful, shouted at all day by self-important upperclassmen, telling us to run here and run there, pick up our clothes, bring in that bedding, put our shoulders back, keep our eyes up, and to keep running, running, running. I suppose that if any time had been provided to sit down and think for a moment, most of us would have taken the next train out. But no one was given much time to think.

Eisenhower made it through that day and four years at West Point and went on to make historic contributions to world history. Like him, thousands of other young people, myself included, have endured that first day at West Point with all its frustrations and self-doubts. Now, years later, as Superintendent of West Point, I can see myself again and again as new cadets enter, each filled with doubts about whether they can do it. But, before even the first day passes, they have surprised themselves by how much they can do. And as they keep trying, their confidence keeps growing. Of course, some don't make it; but it is because they don't want to. Those youngsters who refuse to quit nearly always make it.

Another opportunity for me to see the power of determination is when the West Point cadets sponsor the Special Olympics. The cadets cheer on the young athletes who give their all to compete well, and after the race is run the hugs they share are a simple, deeply-felt reward for their determination. When Special Olympians surpass their innate potential, they have achieved in their own way more than some world-class athletes. And, the cadets who have encouraged these athletes have also achieved something of great worth. Greatness is measured in many ways.

If you try and don't quit, you will achieve great things, I am sure of it. How will you measure that greatness? I hope by how many people you have helped, not by how many things you acquired; by the high moral standards you followed, not by a lack of them; by a humble trust in God, not by avoiding Him. The prophet Isaiah taught us long ago the secret to great achievements: "Even youths grow tired and weary, and young men stumble and fall; but those who hope in the Lord will renew their strength. They will soar on wings like eagles, they will run and not grow weary, they will walk and not be faint."

H.R. Graves

DR. JOHN HAGGAI
Founder & President
Haggai Institute for
Advanced Leadership Training

The son of a Christian immigrant who fled his native Syria during Turkey's harassment in 1912, Dr. John Haggai makes his home in Atlanta, Georgia. But his field of operation is the world. Dr. Haggai, founder and president of Haggai Institute for Advanced Leadership, and his associates (American and Asian) established the institute to provide advanced training for credentialed Third World Christian leaders in culturally relevant methods of evangelization in their own nations. The institute maintains a permanent training facility in neutral Singapore and plans a second major training facility, scheduled to open in 1993, on the Hawaiian island of Maui.

An alumnus of Moody Bible Institute (named Alumnus of the Year in 1975) and Furman University, Dr. Haggai holds four honorary degrees, the latest received in 1991 from Korea's Han Nam University.

His first book, How To Win Over Worry, *has been a best-seller since 1959, eclipsing the two million mark. Additional books include* My Son Johnny, New Hope for Planet Earth, The Leading Edge, The Steward, How To Win Over Loneliness, How To Win Over Pain, How To Win Over Fear, Be Careful What You Call Impossible *and* Lead On!.

Dr. Won Sul Lee, for 13 years the secretary general of the Association of International University Presidents, has dubbed Haggai "the leader of leaders." And as he leads the globe-encircling Haggai Institute, he builds bridges between the East and the West—between cultures, creeds, and countries.

Lovers and Leaders

I define leadership as the discipline of deliberately exerting special influence within a group, to move it toward goals of beneficial permanence that fulfill the group's real needs.

Many people associate the exertion of influence with power. To them, the strong leader so captivates the minds of others that they follow him (or her) without a murmur.

But I doubt if this so-called "strong leader" can be relied upon to select goals of beneficial permanence. Someone who sees strength as the *sine qua non* of leadership will often prefer immediate goals geared to his own self-aggrandizement.

So what motivates good leadership, if not power? My answer is: love.

Love, because the leader deals not with hardware (like a mechanic) or with ideas (like a philosopher) but with *people*. Power-holders (and many leaders today are just that) deal with others on an I-it basis. They aim to gain influence or popularity by being invulnerable. Love-givers (if I may use that term) do the opposite: they serve the needs of the group, and in doing so expose themselves to the danger of rejection.

To talk about love in leadership might sound sloppy. But a moment's thought will show that true leadership is impossible *without* love.

The love I'm talking about goes beyond emotion. It is an act of the will. A world leader once said to me, "John, to do what you do, you must have a great love for the Third World." I replied, "If you're talking about feelings I have to tell you I feel no more love for the Third World right now than I do for this desk. But yes, I have great love for the Third World!"

Love is a military commander risking his life for his men.

Love is a corporate CEO improving safety standards in his factories.

Love is a busy professional using precious time off to look after a neighbor's handicapped child.

Love is practical.

Ultimately, it's only the leader who loves who will gain respect.

Of course love is also a high-risk form of leadership. To love truly (whether your spouse, your children, or your employees) you must accept the possibility of being hurt. I find it highly significant that a person I rate the greatest leader to all suffered exactly this fate, becoming a "man of sorrows, despised and rejected." I mean, of course, our Lord Jesus Christ.

(Continued on page 262)

T. MARSHALL HAHN, JR.
Chairman & CEO
Georgia-Pacific Corporation

A native of Lexington, Kentucky, Hahn graduated Phi Beta Kappa from the University of Kentucky with a bachelor of science degree in physics at the age of 18. He had earned his Ph.D. from the Massachusetts Institute of Technology by the time he was 22—after a two year tour of duty in the Navy.

After graduating from MIT, Hahn held a variety of positions, including head of the nuclear-accelerator laboratory at the University of Kentucky, chairman of the Physics Department at Virginia Tech and dean of arts and sciences at Kansas State University.

He was president of Virginia Tech when he was 35. During his 13 years there, he helped build the university into a major educational center and nearly tripled enrollment.

Hahn was elected to Georgia-Pacific's board of directors in 1973 while still at Virginia Tech. In 1975, he joined the company as executive vice president and was elected president the following year. He became chief executive officer in 1983, and added the responsibilities of chairman of the board in 1984—the titles he holds today.

Hahn has been recognized by industry securities analysts as the top CEO for both the forest product and lumber industry as well as the paper industry in recent years. He is active in business and civic activities at both the national and local levels. He is a director and former chairman of the American Paper Institute, serves on the Business Council of Georgia, and is a member of the Conference Board.

Never Stop Learning

Today's highly structured society has led to perceived decline in the importance of individual responsibility and initiative. Certainly, more than our forefathers, we consider ourselves more members of a group rather than individuals in today's organizations, corporations, and communities. With our problems so complex and our organizations so large, young people may feel that their ideas or individual contributions have little impact. Yet the future of our nation, and perhaps the world, rests with you as individuals.

As most of us have known since we were very young, there is a great deal of social pressure to conform. Yet the major accomplishments in our entire history have been achieved largely by people who were highly individualistic—who did not behave according to the standard of their class, their people, or their time.

That has been the story of many of the world's great scientists, philosophers, and political leaders who started with the courage of their convictions and ended up leading the world into new frontiers of knowledge or accomplishment. Perhaps the most important component of individual success, however, is the ability to inspire others toward accomplishing shared dreams, to enhance individual effort through teamwork.

With our shared goals we have built hospitals, schools, and communities as well as industries, believing that the only way we could succeed was together—as individuals working together to build our great nation.

The ability to fully develop and utilize our skills—both as individuals and as members of a team—begins with education. The most complex challenge facing our nation's educational institutions and its businesses is preparing our workforce and our workplaces for today's and tomorrow's intensely competitive environment. While I am optimistic that the next decade will be a period of great economic opportunity, there is mounting concern that we will not have the traditional abundant supply of effective workers needed to fuel the growth.

Georgia-Pacific's modern plants and mills provide an excellent example. Our facilities are well equipped with state-of-the-art control systems that provide information on quality, production costs, and scheduling. They are systems that require a multi-faceted and well-educated workforce. There is concern because it is estimated that by the end of this decade three of four jobs will require more than a high school education. That means we must have a workforce that is better educated and better trained than any before it, with willingness to change and to continue the educational process.

Our future leaders can not afford to breathe a sigh of relief upon graduation and figure that their learning days are over. Tomorrow's

(Continued on page 262)

MONTY HALL
TV Producer/Humanitarian

Monty Hall was born in Winnipeg, Manitoba, Canada. His show-business career began while he was a student at the University of Manitoba, where he earned his Bachelor of Science degree.

To pay his way through school, Monty worked for Radio Station CKRC singing, acting, writing, emceeing, and engineering. He performed in school productions but found time to become a five-letter man in athletics and was president of the student body in his senior year.

Upon earning his degree, he moved to Toronto, to work for the Canadian Broadcasting Corporation. He created Canada's longest running radio quiz show "Who Am I?"

In 1955, Monty moved to New York City to do a five-year run on NBC's "Monitor" and did numerous other shows including the New York Ranger hockey broadcasts. Hall was New York's first soccer play-by-play man. He then became emcee of "Video Village" and moved to Hollywood with the show.

During a frantic year, he commuted from CBS to NBC studios performing all day on "Video Village" and producing his first show, "Your First Impression," at night. This was followed by his creation of "Let's Make a Deal," which was among the longest-running game shows in television history.

Monty's life away from television has been as important as that on stage. His charitable and philanthropic activities have brought him more than 500 awards.

In 1975, he was elected president of Variety Clubs International, the world's largest children's charity; in 1977, he became chairman of the board, and in 1981 was honored with the lifetime title of international chairman. In 1983, he received the prestigious Variety Clubs International Humanitarian Award.

In 1988, the Government of Canada bestowed on him the highest award that Canada can offer—the prestigious Order of Canada—for his hu-

It Takes Pluck

On my television show "Let's Make a Deal," the contestants depend on luck to select the right door. In the game of life, it takes "pluck" more than luck to be successful.

I found that to be true when I moved from Toronto to New York, in 1955, after early success in radio and television in my native Canada. I spent days and weeks on end, hoping to get an appointment; and even getting appointments found instant rejection. It appeared the American networks weren't holding their breath waiting for me—the rest is history.

I was ready for the challenge. My youth had been one of much illness and poverty. My loving mother nursed me through harsh illnesses and pulled me through some tough times. When I finished high school, we did not have enough money to send me to college, so I took various jobs to raise the tuition.

While working in a clothing firm, I was subjected to some demeaning criticism by the boss. I came home that evening filled with frustration and tears. My mother sat me down and recited the wonderful Rudyard Kipling poem "If" to me—"If you can keep your head while those around you are losing theirs, " etc.

She was a pillar of strength to me and an inspiration. She convinced me that no amount of adversity should ever stop one. In later years, I translated that for some actors who came to me in despair. I told them, paraphrasing my mother's remarks, that "if you believe in yourself, no amount of rejection should deter you from reaching your goals." If someone tells you that you are "not good," don't accept that as gospel. You are "not good" when you yourself think that you are " not good," not when someone else tells you.

Branch Rickey, the famous general manager of the old Brooklyn Dodgers, used to say that "luck is the residue of design." He might have said "the residue of desire," for it is a combination of talent and courage (pluck) that will keep you in the fight, until that "lucky" day when someone recognizes your talent.

Monty Hall

---

manitarian works in Canada and other nations of the world. Monty is married to Marilyn, a writer-producer, and winner of an Emmy Award as co-executive producer of "Do You Remember Love," a drama concerning Alzheimer's disease. The Halls have three children—Joanna Gleason, a star on the Broadway stage, who won the Drama Desk Award and 1988 Tony Award for the best actress in Stephen Sondheim's "Into the Woods;" Richard, a television producer in San Francisco; and Sharon, who is manager of development for BBD&O in New York.

MERLE HARMON, SR.
Chairman & President
Fan Fair Corporation

Merle Harmon broadcast major league baseball for 35 years. He was the voice of the Kansas City A's, now in Oakland, the Milwaukee Braves, Minnesota Twins, Milwaukee Brewers, and Texas Rangers. With the Milwaukee Brewers, he and Bob Uecker became one of the hottest broadcast teams in baseball history. His baseball assignments included playoffs, All-Star games, and the World Series. He broadcast three no-hitters, including two perfect games, and was on hand to describe Nolan Ryan's record setting 5,000th strikeout.

Beyond baseball he covered a Super Bowl, countless bowl games, NCAA championship events, ABC's Wide World of Sports and Sports World Shows. He co-anchored the World University Games in Moscow, where he survived an auto crash, a Russian hospital, and a bout with the KGB.

His evolution from broadcaster to sports retailer was a natural one. Merle was one of the first to realize that fans would eagerly drape themselves in clothing worn by their favorite player or team. Teaming his business and sports experience, he founded his chain of Merle Harmon Fan Fair stores in 1977. Today there are more than 150 of the stores featuring official and personalized gifts for fans of amateur and professional teams. To devote full-time to his new enterprise, he stopped broadcasting Texas Rangers games after the 1989 season. However, broadcasting is still in his blood and he occasionally announces college football and basketball games.

Harmon holds degrees from Graceland College in Iowa and the University of Denver. In 1971, he became the third recipient of the National Association of Intercollegiate Athletics Outstanding Alumnus Award. The two previous winners were President Richard Nixon and Congressional Medal of Honor winner and former American Football League Commissioner Joe Foss.

Merle and his wife of 46 years, Jeanette, have four sons and a daughter. Three of his sons and his daughter are involved in the corporation.

Brighten Someone's Day

I have always admired and, in a way, envied those who work with their hands. Carpenters, artists, mechanics, doctors, and architects, among others. Those who build houses, create paintings, fix automobiles, repair bodies, and design magnificent structures. When the job is completed, they can step back, view their work, and proclaim, "I did that."

For my first few years in broadcasting, I felt that I was not contributing anything worthwhile to society. I could not rationalize that announcing a game on radio or television could be compared to the importance of the work done by those whose hands had saved lives or built a cathedral or skyscraper.

Then one afternoon, after visiting my wife in the hospital where she had delivered our second child, the hospital administrator stopped me in the hallway. He asked, "Do you realize how important your job is to many of our patients?" I was surprised by the question.

He went on to say: "I can walk down this corridor, from one end to the other, and never miss a play when you are on the air. For those few hours you bring listening and viewing pleasure, which may be the best therapy for patients who need to get their minds off their health problems. Some patients have many visitors, others have none, so you may be the one who brightens their day."

I had never thought of my job in that light and his observations had a profound affect on me. Thereafter, every time I sat down in a broadcast booth, I felt a real purpose in what I was doing.

Think back to the last time someone came up to you and, without particular reason, told you how much she or he appreciated what you did, or merely offered a simple and sincere compliment. Remember how it brightened your day?

When's the last time you did that? Why not begin today? It's a habit that will bring you much happiness throughout your life—and you'll make a lot of other people feel good, too.

Merle Harmon

PATRICIA HARRISON
Founder
National Women's Economic
Alliance Foundation

Patricia Harrison began her professional career as a secretary. Today she is co-founder and partner of E. Bruce Harrison Company, a business consulting firm, and president, AEF/Harrison International. The company, founded in 1973, is based in Washington D.C., with offices in Dallas, New York, and Brussels, and is now among the top 15 owner-managed public affairs firms in the country.

Mrs. Harrison was born in New York City and is a former award-winning journalist and author with over 20 years experience in the creation and management of business, industry, and environmental communications programs. In 1983, she founded the National Women's Economic Alliance Foundation, a non-profit organization comprising men and women leaders from business, industry, and government who work together to affirm and increase the benefits and opportunities available within a thriving free enterprise system.

A frequent speaker on economic and management issues, Mrs. Harrison has keynoted forums nationally and internationally. She recently was appointed by President Bush to the President's Export Council, the premier national advisory committee on international trade.

Mrs. Harrison earned a Bachelor of Arts degree from The American University and a Master of Arts in interdisciplinary studies and international transaction from George Mason University.

She has authored three books, including America's New Women Entrepreneurs, *and includes* Washington Woman of the Year *and* Entrepreneur of the Year *among numerous awards and honors she's received.*

Helping Others

In my role, not only as a business owner but as the president of an organization affirming the free enterprise system, I have had an opportunity to meet with men and women throughout the world. Despite differences in education, race, culture, age, and economic achievement, it has become clear to me that a "winner" is a "winner" no matter what language he or she speaks.

There are people who have suffered great deprivation and come back to begin all over again. There are those who never try and complain about lack of opportunity. You Can Do It may be the most powerful sentence in the English language. It is a sentence we need to repeat to ourselves on a daily basis. It is certainly an attitude we must communicate to our children if they are going to thrive in the competitive decade ahead.

The world has witnessed the end of the Iron Curtain. Perhaps we can say that the beginning of the end began when a small outnumbered group of men and women in Hungary made a decision for freedom. Forty-five years later, Hungary has finally rid itself of the scourge of communism. The future is uncertain and the risk is great as individuals must look to themselves and not the state for answers. When I and other business owners met with Hungarian women in the work force it was clear that they wanted to move forward and realize long-deferred dreams, but they were afraid. We listened as they told us what they didn't have, the obstacles they face, the lack of telecommunications, the dearth of capital.

Finally, Sharlyne Powell, president, Women at Large, who had faced her own challenges of poverty, prejudice, and naysayers, said: "You can talk forever about what you don't have. But what I see is a group of people who have education, intelligence, and great spirit. Now, let's talk about what you can do with all of that."

Catherine Marschall, the associate deputy administrator of the U.S. Small Business Administration, a Hungarian who escaped in 1956, talked to the audience in Hungarian and underscored that the Americans were here to help, not because we had all the answers, but because as entrepreneurs we had an understanding of risk, achievement, and a vision of what we wanted to accomplish.

Gail Blanke, senior vice president, Avon Products, and author of *Taking Control of Your life,* talked about the challenges women face when they try to do it all, and how much we have in common with all the women of the world who work and try to raise a family. Her daughter, Kate, who was in the audience, underscored Gail's words when she said, "I love my work but my family, my husband and children, come first." A theme that reassured the family-focused Hungarian women.

At the end of the day, the women who were so reticent to talk to one

(Continued on page 263)

CHICK HEARN
Sports Broadcaster

"You want baseball, you go to Vin Scully. For football, it was the late Ted Husing. But basketball is Chick Hearn." Those accolades came from Jim Murray, the Pulitzer Prize winning columnist of the Los Angeles Times. The occasion was Chick Hearn Night at The Forum, home of the L.A. Lakers basketball team.

Hearn has been the Voice of the Lakers for 32 years. He's broadcast 2,500 games, missing only two—both because of snowstorms. In perspective, he called his first Lakers game when Magic Johnson was one year old!

His first major broadcasting job was doing Bradley University basketball games. This was quite a feat because he had no college education or formal broadcast training. A strong work ethic, determination to succeed, and an understanding wife were his motivation.

In 1951, he was lured to Los Angeles to be USC's football announcer. He also worked for NBC and CBS. His work log includes two Ali fights, seven Rose Bowls and several major golf tournaments. He also has appeared in numerous movies and his star is on Hollywood's Walk of Fame.

Hearn is credited with helping build the Lakers' following, especially in the early years, when the team was a non-entity in an area dominated by baseball's Dodgers. His radio broadcasts, enlivened by his enthusiasm and creative verbiage, caught on. To this day, thousands of fans bring their radios to the game to hear his commentary as they sit courtside. With the advent of television, Hearn inspired introduction of simulcast broadcasting.

His Chickisms have changed basketball's vocabulary. He coined terms like slam dunk, airball, dribble drive, stutter step, give and go, and no-harm no-foul, all now part of every sportscaster's phraseology.

Attitude Is Important

I don't know any hard and fast rules to tell you how to get where you want to go. Life is filled with too many complications and uncertainties for that.

I live in a world of words. There is one word which I feel controls everything we do. That word is ATTITUDE! It will bring us whatever we want, or, will keep us from reaching any of our goals. If I approach a broadcast with a bad attitude, it will soon become evident to my listeners. A poor attitude has killed a lot of promising athletic and business careers. Be assured, attitude will play an important role in any success you achieve.

I encourage you to do something you enjoy by selecting a career suited to your inclinations and talent.

Don't expect or ask for something for nothing. There isn't anything worth having that can be achieved without effort.

Always give more than you get. Keep putting in extra effort and extra thought to make what you do become your best effort—every time.

Never be satisfied. Set high goals for yourself. If you achieve them, set new ones.

Learn your abilities and limitations. You might ponder the famous prayer which says: "God grant me the strength to change those things which can be changed, the patience to bear those things which cannot, and the wisdom to know the difference."

Chick Hearn

ROLAND A. HEMOND
Executive Vice President
and General Manager
Baltimore Orioles

In 1989, in his second season with the Baltimore Orioles, Roland Hemond was named Major League Executive of the Year. It was the third time in his career he'd won the award, the second in the '80s. The honor came in the wake of the Orioles' amazing 32 1/2 game improvement over '88, third greatest turnaround in major league history.

The accomplishment was not new to Hemond. In fact, the energetic executive has engineered three of the major league's ten best turnarounds since divisional play began in '69. As general manager of the Chicago White Sox, Hemond's '71 club improved 23 games over the previous year and his '77 team climbed 26 games above the '76 White Sox.

One of the more active trade makers, he has made 121 trades involving 335 players in his 39 years in baseball. He made 17 trades in his first 17 months with the Orioles as the Baltimore club rebounded as a contender.

Happenstance played a key role in his success. A chance meeting with a blind World War I veteran, Sgt. Leo C. McMahon, led to an introduction to Charlie Blossfield, general manager of the Hartford, Connecticut, Chiefs of the Class A Eastern League. Newly-discharged from the Coast Guard, Hemond accepted a job with the Chiefs, an affiliate club of the Boston Braves.

A subsequent two-week tryout in the minor league office of the Braves ended up being a lifetime baseball career, with the Braves in Boston and Milwaukee through 1960, as scouting and farm director for the California Angels, general manager with the White Sox from 1961 through 1985, a year in the Commissioner's Office, to his present assignment with the Orioles.

Develop Champion Qualities

Baseball is my business, but it's more than that. I love my job and still get the same thrill out of the game I did when I was a kid. That's important. You need to enjoy what you do for a living, whatever it may be.

All players in professional baseball have ability. My job, and that of our manager, coaches, and entire organization, is to develop that ability to capacity. I look for three qualities in each player beyond natural talents.

First, an athlete must believe what he is doing is worthwhile. It is important that a player is aware that he has more responsibility than just putting on a pair of spikes or hitting a home run. Whether he likes it or not, he automatically becomes a role model for our nation's youth. It's true that baseball is just a game, but it has much to offer beyond the baselines. So, a player must believe there is a purpose and dignity in what he does for a living.

The second factor that makes a champion player is his desire to be one. The greatest quality of a championship club is a collective, dominating urge to win. Some great teams have lost the World Series to less talented ones, which simply wanted to win more. It's the same in life—desire drives people to achieve their goals.

Show me a championship team and I'll show you one which has mastered fundamentals—the little things that often spell the difference between winning and losing. Countless players who have the material requisites for greatness—youth, speed, power, even desire—still fail. Why? Because they can't master the basics; a pitcher can't hold a runner on base, a runner doesn't know how to slide, outfielders can't hit the cutoff man, batters can't bunt—just to name a few. Learning fundamentals is essential in sports and business.

Begin early in life to develop these qualities—believe in what you are doing, desire to be the best you can be, and master even the smallest skills required for your vocation. If you do, you'll reach home plate often and score a lot of runs in your life.

THEODORE M. HESBURGH, C.S.C.
President Emeritus
University of Notre Dame

Father Hesburgh guided Notre Dame's destinies for more than three decades after he took office at age 35. He raised the school from a glorified Catholic liberal arts undergraduate institution to a status in academe equal to that of its football team in the annals of sports.

The public-spirited priest became a national figure through his work in religious ecumenicism, with philanthropic foundations, and for the federal government. Father Hesburgh held 14 presidential appointments over the years, which involved him in virtually all the major social issues. He distinguished himself as an ardent defender of academic freedom and as a champion of civil rights.

During the Hesburgh era, he expanded the university's campus and broadened its intellectual horizons. In two historic moves, the university government was transferred from exclusively clerical control to the predominantly lay board of trustees, and admission of women ended Notre Dame's all-male tradition.

He has received 120 honorary degrees and is the holder of the United States Medal of Freedom as well as the prestigious Meiklejohn Award from the American Association of University Professors.

His principal retirement role is to develop two Notre Dame institutes that he was instrumental in founding—the Institute for International Peace Studies and the Kellogg Institute for International Studies.

Father Hesburgh was educated at Notre Dame, the Gregorian University of Rome, and the Catholic University of America, from which he received his doctorate in sacred theology. His autobiography, God, Country, Notre Dame *was published by Doubleday in November, 1990.*

You Can Make a Difference

When one is young, the whole world stretches out ahead, beckoning with dreams and hopes.

Thanks to spending most of my adult life at the University of Notre Dame, I have known many young people who want their lives to make a difference in the years ahead. Many of them have their doubts about whether or not one person can make a difference.

I have always told them: you can make a difference, can help make a better world, more just, more peaceful in the years ahead, if you really believe it is possible, if you try.

I know it is possible because, so often, I have seen it happen. In fact, every step forward the world has made in history may be traced back to one person, or a small group of persons, who had a vision, attracted other dedicated people to share the vision, and then made it come true.

Of course, all this has its costs: one must become educated to the limit of one's capabilities to become competent in one's chosen field, whether it is ministry, medicine, law, science, business, education itself, or whatever.

A man named Albert Schweitzer, a minister and medical doctor, drew the world's attention to the medical needs of sub-Sahara Africa, attracting many talented doctors to help him, winning the Nobel Prize for Peace in the process.

Mother Teresa, a poor Catholic nun, was so touched by seeing elderly homeless people and abandoned infants dying in the streets of Calcutta that she decided to change the scene. Eventually thousands of generous and capable young men and women of many nations joined her to work with the poorest of the poor, all over the world. She, too, won the Nobel Prize for Peace.

Jim Grant, as the new director of UNICEF, the U.N. agency for children, was appalled by the fact that 40,000 children die needlessly every day, mostly in the Third World, mostly through the effects of malnutrition. He organized a simple five point program for child survival. Already it is saving more than two and a half million children who otherwise would have died in the early years of their lives.

John Kennedy asked his brother-in-law, Sarge Shriver, to organize a Peace Corps. It was almost impossible, but Sarge did it. Today, about a quarter of a century later, more than 125,000 young Americans have served poor nations all over the world, seeing their own lives much improved as they did it. Many of them continue to serve, here at home and abroad. One man had the idea, one man made it happen.

One could make a long list of single persons, men and women, who have changed the world for the better. It is still happening. You can do it.!

EDWARD A. HORRIGAN, JR.
Retired Vice Chairman of the Board
RJR Nabisco, Inc.

Edward A. Horrigan, Jr. is the retired vice chairman of the board of RJR Nabisco, Inc., one of the world's leading consumer products companies. He is also the retired chairman and chief executive officer of R.J. Reynolds Tobacco Company.

Horrigan was responsible for the operations of R.J. Reynolds Tobacco Company, which includes R.J. Reynolds Tobacco USA, its domestic operating unit; R.J. Reynolds International, Inc.; R.J. Reynolds Tobacco Development Company, which oversees new product development for both the domestic and international tobacco businesses; and Planters LifeSavers Company. In addition, he was responsible for Sports Marketing Enterprises, Inc., an operating unit that handles all activities related to the corporation's sponsorship of professional golf tournaments, auto racing, and other events. He was also responsible for RJR Nabisco's government relations department and activities.

Before joining R.J. Reynolds, Horrigan was chairman of the board and president of Buckingham Corporation, a subsidiary of Northwest Industries, Inc. From 1961 until 1973, he was with Thomas J. Lipton, Inc., where he served as vice president of sales, and division vice president. From 1958 until 1961, he was general manager of Ebonite Company. Horrigan began his career as unit sales manager of Procter & Gamble in 1954.

He served as an infantry officer in the U.S. Army during the Korean conflict from 1950 to 1954. He was awarded the Silver Star and Purple Heart.

Horrigan has received the Horatio Alger Award and the American Jewish Committee's Human Relations Award. He is a member of the Sovereign Military Order of Malta. The administrative building of Duke University's Fuqua School of Business executive education center, which was completed in 1988, is named Horrigan Hall in his honor.

Learning Is Unending

Let me offer you a few thoughts about the Ed Horrigan school of management.

The first is to repeat an old adage I'm sure you all have heard many times: don't believe everything you read, particularly when it comes to business.

The second thought I would like to leave with you: never think you have any excuse to stop learning. Those who are truly successful in business today are those who are never too proud to admit there is more to learn. In today's business environment the learning process must span your entire career. New techniques, new processes, new technology come on the scene at lightning speed.

Rapid change is the rule in the marketplace. Trends pop up, then perish, almost instantaneously. To meet these challenges you must never be content with the status quo. The history of American business is filled with individuals, and entire companies, that made that fatal blunder.

Anyone who tries to move from the bottom to the top of the ladder without taking steps on some solid rungs in between is most likely to be trampled by those both above and below. The corporate world is not a gentle place. I realized that very early in my business career when I was selling soap in Brooklyn and a grocer once concluded my sales pitch by throwing a meat cleaver at me.

Which brings me to my third point. As a part of this continuing learning process, understand your environment, and be willing to take the carefully calculated risks necessary to seize opportunities. This is the environment that will offer you the opportunity to realize your full potential, if you have the personal courage to accept its challenges and the determination and skill necessary to grow within it.

And this brings me to the final thought I would like to offer you. Strive to be a leader, not just a manager. The need for good managers is becoming greater than ever. By good managers I mean managers who are true leaders. Managers merely ensure that tasks are concluded; leaders begin laying new groundwork for growth. Managers guarantee people stay within the bounds of procedure; leaders enhance potential. Managers control people; leaders inspire them.

The true business leaders I have observed are those who crash through obstacles in search of rewards, rather than fawning behind a safety fence in fear of their jobs. When you do reach the pinnacle of your career, keep this thought in your memory bank: "Don't ever become a legend in your own mind." Wear success well and *humbly!*

Ed Horrigan

BONNIE McELVEEN-HUNTER
President & CEO
Pace Communications

Bonnie McElveen-Hunter was born in Columbia, South Carolina, in 1950, the daughter of a dynamic and determined school teacher and a career pilot in the U.S. Air Force, Madeline and John T. McElveen. She is the eldest of three children. Her brother, Dr. John T. McElveen, is a neurotologist at Duke University, and her sister, Tweed McElveen, is the owner of McElveen Designs & Antiques, an interior design and home furnishings business. She likes to say she had the privilege of growing up rich in every way except money. Those wonderful beginnings equipped her for what she hopes she is doing today in business, and that is making a life—rather than just making a living.

Mrs. Hunter grew up an Air Force "brat" and lived in eight states and Germany. She attended high school in Bellevue, Nebraska, and graduated from Stephens College in Columbia, Missouri, with a degree in business administration.

Today she is president and CEO of Pace Communications, a publishing company she compares to a three-legged stool, the legs representing custom / contract magazine publishing, in-flight magazines, and a consumer / newsstand magazine. Pace Communications currently publishes USAir's and United Airlines' in-flight magazines, Elegant Bride Magazine, Furniture Retailer Magazine, ASTA Agency Management Magazine, IGA Grocergram, and Amtrak Express Magazine.

Mrs. Hunter is a member of the Young President's Organization, the University of North Carolina at Greensboro Business Advisory Board, the Greensboro Board of First Union National Bank, United Arts Council of Greensboro's Renaissance Campaign, as well as the Greensboro Development Corporation.

She feels strongly that her accomplishments have been facilitated by a wonderfully supportive family, divine intervention, and a mother with a low tolerance for failure! She is married to Bynum Merritt Hunter, an

Ten Commandments for Failure

When I was invited to participate in this book, I immediately thought of my mother's "pearls of wisdom:" paint a picture and a child will live up to it, so paint a success story every day; mediocrity is the greatest sin; work is the greatest privilege; and time is precious—use it wisely. In our vocabulary, *can't* was a word that did not exist. In fact, it was written on a piece of paper, put in a shoe box, and buried with full burial rites, never to be used again.

We were taught growing up that two options exist in our lives through the choices we make, success or failure. I decided that since success is an all-too-frequently-used term, I would share with you my Ten Commandments for Failure—for failure is never an ending but an opportunity for a new beginning.

Commandment 1: Thou Shalt Have Little Faith. As a Southern minister put it, fear is like being nibbled to death by the minnows. Fear keeps us from reaching our goals and taking risks. If you are going to lose, fight a battle with a worthy foe—make sure you have been swallowed by a whale!

Commandment 2: Thou Shalt Pick Thy Partners with Wanton Abandon. Why is it we spend more time selecting a car that we will drive for only a short time than we spend selecting the people and the company we intend to keep for a lifetime? I have shared a belief with my business partners and friends of 20 years, Gene Johnson and Bill McGee, that it is more important to "select your partners than to select your business." It has served us well.

Commandment 3: Thou Shalt Make the Quick Buck. As long as we have freedom in our economic system, there will be charlatans looking for the "quick buck." Doing wrong in many cases has been a shortcut to making good, but the "quick buck" is its only reward. It's a lousy way to make a living and, more importantly, a life.

Commandment 4: Thou Shalt Have No Enthusiasm. The definition of enthusiasm is "to be possessed by God," and I can assure you that nothing great has ever been accomplished without it—or Him! Enthusiasm is contagious—try it!

Commandment 5: Thou Shalt Seek Easy Street. Seeking Easy Street is seeking a dead-end street. Work is a privilege. Through work and struggle we find challenge and personal growth. Celebrate the struggle!

Commandment 6: Thou Shalt Do It Alone. Never underestimate the value of teamwork. Lefty Gomez, a great New York Yankee pitcher, was

(Continued on page 264)

---

attorney in the law firm of Smith Helms Mulliss & Moore in Greensboro, North Carolina, and has an eight-year-old son, Bynum Merritt Hunter, Jr., whom she affectionately calls the "Chairman of the Board" of their family.

CONGRESSMAN HENRY J. HYDE
U.S. Representative
Sixth District, Illinois

Congressman Henry Hyde is currently serving his ninth term in Congress, representing Illinois' Sixth District. He serves on the Judiciary and Foreign Affairs committees.

A graduate of Georgetown University, Hyde received his law degree from Loyola University in Chicago. He is a combat veteran of World War II, a former trial lawyer, and in 1987 served on the Iran-Contra investigating committee.

Recognized as one of the Republicans' most competent and motivated legislators, Congressman Hyde has made a difference on a variety of issues, and increasingly on foreign policy from his seat on the Foreign Affairs committee.

He is considered by many as the best debater in the House. In the high-stakes Iran-Contra situation he was the minority's most effective partisan weapon, according to the National Journal, which also gave him a most appropriate accolade: "Hyde's effectiveness may be grounded most of all in his willingness to do his homework and, because unlike many members of Congress, he appears to do his own thinking."

Hyde's rhetorical skills are credited with helping the GOP win over Democrats on key issues. As one fellow Congressman put it, "If you don't have a Henry Hyde articulating your views very forcefully, very well, and with intelligence behind them, it's hard to attract people to come over."

The community-minded Hyde has received honorary degrees from Lewis University, Allentown College, and Midwest College of Engineering. Among the many honors conferred upon the Congressman are: The National Security Leadership Award, American Security Council; Distinguished Service Award, Disabled American Veterans; Exceptional Service Award, American Legion; Alumni Medal of Excellence, Loyola University School of Law; and Alumni Achievement Award, Georgetown University, just to mention a few.

A native of Chicago, Hyde and his wife, Jeanne, have four children and five grandchildren.

Freedom Works

We have just come to the end of what I think must be regarded as one of the sorriest centuries in human history. Thanks be to God, we in the United States have been spared much of the horror of the 20th century. But we—you—should never forget that you shared this century with martyrs: martyrs for the truth, martyrs for freedom, martyrs for faith.

The good news is that, in the providence of God, the 20th century is ending in a far better way than we might have expected. Much of the world, after the travails of two world wars, a 40-year cold war, and innumerable small wars, seems to have learned a great truth: freedom works!

But freedom works only if we know what freedom truly means. Lord Acton, a great Catholic historian of the 19th century, put it best: "Freedom is not the power of doing what we like, but the right of being able to do what we ought."

In this, the 200th anniversary year of the American Bill of Rights, we need to think—you need to think, as citizens and voters who will be responsible for leading America in the 21st century—about this business of rights and obligations. About the most we can bring ourselves to say to someone else is, "I'd prefer that you do such-and-such." And we think of that as a humane, decent way to live in a democracy.

The trouble is, our inability to say to each other, "You ought to do this, or that," could spell the end of this great American experiment in freedom. I challenge all young people: care enough about each other to be able to say, "You know, you really ought to..."

Perhaps the most precious, and least appreciated freedom we posses, is our free will. We are allowed to even choose the wrong way, but we are compelled to make our own decisions in using this God-given gift.

In using your free will, I urge you to remember the soul, the capacity for goodness, mercy, compassion, sacrifice, creativity, and grandeur that is in each of you—and that is in every human being you will meet on your life's journey.

Sometimes that soul is hard to find in others. It's even hard to find within ourselves sometime. But it is there. There is no finer gift you can give to your country, and the world, than if each of you nurtures the soul within you, and to help those around you discover and nurture theirs.

Henry J. Hyde

PAUL JOHNSON
Mayor
Phoenix, Arizona

Paul Johnson was elected mayor by an acclamation vote of the Phoenix City Council in February, 1990, to fill the term vacated by former mayor Terry Goddard. Johnson had been the District 3 representative on the Council since 1986. Though, unusually young as mayors go, Johnson, at 32, subsequently won election with an astounding 99.8 percent of the vote.

A native of Phoenix, Johnson started a construction firm at age 20. After helping the company grow into a successful construction, building, and investment firm, he turned it over to his family to devote his own time to city government.

Johnson lists his priorities as jobs, the environment, and holding the line on government spending.

He attended the John F. Kennedy School of Local and State Government at Harvard University. At age 32, he is the youngest mayor in Phoenix history—and the youngest mayor of a major American city.

Mayor Johnson and his wife, Christa, have two sons, Paul and Justin.

DONALD R. KEOUGH
President & CEO
The Coca-Cola Company

Donald Keough was born near Maurice, a small town in northwest Iowa, the son of a farmer and cattleman. After fire destroyed their home, during the early days of the Depression, the family moved to nearby Sioux City.

Influenced by his mother, Keough had perfect attendance through elementary and high school. When once he signed up for the elective tumbling class, his mother explained, "You won't do much tumbling in your life." She erased tumbling and wrote in debate. The experience helped teach him how to communicate and was valuable preparation for his future. "It shows how a simple act by a caring parent can help shape your life," he noted.

After graduating from high school at 16, in 1944, he enlisted in the Navy. He served two years and upon returning to civilian life enrolled at Creighton University on the G.I. Bill. He majored in philosophy, with a minor in speech and law. Upon graduation, he worked for radio and television station WOW, a large NBC affiliate, where a co-worker was a young announcer named Johnny Carson. "We both made the same salary—the handsome sum of 55 dollars a week," he recalls.

Fascinated by the advertising side of television, Keough became assistant advertising manager for the Omaha-based producer of Butter-Nut coffee. Subsequent mergers and acquisitions brought him into the Coca-Cola organization. The lesson to be learned from his experience, in which four corporate acquisitions required him to make continual adjustments, Keough says, is to be prepared for the unpredictable "twists and turns" of life.

He was elected president, chief operating officer and a director of The Coca-Cola Company in 1981 and became chairman of the board of Coca-Cola Enterprises, the world's largest bottling system, in 1986.

Keough serves on the boards of National Service Industries, Inc., H.J. Heinz Company, and The Washington Post. He is chairman of the board of trustees of the University of Notre Dame and a trustee of several other educational institutions. He also serves on the boards of a number of national charitable and civic organizations.

Make the World Better

As mayor of Phoenix, I am called upon to deliver several commencement addresses each year. The message I give to all young people is always the same—and always brief.

Advice is one thing that all commencement speeches have in common. Most of it you can forget. And most of it you will. Joan Rivers, for example, told a graduating class, "Wherever you go in life, always remember that it's not WHO you know that matters—it's "WHOM." And this is what Bob Hope told a group of graduates: "The whole world is out there waiting for you. Don't go!"

My advice is simple. Joan Rivers is wrong. It's not WHO you know or WHOM. It's WHAT you know and how hard you try to do the best you can. That's what matters. And that's why she's wrong. Bob Hope fares a bit better but he's only half wrong. The whole world IS out there waiting for you. But I say, "Get out there and stare it in the face and make it better. Be visionary. Be adventuresome. Take chances." You simply have to.

WILMA H. JORDAN
President & CEO
The Jordan Group, Inc.

Wilma Jordan formed The Jordan Group in 1987. She oversees the firm's activities which include a full range of investment and advisory services for the publishing industry. Clients include U.S. and international companies.

Ms. Jordan was formerly chief operating officer of the Esquire Magazine Group, which consisted of Esquire and New York Woman magazines, the Esquire Health and Fitness Clinic, Esquire Press and Video divisions.

Fresh out of business school at the University of Tennessee, Ms. Jordan was one of the founders of Collegiate Marketing and Management in Knoxville. The company published publications aimed at college students. Later the company was named 13-30 Corporation, reflecting its specialization in marketing to 13 to 30-year-olds.

In 1979, 13-30 bought then-moribund Esquire magazine. Ms. Jordan and her partners engineered a dramatic turnaround of Esquire, one of the most celebrated success stories in the publishing industry. The achievement earned the 1983 Magazine of the Year Award from the American Society of Journalists and Authors.

Ms. Jordan is a member of the board of directors of the LIN Broadcasting Corporation, Ringier America, and Guidepost Magazine, Inc. She is a member of both The Women's Forum, Inc., and Advertising Women of New York, was inducted into the YWCA Academy of Women Achievers in 1985, and serves on the University of Tennessee College of Business Advisory Council.

In addition, she is an active fundraiser for the Patricia Neal Stroke/Trauma Rehabilitation Center in Knoxville, and chaired the first Patricia Neal Center Ball at the Waldorf-Astoria in 1987.

Courage and Tenacity

I believe courage and tenacity make a winner—every time.

It is easy to be safe, to follow the road taken by others; but what of significance has ever been achieved by a concern to be safe? I like the advice that John D. Rockefeller gave to young people, when he said: "Strike out on new paths rather than travel the worn roads of accepted success." That takes courage.

Too many people think of security instead of opportunity. That's a natural tendency. Whenever you have a choice between going forward and playing it safe, my advice is to go for it. Use common sense in deciding your course of action, then put everything you've got into it.

A half-hearted effort won't get it done. It might carry you a little way toward your goal, but it will never get you far enough to reach it. Be tenacious, no matter how rough it gets; be determined to stay with it—and you'll become a success, too!

Wilma H. Jordan

"You Can Do" Philosophy

"You can do it!" For some people, this is little more than a tired cliche. For many of us, however, it is a statement that is both real and empowering.

For me, in fact, it addresses a basic reality of life—that we are put here "to do," and very little of what we "do" can be limited to who we "are." The "you can do" philosophy is a truth I have learned one day at a time over more than six decades.

People arrive at a certain position in life not by chance or luck. To a large degree, it is the result of having the will to succeed and being totally committed.

As president of The Coca-Cola Company, I have the good fortune to help lead a business that sells the best known product in the world, Coca-Cola. It is sold in nearly 170 countries, and every day there are new and wonderful challenges to meet.

But selling Coca-Cola is also a job that has very little in common with selling coffee in Omaha, Nebraska, which was exactly how my career began back in 1950.

Did I know back then that eventually I would assume the responsibilities and face the challenges that I enjoy today? Of course not. I did know, however, that selling coffee was a good opportunity for me and that with a little hard work it was something I could be good at and even master.

In life, it is so important to set short term goals so as to enjoy periodic achievement. It is difficult, if not impossible, to move from an entry level position to chairman of the board in one giant stride. It is possible, though, to set interim goals and move up the ladder in smaller steps. If you work hard you can achieve a goal and be ready for your next goal and next victory. Before you know it your ultimate objective will be in sight.

By joining that little coffee company, it was like I had jumped into a small creek and started swimming. That creek turned into a river, and that river turned into a gulf. Finally, I found myself in an ocean of opportunity called The Coca-Cola Company. All I have ever done is just kept swimming as hard as I could, and today I am swimming harder than ever.

Taking the first plunge into that first creek is often the toughest challenge. But once you feel the water on your skin and learn that you are not going to drown, you will grow stronger and stronger. Before long, you are well on your way toward the ocean, and the realization that you can indeed do it!

Donald Keough

HENRY (HANK) KETCHAM
Cartoonist Creator of
Dennis the Menace

Hank Ketcham created Dennis the Menace in October, 1950, and it was syndicated to 18 newspapers the following March. Today Dennis the Menace, who marked his 40th birthday in 1990 while remaining a lovable five, is distributed by North America Syndicate to more than 1,000 newspapers in 48 countries and is translated into 19 languages.

Ketcham was born March 14, 1920, in Seattle, Washington. He became interested in drawing at the age of seven when a local art director doodled cartoon sketches to amuse him. The bug bit him and Ketcham practiced cartooning in every spare moment of his school years.

He entered the University of Washington in 1937, as an art major, but after a year the cartooning urge lured him to Hollywood and the Walter "Woody Woodpecker" Lantz animation studio. Moving to the Walt Disney studios, he worked on "Pinocchio," "Fantasia," and other Disney productions until World War II, when he enlisted in the U.S. Navy.

After the war, he plunged full-time into the highly competitive free-lance cartooning market. He quickly became one of the country's most successful and prolific cartoonists, selling his work regularly to Collier's, The Saturday Evening Post, Ladies Home Journal, Liberty, and The New Yorker, as well as to advertising agencies. By this time, Ketcham was also married and the father of a boy named Dennis.

Since the early days, Ketcham has expanded his lovable imp's popularity through a variety of other media. The hit network television series which ran from 1959 to 1963 still appears on stations around the country.

Dennis' civic mindedness has made him a popular spokesman for many worthy causes, including The Boy Scouts of America, UNICEF and the International Red Cross. His image appears on myriad licensed products, from lunch boxes to greeting cards. The Dennis the Menace Playground

(Continued on page 258)

I discovered this anonymous message many years ago. It has been an inspiration to me ever since. Without persistence, Dennis would not have endured all these years. I share this message with you, hoping it will motivate you to diligently pursue all your goals in life.

Nothing in the world can take the place of persistence.

Talent will not; nothing is more common than men with talent.

Genius will not; unrewarded genius is almost a proverb.

Education will not; the world is full of educated derelicts.

Persistence and determination alone are omnipotent.

Hank Ketcham

TERESA KETTELKAMP
Assistant Deputy Director
Illinois State Police

Teresa Kettelkamp is the highest-ranking female State Police officer in the nation. In her position, she carries the rank of lieutenant colonel and is now second in command in the Division of Administration.

Teresa is a graduate of Quincy College, B.A. political science, State Police Academy, and the FBI National Academy. While in graduate school at the University of Illinois–Chicago studying sociology she planned to go to law school when she became interested in the Illinois Bureau of Investigation.

From school, she joined the IBI in a clerical function, but found the investigative end more interesting. She soon became a special agent working on the Organized Crime Squad, General Assignment Squad, and Covert Squad, doing undercover work, before joining the Operational Services Command.

Prior to her present position, she worked in the Division of Criminal Investigation, Division of State Troopers, and Division of Internal Investigation.

Teresa keeps fit playing tennis, swimming, and jogging. Music is one of her diversions. Among her favorites is Phil Collins' "Another Day in Paradise," about the homeless, one of her concerns.

Work Hard, Have Faith

When my daughter was born, I made a banner for her bedroom which read: *Girls Can Do Anything.* I wanted to start her out in life with this positive affirmation because, as I looked at this precious newborn, I wanted with all my heart for her to always feel that life's opportunities are limitless. I truly believe that what any person believes in his or her heart can be achieved. I've always like what Henry Ford said, "Whether you think you can or think you can't, you're right." I believe this to be true.

The older I become, the more reflective I am about who I am and how I was able to achieve the success I have. My not-so-secret secret is that I am where I am because I worked hard and have faith in a faithful God. Some other beliefs I hold which I think will benefit young people are:

- Learn early in life that validation of your worth comes from within yourself—never externally. Get to know yourself and know that you can believe in yourself.

- Life should be lived one day at a time. Living in the past and/or worrying about the future eliminates your today. In keeping with this, learn to forgive those who do you harm. Law enforcement is constantly facing crimes based on grudges and revenge.

- Time and good health are precious—manage them wisely.

- It is important to achieve and maintain a balance between work, family, play, and your spiritual life. Reading the Bible daily will help you accomplish this personal goal.

- You should treat others as you want to be treated. There will always be people in your life who can use your help—particularly children and the elderly.

- A God does exist—make God an integral part of your life. If you don't, you're doing too much yourself.

A career in law enforcement is worth considering because it can positively touch so many lives. There are many levels of law enforcement (city, county, state, and federal) and much diversity within each level that make it a very rewarding career. Law enforcement is also filled with many challenges for you to use your God-given talents to make the world a better and safer place. How can you beat that?

HEYWARD L. KING, JR.
Chairman & CEO
W. Lee Flowers & Co., Inc.

Heyward King is a successful businessman who prefers to be known as a Christian. Despite climbing to the top of the corporate ladder, his greatest satisfaction has come in serving his church and community.

After he received his B.S. degree in education from the University of South Carolina, he joined the family wholesale grocery business. He's run the gamut, from floor sweeper to head of the company.

A motto of his company, which is affiliated with IGA, is Hometown Proud. King is heavily involved in civic work as a board member and chairman of the Lake City School District for 12 years. He is chairman of the board of visitors at the University of South Carolina, where he also served as an adjunct professor in the school of business in 1988.

His competitive nature stems from being a 17-letterman in high school and a football and track monogram winner at USC.

He chairs the Florence County for Progress Board which under his leadership has brought tremendous growth to the county. His leadership in the county has been recognized by the governor of South Carolina, the county and city on several occasions.

Heyward has been chairman of the board of Lake City United Methodist Church for two 5-year terms, during which time he raised more than $600,000 for the small church.

He has gained prominence in the food industry serving as a director of the Independent Grocers Alliance (IGA), National Wholesale Grocers Association and the Food Marketing Institute.

King and his wife, Susie, have been married for 32 years. They have four children and two grandchildren.

Fundamentals

This is what I would tell you if you were sitting in my office and had asked for my advice. I hope you will follow these guidelines—and the advice others have given you in this book. All of us want to see you succeed because you are important.

First of all, believe in the principles of your religion, your parents, your country, in people and, particularly in yourself. If you believe that you were born for a special, useful purpose, you will succeed beyond your dreams.

As early as possible, decide what you want to do with your life. Set short and long range goals in writing and review them regularly.

Youth is a time for great dreams but use your common sense. Study the things going on around you and think about what they mean.

Honesty is not only a good policy, it is the ONLY policy. It is not always easy to be honest, but if you are honest with yourself first, you will have to be honest with everyone else.

Whenever you are faced with temptation, ask yourself, "Is it right or wrong?" and act accordingly.

Be compassionate. At all times treat your fellow-man as you would want to be treated—the Golden Rule will never go out of style.

Share as best you can your time, your talent, and your possessions, with those who need and deserve your help. Bread cast upon the water brings big returns. This is one of the important facts of life.

The Almighty is with you at all times, remember this, and He will guide you along the right path. You are a child of God. Stand by your church and your faith and God will stand by you.

Leymard King, Jr.

PHILIP H. KNIGHT
Chairman & CEO
NIKE, Inc.

Phil Knight was selected Oregon's Business Person of the Decade by business leaders from throughout the state, who made him their unanimous choice for the honor.

Knight holds a BA business degree from the University of Oregon and an MBA from Stanford University. He is a certified public accountant and spent two years as an assistant professor of business administration at Portland State University.

At the University of Oregon, where he was a star middle distance runner, he and his coach, Bill Bowerman, liked to tinker with shoe designs. They chipped in $500 to start Blue Ribbon Sports in 1964, concentrating on distributing Japanese made shoes in the USA.

Seven years later, BRS started making its own shoes and, in 1972, marketed its first NIKE products in time for the Olympic trials. Knight combined economical Far East production with innovative designs and adroit marketing to turn athletic shoes into a major growth industry. He still runs 20 miles per week and personally tests new NIKE shoes.

Knight serves on numerous boards, and is a member of various civic, corporate and education committees. He is married and the father of two children.

Simple Advice

My best piece of advice is very simple: Don't be afraid to fail—the only time you have to succeed is the last time you try!

JACK D. KUEHLER
President
IBM Corp.

Jack D. Kuehler, president and IBM director, and member of the Executive Committee, the Corporate Management Board, and the Management Committee, joined IBM as an associate engineer at the company's San Jose, California, Research Laboratory in 1958.

He came to IBM with a B.S. degree in mechanical engineering from Santa Clara University, a year's experience designing jet engines for General Electric, and three years in the Army assigned to the Atomic Energy Commission.

Kuehler advanced through various technical and managerial positions. By 1981, he was group executive of the Information Systems and Technology Group. The following year he became an IBM senior vice president, and in 1985 assumed executive responsibility for the worldwide development and U.S. manufacturing for IBM's technology and computer systems. He was elected to the board of directors in 1986, became an executive vice president in 1987, vice chairman of the board in 1988 and president in 1989.

While working full time as an IBM manager, and later as an executive, he earned a master's in electrical engineering from Santa Clara University. Kuehler also has two honorary doctorates of science from Santa Clara and Clarkson Universities.

Among many other activities outside IBM, Kuehler is a Fellow of the Institute of Electrical and Electronics Engineers, a Fellow of the American Academy of Arts and Sciences, a trustee of Santa Clara University, a member of the board of directors of Olin Corporation, the National Association of Manufacturers, National Action Council for Minorities in Engineering, and the New York State Business Council. He is also a member of the National Academy of Engineering.

Jack and his wife, Carmen, live in Connecticut. They have five children.

Like What You Do

Not many of us know early in our lives exactly where we're headed in our careers. But that's really not very important. What is important is that we work at something we like, work hard at it, and do it to the best of our ability. Liking what we do and doing it well usually go hand in hand.

What if our very first job doesn't work out? That's no catastrophe. There's always a second chance, and anyone who says there's only one is just plain wrong.

It seems to me that at least three things are important to living a fulfilled life.

First, become involved—in your church or synagogue, your neighborhoods, your schools, in protecting our fragile environment —wherever your interests and your talents lead you.

Second, believe in yourself, and set your sights high. And remember, history has told us over and over that one person really can make a difference.

And third, have some fun along the way. Take time to drink in the sunshine and smell the roses. We can't know the end of this fascinating journey. But rather than curse the inevitable bumps and the twists and turns, relax and smile at the infinite delight and wonder along the way.

Jack D Kuehler

W. DANIEL A. LAMEY, CAE
Secretary General
Junior Chamber International

Dan Lamey was born in Stellarton, Nova Scotia, Canada. He graduated from St. Mary's University in Halifax with a Bachelor of Commerce degree. Virtually all of his working life has been spent in the ever growing field of voluntary association management. In 1989 he earned the field's professional designation of Certified Association Executive (CAE) from the American Society of Association Executives (ASAE).

In the midst of his university education, he took leave from his full time studies to take his first association job, working for the Association of Student Councils student travel co-op from 1972 to 1973, by running their office which served students in universities and colleges of the Atlantic Provinces of Canada.

After graduation he became a management trainee for the Bank of Montreal. After three years of what he feels was excellent practical management training, he became national Executive Director of the Canadian Junior Chamber, also known as the "Jaycees".

Having originally intended to return to the "normal" business world, he found that the vocation of association management was where he wanted to build his career in a broad field with endless opportunities. In 1980, he became national Executive Director of Canada's largest national service club, The Association of Kinsmen Clubs. He gained international experience by serving the World Council of Young Men's Service Clubs, of which Kinsmen was a member, as General Secretary. He also managed the international development projects which the Kinsmen organization funded, in such countries as Zambia, India, Bangladesh, Panama, Mauritius, The Philippines, Kenya and Ethiopia, all of which he visited.

In 1986, his career path led him to the United States, when he accepted the position of Secretary General of Junior Chamber International, an organization based in Coral Gables, Florida, that counts over 420,000 member "Jaycees" in 105 countries and territories.

Lamey's voluntary involvement is extensive and includes several organizations in the business, professional and charitable fields.

138

Let the World Come to Your Life!

It is, perhaps, a cliche to say that the world is getting smaller. Of course, the distance around the equator or between Memphis and Tokyo is the same as it was 75 years ago. But, in a communication sense or in terms of time, the world is truly getting smaller—a fact that can change your future.

Remember that when you were three years old your "world" was a big place, even though it may have been confined to your house or apartment? That world was nonetheless interesting, sometimes mysterious and often exciting. A closet or a basement was only to be explored by the most adventurous of spirit.

As you grew older, your "world" also grew. Growing beyond your neighborhood, even your hometown or city—you came to feel comfortable in this bigger—yet still interesting and mysterious world of yours. If you are like the average young American, however, you may set limits on your known world that do not go beyond the boundaries of your city or state, but in all likelihood, definitely do not go beyond the boundaries of your own country (visits to Tijuana, Mexico or Niagara Falls, Canada notwithstanding).

News reports, National Geographic studies and countless other commentaries attest to the fact that young Americans are less informed about the world outside their own country than earlier generations. Even more critical is the fact that they are much less informed than similar young people from other countries. While there is more information about the rest of the world available than ever before, too many tend to ignore it and, as a result, their known world stops growing at an early age.

The world outside our country is not maps, capitals and governments; it is people—people who are pursuing their own future, building their own lives and facing many of the same-or-greater-challenges as you. To be truly successful in coming decades you and countless millions of other young Americans are going to have to tune in to this larger world—expanding your comfort zone beyond the borders of your own state and country—becoming a person who really lives life in the world beyond the United States—someone for whom the world is a part of daily life.

The skills needed to succeed in understanding the world and its impact on life are not that special, although the ability to learn and speak a foreign language is not something you should ignore. The same natural inquisitiveness that helped you explore a new house, a new school or a new town, will work for you just as well when it comes to another country or even simply an encounter with a person from another country.

I have always felt that empathy—the ability to deeply understand the thinking or situation of another person—is an especially important skill in my life. The ability to walk in another's shoes and really understand

(Continued on page 263)

STEW LEONARD
Chairman
Stew Leonard's Inc.

Sam Walton, founder and chairman of Wal-Mart, calls Stew Leonard one of the most innovative and outstanding merchants in America.

Stew Leonard, a graduate of the University of Connecticut's School of Agriculture, began with his roots in a family dairy business. His dream was to build a retail store with a large barn. Inside would be a modern dairy plant. Children could watch their milk being pasteurized and packaged while their mothers shopped in the farm-like atmosphere. The business would enjoy the solid foundation of value, based on a no middleman concept.

In 1969, with the help of SBA Financing, his dream came true. His slogan became, "You'd have to own a cow to get fresher milk."

Today, Stew Leonard's original dairy store has been expanded 29 times. Its sales per square foot are 10 times the food industry average. With annual sales of 100 million dollars, it will soon be featured in the Guiness Book of Records as the highest grossing food store in the world on a sales per square foot basis. It has been featured in Ripley's Believe It or Not as the World's Largest Dairy Store. Each week over 100,000 people flock here. To put that figure into perspective, the Rose Bowl holds 100,000 people.

When President Reagan invited Stew to the White House to receive the Presidential Award for Entrepreneurial Excellence, Stew said, "Only in America could a guy start out as a door-to-door milkman and end up shaking hands with the President of the United States."

My Dad's Advice

If I knew how badly you wanted to succeed, I could tell you whether or not you're going to make it.

Half way through my senior year in high school, a questionnaire was passed out to the members of the senior class by our yearbook staff. They were collecting material for the copy that would go under each graduate's picture in our class yearbook.

Most of the questions were easy: What's your nickname? What are your hobbies, sports activities, clubs? The last question was: What would you like to become in your life?

I knew in my heart that I desperately wanted to be a success. My dad was my idol and he had risen from poverty to owning his own dairy business. He had always stressed to me one piece of advice—"You can become anything you want in this world, if you want it bad enough, stick to it long enough, and are willing to pay the price."

To me at that time money was the symbol of success. So I thought about that last question for a minute, then wrote down that my goal was to become a millionaire. I handed in the questionnaire and promptly forgot all about it.

A few months later, a group of my friends approached me in the hall between classes. They were laughing loudly holding a copy of the just-published yearbook. When they got to me I discovered why they were laughing.

The book was open to my picture and they began to shout, "Ha, ha, ha, you want to be a millionaire? What a joke! You don't have a chance! You're not even the smartest one in the class, why you only got a 'C' in Chemistry! Talk about crazy dreams! You'll never do it! Ha, ha, ha."

Naturally, I was humiliated. I knew that on the surface everything they said was correct. But there was one thing they didn't know. They didn't know how badly I wanted to succeed.

Today, it's 45 years later and, though I no longer equate money with success, my dream has become a reality. The point of this little story is to stress to you the importance of my dad's advice. It's the best advice I've ever gotten in my life and it works like magic! "You can become anything you want in this world, if you want it bad enough, stick to it long enough, and are willing to pay the price."

My dad's advice is just as good today as it was then—YOU CAN DO IT!

Stew Leonard

EUGENE LOOPER
Banking/Financial Consultant

It's a long way from a tenant farm in rural South Carolina, in the shadow of Appalachia, to the halls of academia and banking's leading institutions. Charles Eugene Looper made that journey and today is one of the nation's leading banking/financial consultants.

His trek took him to Furman University, where he earned a B.A. degree and won a fellowship to Louisiana State University where he received his Master of Arts degree.

After a three year hitch in the U.S. Navy, primarily at sea on a destroyer as a Lieutenant Senior Grade, he resumed his education at Georgetown University, where he earned his Ph.D. in public law.

Prior to entering the banking field, he served as an instructor in Georgetown's School of Foreign Service and as professor of political science at Furman University. Later, while studying monetary theory at London University's School of Economics, he realized that an education without capital was unproductive, which led him into banking.

He began at Wachovia Bank & Trust Company, in Winston-Salem, before becoming vice president at the Southeast Banking Corporation in Miami, Florida. At the same time, he served as a part-time professor in the School of Administration at the University of Miami.

Mr. Looper has received scores of honors and has been active in civic, philanthropic and political activities throughout his career.

He has authored numerous publications, including a prophetic article in The Bankers Magazine in 1981 titled "Early Warning Signs of Banking Trouble."

Capital and Savings

The shades of night were falling fast
When through an Alpine village passed
A youth who bore mid snow and ice
A banner with a strange device,
Excelsior.

You may have read Longfellow's poem "Excelsior" and wondered where the ambitious, self-denying, courageous young man carrying the banner with the strange device was going. Many people carry banners with strange devices but with no well-formulated goals, no direction, and gain little achievement. Well-formulated goals are those which enhance the essential elements for achievement: knowledge and capital.

The catalyst is monetary capital. With knowledge you formulate ideas and plans; with monetary capital you purchase resources and energy for conversion of knowledge into products and services.

Knowledge capital is created by education and thinking. Monetary capital is created by savings. At this writing, our country is in a recession. Individuals who have not cultivated the habit of savings find themselves in a precarious position. Installment buying has been made so easy that it is common to spend out of proportion to one's income. Early habits cling to us through life, so, learning to save should be embraced as soon as an individual becomes an income producer. It is essential to personal success.

Thus, a great imperative in a free society is the obligation to save a portion of what is produced or earned. It is no surprise that the countries with the highest savings rate are the most productive and the most democratic. Underdeveloped countries are those deficient in both knowledge and monetary capital which consequently fail to provide the essential of freedom; adequate production of goods and services required for individual mobility.

So it is with the individual—knowledge not energized by capital is academic and frequently misdirected as empty and frustrated idealism. Growth and development for such individuals and countries depends largely upon the quality of education afforded and the acceptance of the necessity to preserve a portion of what is produced. The squirrel who fails to store a part of the fall harvest of nuts seldom survives the winter.

BEN H. LOVE
Chief Scout Executive
Boy Scouts of America

The top professional leader of the Boy Scouts of America since 1985, Ben Love directs the administration of the organization which includes more than 10,000 employees and 1.5 million adult volunteer leaders who deliver Scouting to more than four million young people across the nation.

Scouting Experience

Love has been active in Scouting since his youth, and held adult volunteer positions of Scoutmaster and neighborhood commissioner. His professional career includes service as a district executive, Scout executive, and national staff positions as director of the Boy Scout Division and regional director. He received the Vigil Honor of the Order of the Arrow and three bead in Wood Badge. Other honors include the Shofar (Jewish), the Allaha Akbar (Islamic), and the Saint George Award (Catholic) religious awards; a special recognition from the European Region of the World Scout Bureau: and the Inter-American Region of the World Organization of the Scout Movement's Youth of the Americas Award.

Education

Love attended Vanderbilt University and graduated from Lambuth College in Jackson, Tennessee, with a bachelor of science degree. In 1986 he was honored with a doctor of humanities degree by Lambuth College, where he is a member of the President's Advisory Council. In 1987 he received an honorary doctor of philanthropy degree from Pepperdine University.

Activities and Affiliations

Love serves as a director of La Cima Club, Las Colinas, Irving, Texas, and is a member of the Board of Directors, Council for the Advancement of Citizenship; he is a former director of the Utica National Insurance Companies. He was awarded the Gold Medal from the Sons of the American Revolution and the Flame of Light Youth Leadership Award.

It Takes Determination

It doesn't matter where you come from in America, where you were born, where you were raised, where you went to school. You can achieve your dreams, your goals, your ambitions regardless of the circumstances in which you were raised.

This means that a poor youth can achieve great positions if he or she has the desire to reach the top. It also means that one who has been raised in riches can achieve the humility to attain great accomplishments on his or her own terms.

That is what is great about America—we are all elevated to a common denominator. Each of us reaches our goal by setting our own standards and values. The Scout Oath and the Scout Law are value driven, and attainable by all regardless of circumstances.

I speak from experience as a poor boy raised in rural Tennessee when I tell you that if it is your objective to become Chief Scout Executive, you can do it. Or, if you want to be President of the United States, you can do it. Or, if you want to be a doctor, lawyer, engineer, nurse, butcher, baker or candlestick maker, you can do it.

There are no limitations to our desires. All we need is the determination to reach our objectives. This book is replete with stories of people who overcame adversity to reach their goal. Be determined and you can do it, too!

Ben H. Love

Love is a veteran of the United States Army, having served in the Korean War. He is an elder in the Presbyterian Church.

Family

Married to the former Ann Hugo, of Dyersburg, Tennessee, the Loves have four grown children - Philip and Mark are Eagle Scouts and Ben, Jr. is a professional Scouter. Mr. and Mrs. Love live in Colleyville, Texas.

SID LUCKMAN
NFL Football Great
Business Executive

The most-fabled quarterback in Chicago Bears history, Sid Luckman has achieved equal success in the business world.

Brooklyn-born, his high school team won the New York City championship. He was an All American at Columbia University, where despite the athletic schedule, he made time to work several jobs to pay his way enroute to a Bachelor of Arts degree.

Bears owner-coach George Halas handpicked him as the team's No. 1 draft choice in 1939 to make him quarterback of the intricate new T-formation, which only the Bears used. With the T, Sid led the Bears to world championships in 1940, 1941, 1943 and 1946.

He played 12 years for the Bears making All Pro eight times and was the NFL's most valuable player three times. His records include seven touchdown passes against the Giants and five in the World Championship game against the Washington Redskins, still a record. He's a member of both the College and Pro Football Hall of Fame.

After retiring as a player, he served as a Bears assistant coach and was a vice president of the team, as well. He also assisted Notre Dame, West Point, Columbia University, the University of Pittsburgh, Maryland University and Holy Cross to acclimate them to the T-formation system.

Formerly vice chairman of Cellu-Craft, a manufacturer of flexible packaging, he now serves the firm in sales and consulting. Sid also serves on the boards of various corporations.

He founded the Estelle Luckman Foundation for cancer research in memory of his wife, Estelle, his high school sweetheart, who died in 1981. His three children and various civic and philanthropic endeavors take up his time, when he isn't watching his beloved Chicago Bears.

Spend Your Time Well

Football fans continue to marvel when a quarterback runs a two-minute drill at a crucial time in a game. This studious use of time is often the difference between victory and defeat. People tend to forget it took hours of practice to achieve the coordination it takes to make it work when the game is on the line.

In life, not a minute should be wasted. Time is one of our most precious, mysterious and unappreciated possessions. Precious because none of us knows how much time we've been allotted in this life.

Mysterious because, despite being the only truly constant in our lives, (there will always only be 60 seconds in a minute), time somehow quickly slips away. I'll always remember what the late George Halas, my dear friend, coach and hero, told me shortly before he passed away: "It seems like only yesterday when we were winning all those championships for the Chicago Bears." An avid reader, he quoted Thomas Aldrich who wrote: "All the best sands of life are somehow getting into the wrong end of the hourglass."

Time is unappreciated, because we seem to forget that each minute can be used only once—then it's gone forever. We have no control over the passage of time—the clock keeps ticking—whether we're wasting it or doing something worthwhile with it. So, it's up to you what you'll do with yours.

Unlike the movies, which back-peddle in time, or, fast-forward into the future, we must live life one second at a time. If we could live every 120 minutes as a two-minute drill, as we try to reach one of our goals, we'd never waste one precious moment.

Inevitably, time does slip away. For some, it simply disappears and nothing is left behind. For others, like Mr. Halas, who helped found the National Football League, when time is gone—monuments remain.

What will you have left, when time runs out for you?

Sid Luckman

MANUEL LUJAN, JR.
Secretary of the Interior

Sworn in February 3, 1989, as the 46th Secretary of the Interior.

Served in the House of Representatives from New Mexico 1969-1989. Was senior Republican on the House Interior and Insular Affairs Committee and the Energy and Environment Subcommittee; vice chairman of the House Science, Space and Technology Committee; member of the President's National Commission on Space. Received National Science Foundation Distinguished Service Award.

In Congress, was a leader in battle against wasteful government spending, co-sponsor of seven major environmental protection bills including the Clean Air Act of 1970 and the Clean Water Act, promoted education through support of student loan programs, and backed scientific research to help meet the challenges of the 21st century.

Raised in Santa Fe, N.M., and earned a B.A. from the College of Santa Fe. Also attended St. Mary's College in California. Has received five honorary Ph.D.s.

Organized private sector fund that has provided hundreds of $500 scholarships for students attending college in New Mexico.

Personally inspected cleanup efforts of Exxon Valdez tanker spill in Prince William Sound and serves as a Federal Trustee in assessment of damages. Took steps to improve transportation of oil, insure continued safety in federal offshore programs, and increase cooperation with industry to step up oil spill cleanup research.

Married to the former Jean Couchman of Santa Fe. The Lujans have four children.

Take Pride in America

As Secretary of Interior, I am responsible for the protection of much of America's natural heritage—our parks, wilderness areas and public lands.

Our public lands give Americans some of the best recreation opportunities anywhere in the world including camping, hunting, fishing, sightseeing and just plain relaxation. Today these lands are being threatened, sometimes by the very people who use them. We have problems with litter, vandalism, pollution and overcrowding. And with more than 500 million acres to protect, there is no way that only Interior employees can be effective policemen for these treasures.

But there is one thing I know for sure, Americans love their land and are willing to work to protect it. So, we have started a program at the Department of Interior called Take Pride in America. It is a very simple and practical program. Its message is that public lands are your lands. If you want to continue to enjoy them and assure they'll be around for generations to come, you are going to have to help take care of them.

This challenge has gone out to America. The response has been amazing. From a small town garden club to major corporations, the country has responded. We have clean-up drives, recycling programs, volunteers repairing trails and painting buildings. There is an ever-expanding outreach to people everywhere showing them how heartfelt pride in God's gifts to America can assure these gifts will be here to bless future citizens with special joys of a bountiful and beautiful land.

The invitation to Take Pride in America is addressed to everyone. Accepting it is the best gift people of all ages can give to our blessed land. I especially encourage young people to heed this call by making your lands part of your life.

Manuel Lujan Jr.

GERALD L. MAATMAN
President & CEO
Kemper National
Insurance Companies

Gerald Maatman joined Kemper in 1966 as director of Loss Control Engineering after serving on the faculty of the Illinois Institute of Technology, from which he earned his bachelor of science degree. He earlier has served as an executive with the Illinois Inspection and Rating Bureau. He directed the 1968 formation of the Kemper Corporation subsidiary National Loss Control Service Corporation and was its first president.

Before being elected Kemper National president in 1987 and chief executive officer in 1990, Maatman was executive vice president in charge of Kemper Corporation's regional property-casualty insurance companies and Kemper's Information Services Group. He is also a director of Kemper National and chairman of its executive committee.

Maatman is co-chairman of the Advocates for Highway and Auto Safety, a coalition of insurers, consumer groups and others interested in promoting auto safety. The group will attempt to reduce deaths, injuries and economic costs associated with motor vehicle crashes and fraud and theft involving motor vehicles.

He is also a director of the Institute for Civil Justice, National Commission Against Drunk Driving, the National Fire Protection Association, Junior Achievement of Chicago, National Down Syndrome Society, and Underwriters Laboratories, Inc. He is also on the Leadership Council of the Network of Employers for Traffic Safety and is a member of the Society of Fire Protection Engineers.

Born in Chicago in 1930, he now lives in North Barrington, Illinois, with his wife Bernice. They have two grown children.

Outwork Your Peers

The next decade or two will be a time of great challenge for both business concerns and their managements. Communication advances, increased competition in world markets and greater volatility of our financial systems are but some of the factors which will make it increasingly difficult to achieve future business success.

On a personal level, young aspiring professionals will continue to be faced with competition from increasing numbers of well educated peers. What then can a young adult do to maximize his or her chances of achieving a significant level of business success?

Without question, the single most important ingredient for success lies in "out-working" your peer group. This includes not only mastering the elements of your current job and performing in a superior manner, but also remaining alert to ways in which your group's operations can be further improved.

The ability to handle and lead other people is a second most important element in this picture. Aside from developing effective verbal skills to assist you in selling your ideas, it's important to gain a good understanding of human nature (i.e., learning why people act differently under varying circumstances) and to develop the knack of creating "win-win" situations where both yours and the other party's personal goals can be satisfied. Another important characteristic of any good leader is the ability to lead by example and also to be able to put oneself in the other person's shoes and to act accordingly.

The chances of advancing upward into senior levels of management can be improved measurably by developing a good ability to step back and understand the "big picture". You need to recognize how your job fits into your unit's operations—how the unit supports the company's goals—and how corporate goals and strategies give it a competitive advantage in your industry's marketplace.

Finally, it's very important that a young person decide on long term personal goals and then develop and maintain the inner discipline to keep focused on these multi-year objectives.

An overriding consideration in any young person's business pursuits should be a complete and total commitment to honesty and integrity. Being true to oneself and acting accordingly must be a given in a person's daily life. The ultimate test should be "can I look in the mirror every morning and feel comfortable with myself?" Although a short term advantage can sometimes be gained by acting otherwise, over the long run, such a person is almost certain to fall by the wayside.

151

ROBERT S. MacARTHUR
President
American Youth Foundation

Over the years Bob MacArthur has been employed as a steel worker, a minister, a farmer, a dean, an administrator, and an executive. He has climbed mountains, coached baseball, milked cows, composed music, and recorded a folk mass. He has been a classroom teacher, preacher, and a pastoral counselor. And, he is a cheerleader for his wife, Peggy, and their four children.

After graduation from Dartmouth College, Bob attended Berkeley Divinity School at Yale and served for two years in the parish ministry of the Episcopal Church. Exploring further his interest in intentional community life, he worked in the mountains of North Carolina on a farming cooperative patterned after Danish folk schools.

For 12 years he directed the Outward Bound Center at Dartmouth College, helping students relate the individual and team challenges of the wilderness to their formal and informal education. While at Dartmouth, he taught freshman writing courses and served as acting dean of the William Jewett Tucker Foundation, an endowment established to further the moral and spiritual growth of undergraduates.

Today, inspired by William H. Danforth's philosophy, Bob leads the American Youth Foundation in its efforts to motivate young people to achieve their best, live balanced lives, and serve others. Mr. Danforth's book, I Dare You, *is still available from the foundation.*

I Dare You

As a small boy, William H. Danforth was a sallow-cheeked and sickly student. One day in class his teacher looked Danforth straight in the eyes and said, "I dare you to be the healthiest boy in the class." That dare was enough to launch a lifetime of achievement and service.

Danforth changed his diet and began a regimen of physical exercise. He grew robust and healthy. As an adult with tireless energy and the talent to motivate others, he founded Ralston Purina, a company that has grown to worldwide prominence today. He never missed a day for sickness and outlived most of his classmates.

In 1931, Danforth shared the philosophy of his success in a book called, *I Dare You.*

> The only reason you are not the person you should be is because you don't dare to be. Once you dare, new powers harness themselves for your service.

Danforth dared everyone to discover and harness the hidden powers of our mental, physical, social, and spiritual gifts. Living this four-fold life, he dares us to be "my own self, at my very best, all the time." And, he dares us to share ourselves in service to others.

From my work at the American Youth Foundation, I know that young people accept the dare today. They are taking control of their lives, motivating their peers, and inspiring younger students. By establishing these habits now, they are preparing for their roles as active citizens and community leaders in their adult years.

As an underclassman Tony was also an underachiever. After attending the AYF's National Leadership Conference he accepted the dare to seek his best and serve. Now in his senior year, he is president of the student council, captain of the football team, and a role model to seventh graders whom he is mentoring.

As part of the AYF Youth Leadership Compact team in her school, Michelle helped organize a Special Olympics Day for 250 disabled children. She and her team enlisted the help of 550 of their fellow students and teachers. The event was a great success, reminding us that the efforts of a few can achieve an impact many times their number.

Danforth concluded his book with a timeless dare:

> Never give up until you have released your unused capacities for service and shared your gifts with others. One enkindled spirit can set hundreds on fire.

Tony and Michelle are but two examples of hundreds of young people with "enkindled spirits" who are making a difference. Regardless of our

(Continued on page 265)

ABRAHAM LINCOLN MAROVITZ
Senior Federal Judge
Northern District of Illinois

The rich and colorful life of Senior Federal Judge Abraham Lincoln Marovitz is not only one but a multitude of Horatio Alger stories. His life is one of abiding faith and love for his parents and everyone around him. A man who rose from poverty to become one of the Chicago's most respected citizens.

At birth he was named Abraham Lincoln because his mother had learned about the American president at a settlement house following her immigration from Czarist Russia. She made a promise to herself that someday she, too, would have an Abraham Lincoln of her own.

Little did she realize that her son would one day walk local, national and international corridors with such notables as the late prime ministers of Israel, David Ben Gurion and Golda Meir, Governor Adlai E. Stevenson, Senator Hubert Humphrey, and the late Mayor Richard J. Daley, among many others.

Judge Marovitz was the first professing member of the Jewish community to be elected to the Illinois State Senate. In 1942, at age 38, he joined the U.S. Marines. After the war, he returned to the State Senate, serving 11 years before becoming a Superior Court judge. He received an award as the "most outstanding legislator" for his courageous stand on civil rights. Later, he was elected chief justice of the Criminal Court.

In 1963, following his nomination by President Kennedy, he was sworn in as a United States district judge for the Northern Illinois District. Among his many honors is a Doctorate of Humane Letters from Lincoln College, the first annual Lincoln the Lawyer Award from the Abraham Lincoln Association, and the Spirit of Lincoln Award from the Anti-Defamation League of B'nai B'rith.

In observance of the great distance he came from poverty to prominence, Judge Marovitz was presented the Horatio Alger Award in 1979. To his legion of friends he has remained plain "Abe."

Do the Right Thing

I believe that success and greatness is in the kindness, understanding, courage, faith, compassion, and desire to aid others that lie within a man's heart and in the way he uses those qualifications in all of his relations with other persons.

I was born in 1905, in very poor (monetary) circumstances. I was raised in a tough area of Chicago and was a mediocre student at best. In 1963 I was appointed to the U.S. District Court by the late President John F. Kennedy.

My chambers are filled with Lincolnia and memorabilia which prompts questions from the groups of children who visit me there. I tell them that I attribute what modest success I have achieved to first: the lessons I learned from my beloved parents who were uneducated, immigrant people possessed with native intelligence, common sense and high moral principle. My mother was the kindest person I have ever known and my father was the most honest man I have ever known.

I was also blessed with a lot of help during my lifetime; a little push from some, a big push from others. I have never met a self-made man or woman, everyone needs help. Helping people is my greatest concern. I find that I can't do any "big" things, but I can do a lot of "little" things. It is my practice to endeavor to do a "mitzvah" (good deed) every day and if I don't, I feel the day has been wasted and I try to make up for it the next day. I always encourage young people who visit me to follow the practice of doing something nice for someone each day.

Another thing I tell young people, perhaps the most important lesson I learned from my parents, is: "You must stand for something in this world and wherever you go, take along your self-respect—then be sure you leave with it."

There are many plaques on my chamber walls with sayings to which I give credence. One, written by Archer G. Jones, sums up my philosophy: "There is but one rule of conduct for a man—to do the right thing. The cost may be dear in money, in friends, in influence, in labor, in a prolonged and painful sacrifice, but the cost not to do right is far more dear; you pay in the integrity of your manhood, in honor, in truth, in character. You forfeit your soul's content, and for a timely gain, you barter the infinities."

Live by this rule and your life will be a success.

Abraham Lincoln Marovitz

N. LYNN MARTENSTEIN
Vice President of
Corporate Communication
United Air Lines

Lynn Martenstein directs United Airlines' external communications, creative services, employee communications and contributions. She also sits on the editorial board of Vis-a-Vis, the airline's in-flight magazine.

Prior to joining the airline, she was director of external communication for the national headquarters of the American Red Cross, Washington, D.C. She also served as liaison to the White House.

Prior to the Red Cross, the communication executive worked as director of public affairs for the national headquarters of the American Automobile Association.

Martenstein's work in public relations and advertising has been recognized by the Television Academy Emmy Awards, Clio Awards, American Society for Association Executives, Public Relations Society of America, International Association of Business Communicators, and Outdoor Advertising Association.

Lynn currently serves on the board of directors of the American Red Cross Mid-America Chapter and the Goodman Theatre in Chicago. She is a member of the National Press Club and the Public Relations Society of America.

Martenstein is an honors graduate of Hollins College and holds a masters degree in business administration from American University. She is married to Richard F. Hebert.

Believe in Yourself

My parents had high expectations of me. If I expressed interest in becoming a nurse, they suggested I become a doctor. If I leaned toward office work, they encouraged me to become president of the company.

Predictably, perhaps, I played business as a child, at various times, selling seashells, original poems and drawings, rides around the block on a foot-pedaled surrey, even groceries back to my parents. My father was always my best customer.

Gradually, my parents' confidence in me took hold. And *I* came to believe I could achieve whatever I put my mind to. My advice to young people? Believe in yourself. And surround yourself with family and friends who also believe in you.

MICHAEL H. McCAIN
President & CEO
McCain USA Inc.

Michael McCain started at the bottom of his company's ladder and worked his way up through sales, marketing, information systems and management. At age 32, he now heads a major U.S. company.

The McCain heritage began with Michael's father and uncle, who were pioneers in the Canadian frozen food industry. In 1975, the company expanded into the U.S. market, and Michael earned the right to lead the company in 1990.

Building a team of experts in the organization, Michael encouraged his employees to put forth entrepreneurial efforts in response to emerging consumer opportunities. As a result, the company has developed new products that have established a solid base in the U.S. marketplace.

McCain is a graduate of Mount Allison University and the University of Western Ontario. An avid skier and tennis player, he most enjoys spending time with his wife, Chris, and their four children at their suburban Chicago home.

Age No Handicap

It's interesting how our culture looks at age. In a racehorse, three or four years is ideal. The careers of many fashion models peak at age 19 or 20. Professional athletes are usually considered "over the hill" by 35.

Coming out of college, I was anxious to make my mark. I was filled with the confidence and enthusiasm of youth that is ready and willing to change the world.

However, in the world of business where I've thrown my lot, age is viewed in an entirely different perspective. Our gymnastics are mental. We may have to be quick thinkers and fast talkers, but the race is not usually won by the speediest runner. Youth is sometimes viewed as an affliction which is best cured by time. "You have to put in your time" and "experience is the best teacher" are common themes. Champions of business traditionally are honed through years of practice. For the young graduate, it can be discouraging at times.

I've always been a little impatient about standing in line. I believe in serving my time, but I like to speed up the clock if I can. To make a faster turn on the learning curve of my career, I've tried to know my business from the inside out—better than my contemporaries and as well as anyone, regardless of their years in the industry. My goal: to compress my professional learning process and demonstrate that ability is not a matter of age, but a function of mental maturity and an accumulation of life experience.

Over the past 12 years, more than one person has been a "nay sayer" based on age or family connection. Fortunately, I have always accepted the challenge to prove them wrong where necessary. That's why I run a large business at age 32.

There are still people in the world who look at businessmen like bottles of wine—believing that our real potential won't be tapped until we're over 50. I have found that the best solution to this discrimination is to not be sensitive to it. Simply ignore it. Go on to be the best you can be at whatever age.

If my dozen years in business have taught me one valuable lesson, it's that what you think about yourself is most important. The key to success is, no matter what anyone thinks, that you know you can do it.

WARREN E. McCAIN
Chairman of Executive Committee
Albertson's, Inc.

Warren McCain was born in Logan, Kansas. He was raised in Payette, Idaho, where he graduated from high school before serving in the U.S. Navy during World War II.

While attending the Illinois Institute of Technology in Chicago, he worked at the National Tea Company to make ends meet. This piqued his interest in the grocery business. He next studied at Oregon State University from 1946 to 1950 before a second hitch in the Navy during the Korean War.

Upon returning home, he pursued a career in the grocery business at Mountain States Wholesale, where he spent eight years gaining broad experience in many facets of the food business. In 1959, he joined Albertson's, Inc. in Boise, Idaho, as general merchandise supervisor. He climbed the corporate ladder to the top, becoming president, chairman, and chief executive officer.

His outstanding success is reflected in some of the honors he's received:

University of Southern California Industry of the Year Award (1985).

The Wall Street Transcript selected him Best Chief Executive of Retail / Supermarkets & Food Chains (1987, 1988, and 1989).

First Place Award from Financial World as CEO of the Year / Grocery Industry (1990).

Named Retailer of the Year, Mass Marketing Retailing (1991).

In 1985, he received an honorary law doctorate from the College of Idaho. He was named Business Man of the Year by Alpha Kappa Psi Fraternity, Idaho State University, and was the recipient of the Leadership for Public Education Award from the Idaho Association of School Administrators.

Warren was inducted into the Horatio Alger Association of Distinguished Americans in 1991.

He serves as a director of Albertson's, Inc., Portland General Corporation, and Pope & Talbot, Inc., and is a member of the Board of Trustees, College of Idaho.

Lessons to Follow

Back in 1945 I was aboard a Navy ship off the coast of Nagasaki, Japan, shortly after the atomic bomb had been dropped on that city. I was 20 years old, confused, and full of anxiety. I was thinking about what I was going to do with my life when I returned to the United States.

I was a small-town kid from Payette, Idaho, who didn't have a family that could afford to send me to college. I'd had enough exposure in the Navy to know I was capable of doing something beyond pumping gas in the local service station, and my high school education had given me a good base in mathematics and English.

During this time I read a book that made a big impression on me. I adopted some philosophy from that book, *Magnificent Obsession,* written by Lloyd C. Douglas, the world-famous novelist who also wrote *The Robe* and other bestselling books.

Two of the important lessons I learned from Mr. Douglas were to never try to run away from troubles, and to always repay your benefactors and mentors by doing the same for other people.

The first point he made was that you must face your troubles; overcome them, right where you are. Instead of trying to escape from frustrations, you need to triumph over them; otherwise, they'll be with you wherever you go.

I have been fortunate to be in a position to repay the 12 persons, not including my family, who had a significant impact on my life and career. I have attempted to repay each of these individuals in various ways. Three of them were high school teachers in whose honor I sponsor 16 four-year full-ride scholarships for students otherwise unable to attend college.

As for guidelines to success, I encourage young people to answer several basic questions before making decisions on their careers. Do you want to be with a small company or a large corporation? Do you want to travel, and where would you prefer to live? After you make those decisions and you begin working for a company, I think you have to be an extremely good listener. Then, you can't be too impatient for promotions and moving ahead. Worry about the job you're in today, then when the next job comes along, you'll be prepared for it. You have to be a good team player, set high goals for yourself, and you absolutely must practice great discipline in everything you do.

Warren E. McCain

DRAYTON McLANE
President & CEO
McLane Company, Inc.

Drayton McLane received a bachelor of business administration degree from Baylor University and a master of science degree from Michigan State University.

He is president and chief executive officer of McLane Company, as well as vice chairman of Wal-Mart Stores, Inc. McLane serves on the board of directors of Wal-Mart Stores, Inc., Central and South West Corporation, and Scott & White Hospital. He has served as chairman of the National American Wholesale Grocers' Association and the Texas Wholesale Grocers' Association. He is vice chairman of the board of governors for the National Children's Miracle Network. He has served as president and as campaign chairman for the United Way of Central Texas.

He was the recipient of the National American Wholesale Grocers' Association's 1990 American Achiever Award. He also won the Arthur Young / Venture Magazine Entrepreneur Award of the Year in 1987. The Boy Scouts of America honored him in 1985 with the Boy Scouts of America Silver Beaver Award; and in 1989, he received their Distinguished Citizen's Award. McLane, who received the Herbert H. Reynolds Award and the 1991 Baylor Distinguished Alumni Award, was president of the Baylor Development Council in 1981.

He and his wife, Elizabeth, have two sons, Drayton and Denton. They are members of Temple First Baptist Church, where McLane is a deacon and past chairman of the deacon board.

You Need a Goal

Youth is like an unwritten book and you are the author. What a marvelous opportunity! As the pages of life have unfolded day by day, year by year, I have discovered there are some very practical and applicable keys to success and happiness.

The primary key to success and happiness is to get a goal for your life. This includes both short range and long range goals. These will change periodically throughout one's life as goals are achieved, new opportunities arise, and we seek new directions. However, once you have identified and set your course, then charge forward. Be a leader, be courageous, believe in yourself, and be confident in your abilities.

Leadership requires one to set an example of high standards in both the quality of your performance and morally. Take the appropriate steps to accomplish your objectives with strong integrity, determination, commitment, and a winning attitude. You can make it happen through perseverance and keeping your mind set on achieving goals.

Courage is the inner strength one attains through his conviction and belief in what he is trying to accomplish. Leaders are also able to motivate others with enthusiasm and a well defined plan of action. Be a cheerleader and rally others around your cause.

Christopher Columbus was a great example of leadership, courage, conviction and determination. He developed an idea, turned it into a goal, defined a plan of action, pursued and motivated a group of teammates, rallied them around his cause, and set out to accomplish his objectives. Many historians have written volumes of books on his life, but he was the original author. You can do it, too!

Drayton McLane

HARRY A. MERLO
Chairman/President
Louisiana-Pacific Corporation

Harry Angelo Merlo was born March 5, 1925, in the little sawmill community of Stirling City, California. Those early years were filled with lessons of dedication, hard work and honesty, the foundation of his rise to success within the free enterprise system.

Since its formation in 1973, Harry Merlo has guided the growth of Louisiana-Pacific to become one of the foremost forest products companies in the world today.

Enjoy Serving Others

Personal excellence every day of our lives is what my loving Mother held out to her family as the goal worthy of our pursuit. She told us, "Because we are foreigners, we must work harder to be worthy of America. We must earn the right to be Americans."

As I grew up my Mother's teachings became for me the spirit of Yes, We Can! The thinking is basic and timeless. To succeed, each of us must make a difference in everything we undertake. For ourselves, our families, our community and our country.

Everybody has his own formula, but for me life has always been rather simple because I am thrilled to serve people. My philosophy is this: "Alone we're nobody, but as a team we are important." You give your energy and ability unselfishly for your fellow worker and don't worry about yourself. If he does the same, your team will win and all will share in the victory. You know, the Good Book says: "He among you who shall lead will be a servant to all." If you enjoy serving others, I guarantee you will be a success.

Harry A Merlo

JERRY D. METCALF
Chairman & CEO
Scrivner, Inc.

Born in Manhattan, Kansas, Jerry Metcalf was one of seven children.

He chose his career early in life. When Jerry was in high school, he accepted a job stocking groceries in a friend's father's grocery store and then worked his way through college. He graduated from Kansas State University with a degree in business. By this time, he realized that he enjoyed the work so much that he wanted to remain in the grocery business.

Recognizing his talent with the public, a large wholesale food distribution company asked him to step out of the grocery store and into the wholesale business. He accepted the offer, and after eight years with the company, was placed in charge of a $200 million operation. At age 31, Jerry was the youngest person to ever preside over a distribution center for the company.

Over the years, he continued to work his way up, and now serves as Chairman and Chief Executive Officer of Scrivner, Inc., one of the largest wholesale/retail food distributors in the country.

On his climb up the corporate ladder, Jerry has always remembered the less fortunate—success has not diverted him from reality. His philanthropic interests are many, with special focus on children's education and the homeless.

Although he is a hard-working businessman, he is also a devoted husband and father. He resides in Edmond, Oklahoma, with his wife, Jaynie. His son, Jeff, and daughter-in-law, Wendy, live in Chicago.

Even though Jerry is at the top, his work ethic has not slackened. He is still as driven as ever. He maintains a business schedule that keeps his days booked, which goes with his philosophy: set a goal, work hard and never give up.

Hard Work and Determination

Hard work and determination. That may sound like a cliche, but it isn't. Growing up in a large family, I learned to share and that there is no substitute for hard work and determination. Striving to be the best at whatever you do is the highest personal goal you can set for yourself.

I am a firm believer that the Lord gives us the tools to be whatever we are in life. What we do with those tools is up to each of us individually. You have to set a goal and then work diligently to achieve that goal. Once you do, set another goal and work just as hard to meet the next challenge. When you achieve success you'll know that you are using the tools given you properly.

As you seek to balance your life, with private and personal objectives, bear in mind that others have the same aspirations. Be considerate of them. No one becomes successful without the help of fellow workers and business associates. You only earn their respect and support by your actions.

Keeping that in mind, I believe that determination breaks down all obstacles. If you want to do something badly enough you can figure a way to do it. It takes focused thoughts, hard work and determination. Never give up.

RAY MEYER
Legendary Basketball Coach

Perhaps the greatest compliment a person can receive is to be recognized in public. Ray Meyer is complimented often. More than seven years since he last coached DePaul University's Blue Demons basketball team, he is still recognized from coast to coast as "Coach."

After leaving the coaching ranks in 1984, Meyer turned his attention to a dual role as a special assistant to DePaul President Rev. John T. Richardson, C.M. and Athletic Director Bill Bradshaw working on fund raising and other special projects.

One of basketball's most respected authorities, he also serves as color commentator for DePaul broadcasts on WGN Radio. The Great Midwest Conference, formed in 1991, has named its Coach of the Year trophy the Ray Meyer Award.

Meyer knows basketball from all sides. An All-American player at Notre Dame, he served as team captain for two years and earned his bachelor's degree in sociology in 1938. He is only the fifth major college coach to record at least 700 career victories and remains among the all-time NCAA Division I leaders in wins. Meyer's record of 37 winning seasons in 42 years is testimony to his reputation as the consummate teacher. He fashioned a brilliant 180-30 (.857) record and guided the Blue Demons to seven consecutive post-season tournament appearances in his final seven years at the helm.

Meyer was elected to the Naismith Hall of Fame in 1979, earned four national coach of the year awards in a six-year spann was named Man of the Year by the National Basketball Coaches Association in 1980, and is a member of the Illinois Sports Hall of Fame.

As decorated as Meyer is, his greatest honor comes regularly when he's recognized publicly by fans as simply "Coach."

Be Dedicated

If I had to pick a role model for young people my choice would be George Mikan, a great basketball player and a fine human being.

When George enrolled at DePaul he was 6'9" and about 230 pounds of raw talent. At a time when basketball featured small speedy guards and fast forwards, he was clumsy and lacked agility. The moment we met I told him he could become as good as he wanted to be. He readily accepted a rigid regimen I programmed for him. George spent hours jumping rope, doing vertical leaps, handling a medicine ball and doing drills to improve his foot work, in addition to the rigors of regular team practices.

Because of his dedication, he became an All-American and went on to an outstanding professional career culminated with his selection as basketball's "Player of the First Half of This Century." He also was an excellent student and today is a leading corporate lawyer. His success can be summed up in one word "dedicated."

I coached two years as an assistant at Notre Dame, my alma mater, and forty-two years at DePaul. I've seen countless players with natural ability waste their talent because of a lack of dedication. Whether you are an athlete or not, you must set high goals for yourself. Goals you need to stretch to reach and you must believe you can do it. Believing in yourself is half the battle. The harder you work to succeed—the harder it is for you to fail. You are never defeated unless you admit it. You are not going to be successful all the time. There will be setbacks and detours. The supreme test is not in your successes but in your failures. You must have the courage to overcome disappointments.

When things get difficult, in a game, or, in life, you must force yourself to do the things you have to do. One can't improve or succeed without desire, dedication, self-discipline and perseverance.

Don't always look for someone else to motivate you. Even a coach is limited in motivating. Sometimes a pep talk will work. Other times an old-fashioned chewing out will do it. Most often, it is the individual who ultimately is responsible for motivation. The successful person, on the basketball court, in business, or simply as a human being, is the one who makes a commitment to be the best he or she can be.

If it can be done, you can do it—if you dedicate yourself to the task.

Ray Meyer

JAMES R. MOFFETT
Chairman & CEO
Freeport-McMoRan, Inc.

Jim Bob Moffett was born in Houma, Louisiana, the son of a transient oil field worker who left the family when Moffett was five years old. He spent his youth in Houston, where during high school, he worked all sorts of jobs to help support his mother and sister. He bagged groceries, delivered newspapers, pumped gas, sold shoes but still found time for sports, the Boy Scouts, and became a member of the National Honor Society.

When he graduated from the University of Texas, he received an award for excellence in geology and was the football player with the highest scholastic average. While a senior he married his high school sweetheart and after graduation went to work for Ken McWilliams, his mentor. After putting in a day's work, he attended night classes at Tulane University and earned his master's degree in geology.

Eventually, he and McWilliams formed a partnership which was to grow into today's Freeport-McMoRan, Inc. By 1980, Moffett was chairman and chief executive officer. Known as one of the best financial minds in the energy business, he reconstructed the corporation by forming a complex web of companies and master limited partnerships, which resulted in worldwide company growth.

In 1991, he was honored with a tribute in the Congressional Record to acknowledge his leadership in making the company the ideal corporate citizen. Freeport-McMoRan gives between $6 million and $10 million a year to charities, the arts, conversation, education and research. Moffett gives another $1 million out of his own pocket.

Jim Bob was named New Orleanian of the Year in 1992 for setting the standard for corporate citizenship by giving back. "Giving goes with success," he says. "It's as American as apple pie and baseball. If you're successful, you should give back to the community and encourage others to do so." Beyond monetary contributions, he is most proud of his employees, who give thousands of hours yearly volunteering in support of community programs.

Never Give Up on Yourself

Everyone can have an impact on the quality of life in the world. No matter what your I.Q., size, shape or race, do the best you can do every day. Out-work and out-think the other guy and success will follow. Be patient—good things don't happen every day or every year, but they will happen. There are no short cuts to success to replace honest, hard work. Never give up on yourself!

THOMAS S. MONAGHAN
Founder/Chairman
Domino's Pizza, Inc.

Thomas S. Monaghan was born in 1937 in Ann Arbor, Michigan. His father died four years later, ushering in a childhood of foster homes and orphanages.

After graduating from St. Thomas High School in 1955 and enrolling at Ferris State College in Big Rapids, Michigan, Monaghan enlisted in the U.S. Marine Corps in 1956. Receiving an honorable discharge in 1959, he returned to Ann Arbor and enrolled at the University of Michigan.

While attending college, Monaghan and his brother James borrowed $900 and bought a small pizza store called DomiNick's in Ypsilanti. In less than a year Monaghan bought his brother's share of the business and formed another partnership, opening additional stores in Ann Arbor and Mt. Pleasant, Michigan.

The story behind Domino's Pizza, of the many obstacles Monaghan conquered throughout the years and the path he took to success, was compiled for the first time in his 1984 autobiography, Pizza Tiger, *co-authored by Robert Anderson.*

Monaghan pioneered several innovations in the pizza industry that have set standards among other operators. Monaghan is credited with developing dough trays, the corrugated pizza box, insulated bags to transport pizzas, the pizza screen, a conveyor oven and a unique franchise system.

As Domino's Pizza grew into the world's largest pizza delivery company, Monaghan's enterprising spirit allowed him to set his sights on other endeavors. As a boy, Tom always looked forward to the annual orphanage outing: a Detroit Tigers game. In 1983, he purchased his dream team for $53 million; in 1984 they won the World Series. He is now taking time to pursue philanthropic interests involving charitable organizations. Monaghan is married and has four daughters.

Priorities to Ponder

The management techniques I applied in building Domino's Pizza were developed mostly by trial and error. But all of them were based on homemade philosophy I call my five personal priorities. My five priorities are spiritual, social, mental, physical, and financial, in that order:

Spiritual

My background makes concern about spiritual matters as natural to me as breathing. My religious faith is strong. I know I would not have been able to build Domino's without the strength I gained from my religious faith. When it comes to secular matters of business, my spiritual priority is expressed in the Golden Rule: Do unto others as you would have others do unto you.

Social

A loving wife and family are to me, essential for a happy productive life. After family on my scale of social relationships come friends. Nobody can succeed in business without the help of friends.

Mental

The key factor in maintaining a healthy mind is a clear conscience. This means you have done your best to live up to your own expectations. A clear conscience fosters self-esteem, a positive attitude, and an optimistic outlook, all of which promote success in business.

Physical

It may sound corny but I subscribe to the idea that the body is the temple of the soul. If I lost my health, I'd give every penny I had to get it back, and I don't know anyone who wouldn't.

Financial

The financial priority is last on my list because it arises from the others. I know that if I attend to the first four properly, financial success will follow.

Another important principle I've stressed over the years is have fun in the work you do. I believe that if you've chosen the career that is right for you, it will give your life a feeling of purpose.

Thomas S. Monaghan

SAM MOORE
President
Thomas Nelson Publishers

Sam Moore is a card-carrying theologian who worked his way through the University of South Carolina selling Bibles door-to-door. He had arrived in this country from Lebanon in 1950 under the sponsorship of a Baptist missionary. His initial customers laughed at his foreign accent, and his first week's earnings were $19!

Today, he heads Thomas Nelson Publishers, the world's largest Bible publisher and a leading independent publisher of Christian and inspirational books.

He graduated with a degree in economics and a minor in accounting. Moore also has an M.A. degree from Columbia Bible College and Seminary.

In 1957, he moved to Nashville determined to start his own business. He began by borrowing money to buy Bibles and trained college students in the door-to-door techniques that had proven successful for him. Subsequently, he began to publish Bibles himself.

Then, in 1969, Moore purchased Thomas Nelson and Sons, a venerable British Bible publisher, which wanted to sell its U.S. distribution network and its collection of Bible plates. This made Moore's company the largest Bible publishing firm in the United States. It became the world's's largest when Moore spent $4 million to have 150 biblical scholars write the New King James Version, first published in 1982, which to date has sold more than 22 million copies.

The energetic Moore, utilizing his network of more than 7,500 Christian bookstores, has most recently sharply increased his company's revenues with a line of Christian music cassettes, including tapes by Johnny Cash and Barbra Streisand, along with other gift items.

Work Ethic

In recent months the American work ethic has been challenged. While the accusations may be accurate in some cases, I believe most people still recognize the value of honest work.

We all have to work. It is a key element to a satisfying life. Work sometimes is difficult and tedious. We'd all be happier if we could find some satisfaction in our work other than just financial reward.

In this high-tech era, we've become computerized workers and clock-watchers. There's no romance in working overtime, and leaving on time has become a daily routine. If you measure your performance by the clock, it usually indicates you're putting in the least effort. Personal satisfaction at day's end comes in knowing you have put forth your best effort.

In our Varsity Internship Program at Thomas Nelson, we have several hundred college students each year who save in excess of $1,000 per week (after expenses) for a period of 10 to 12 weeks during the summer. Many of the students work over 85 hours per week to earn money for their college education and at the same time earn college credit in the area of marketing. I am gratified to see this renewed work spirit in America's youth.

The great philosopher Elbert Hubbard made a remark that's still timely: "Folks who never do any more than they get paid for, never get paid for any more than they do."

Throughout this book you'll read about successful people who began with little or nothing, but with the right work ethic they have achieved what at one time might have seemed like unreachable goals. I have found successful executives are usually on top because they tried a little harder, worked a little longer, and gave more of themselves.

Many of these business leaders have learned that serving God is the greatest career in the world. Always remember that if we spend part of our lives furthering His kingdom, it will bring us restorative powers and joy to our souls.

Sam Moore

JEAN NIDETCH
Founder
Weight Watchers International, Inc.

Jean Nidetch has helped to change the shape of millions of overweight men and women throughout the world.

In 1961, after a lifelong struggle with overweight, she found a diet on which she shed 72 pounds. As she lost weight, Jean shared her success with friends. Little did she realize that a meeting with six overweight women in her Queens apartment was a prototype for a business.

At a time when support groups were non-existent and self-help was unknown, Nidetch's idea caught on. Within three months, 40 people were squeezing into her modest apartment for weekly meetings. Within a year, Weight Watchers expanded beyond her home and later became a public company. Nidetch knew she had succeeded beyond her dreams when 17,000 Weight Watcher members from around the world gathered in Madison Square Garden to celebrate the enterprises tenth anniversary.

Jean, with the help of a board of directors, took the company public in 1968. In 1978, after 15 years of phenomenal growth, they sold Weight Watchers to H.J. Heinz & Co. for $72 million.

She now serves as a consultant to Weight Watchers International, travelling as much as 10 months a year to spread the Weight Watchers message, including regular summer visits to camps for children. She encourages overweight youngsters to reach their weight loss goals and speaks about the emotional and behavioral changes that will take place when their goals are met.

Jean's commitment to both self-improvement and higher education is apparent. She has established the Jean Nidetch Foundation to benefit economically disadvantaged teenagers who wish to continue their education, and a UCLA scholarship has been established in her name to support postgraduate education in political science for deserving college students.

Nidetch has received hundreds of awards and accolades. The Ladies Home Journal honored her as one of "The Most Important Women in the

Whenever I speak to a group of youngsters I tell them: "If you have a dream—go for it!"

Since I am usually talking to those with weight problems, I add what may be the most important suggestion for them to ever attain any kind of success—Stay Healthy!

Modern medicine, health clinics and spas can help keep us in shape, but there is little that can be done if we are not willing to personally commit ourselves to a responsible program of personal health care.

Let me caution you to learn early-on that you are what you eat. Make no mistake about that. Our most dreaded diseases including cancer, heart trouble, diabetes and kidney problems are all affected by faulty diet.

It is also well to remember that health care, like anything else, should be done in moderation. Too much exercise is as harmful as never exerting ourselves at all. The same goes for eating which calls for a balanced diet. Healthy persons carefully balance their physical, mental and spiritual well-being into a fully integrated way of living. The responsibility of healthy living rests with each of us.

An old proverb sums it up well: "He who has health has hope; and he who has hope has everything!"

Jean Nidetch

U.S." She became the first woman to become a member of the New York Chapter of the Young President's Organization. In 1989, she received the prestigious Horatio Alger Award, and in 1991, she became a member of the Horatio Alger Association board of directors. Her autobiography, The Story of Weight Watchers, *sold over 2 million copies.*

Throughout her remarkable career, Jean Nidetch has realized her goals and potential and serves as a continuous source of inspiration for others in reaching theirs.

HUGH O'BRIAN
Founder
Hugh O'Brian
Youth Foundation (HOBY)

Motion picture and television star Hugh O'Brian mastered his craft across the entire spectrum of show business. His seven-year starring role as "Wyatt Earp" is a television classic and he appeared in scores of other stage, television and movie roles. But along with his success in his chosen field, he never lost sight of his civic and philanthropic responsibilities.

For the past 33 years, O'Brian has put his "guts, bucks and time" into the Hugh O'Brian Youth Foundation (HOBY). He walked away from a lucrative career in movies and television to devote his life to this effort. Its format is simple: bring a select group of high school sophomores with demonstrated leadership abilities together with leaders who are on the firing line in business, government, education and the professions—then let them interact.

Next spring, more than 13,000 high school sophomores selected for their leadership potential will attend 92 HOBY Leadership Seminars in all 50 states, the Bahamas, Mexico, Jamaica, and Canada. All seminars have the theme "America's Incentive System," and are all conducted by volunteers. Funding comes entirely from the private sector.

In recognition of the outstanding work he has done with youth, O'Brian has been awarded four honorary degrees and many awards. Most recently, in 1989, he received the 60th Annual American Education Award presented by the American Association of School Administrators. This award is the oldest and most prestigious award that the education profession bestows. In 1990, the Los Angeles Business Council awarded him its 6th Lifetime Achievement Award. The Freedom Through Knowledge Award, sponsored by the National Space Club in association with NASA, one of the nation's highest awards, is among the other honors he's received.

Freedom to Choose

In 1958, I was privileged to spend nine inspirational days in Africa with Dr. Albert Schweitzer which changed by life. Dr. Schweitzer's strong belief that "the most important thing in education is to teach young people to think for themselves" motivated me to form the Hugh O'Brian Youth Foundation (HOBY). The Foundation's goal is not to teach these future leaders what to think, but how to think. HOBY's purpose is to seek out, recognize, and develop leadership potential in high school sophomores.

I do NOT believe we are all born equal. Physical and emotional differences, parental guidelines, varying environments, being in the right place at the right time, all play a role in enhancing or limiting an individual's development. But, I DO believe every man and woman, if given the opportunity and encouragement to recognize their potential, regardless of background, has the freedom to choose in our world. Will an individual be a taker or a giver in life? Will that person be satisfied merely to exist or seek a meaningful purpose? Will he or she dare to dream the impossible dream?

I believe every person is created as the steward of his or her own destiny with great power for a specific purpose, to share with others, through service, a reverence for life in the spirit of love.

You have the freedom to choose what you will do with your life.

Hugh O'Brian

ROBERT ORBEN
Author/Humorist

*Bob Orben is the author of 46 books of professional humor for show
business and speakers. Known as the Orben Comedy Series, these books
have been used as a basic source of humor by most professional entertainers and public speakers. The first book in the series,* The Encyclopedia of
Patter, *was written in 1946 when Bob was 18 years old.*

*For many years, he was editor of "Orben's Current Comedy"—a humor
service providing topical new laugh material for public speakers, entertainers, emcees, toastmasters, and business, political and community
leaders.*

*Orben was in Hollywood from 1964 to 1970 where he wrote for the Red
Skelton TV Show. From 1962 to 1963, he was a writer for the Jack Paar
TV Show in New York.*

He wrote for Dick Gregory for six years and edited Dick's first two books,
From the Back of the Bus *and* What's Happening?

*In recent years, Bob has also served as speechwriter for leading business
and political figures. In early 1974, he was a speech consultant to Vice
President Gerald R. Ford. In August of 1974, he became a speechwriter for
President Ford—and in January 1976, he was appointed special assis-
tant to President Ford and director of the White House Speechwriting
Department.*

*Orben is now active in the speaking field and also conducts workshops and
seminars on public speaking, speech writing, and the uses of humor in
business communication.*

180

Offer the Framazan

Many years ago, I heard this story: A young man was on a commuter train returning home from work. He couldn't help but overhear a conversation going on between two executives near him. One of them was saying, "It's ridiculous. We urgently need a new framazan, but you know what they're asking for it? $50,000 for a framazan and they won't be able to deliver it until July."

The young man turned to the speaker and said, "I can get you a framazan for $30,000—and what's more, you'll have it next week!" The businessman's eyes opened wide and he said, "$30,000 for a framazan with next week delivery?" The young man nodded. The businessman said, "You got a deal!"

A half-hour later, the young man got home, picked up the phone, called his neighbor and asked, "What's a framazan?"

Why am I resurrecting this story?

One of our greatest deterrents to action and advancement is the fear of failure—prompted by the fear of the unknown. When presented with opportunity, we often ask ourselves, "Do I know enough? Am I qualified? Can I handle it?" And sometimes we hesitate while others less capable walk in and succeed.

One of the great lessons in life I have learned is that it is always possible to find out what a framazan is and how to deliver it. We grow and we prosper in a direct relationship with our willingness to face and overcome the fear of the new.

So stand up and offer the framazan.

You can do it!

Bob Orben

PETER M. PALERMO
Vice President/General Manager
Consumer Imaging Division
Eastman Kodak Company

Peter Palermo began his career with Eastman Kodak Company in 1963 and held various management positions in Kodak's international operations as well as worldwide business units. In addition to his assignment as marketing manager for Kodak Caribbean operations, he has served as general manager for Kodak in the Philippines and Mexico.

In 1984, he was elected a corporate vice president and appointed general manager of Kodak's Health Sciences Division. In 1986, he was named general manager of Kodak's worldwide Consumer Products Division, and in 1989 became the head of the newly-formed worldwide Consumer Imaging Division.

Palermo holds a bachelor of arts degree in psychology and English from Bowling Green University, and an MBA degree in economics from the Graduate School of Management at the University of Rochester.

Palermo has been recognized as one of the "Outstanding Young Men of America" (1973), and is the recipient of the Catholic Archdiocese of the Philippines Award for Humanitarianism presented by Pope John Paul in 1981.

He has served as a director of the Photographic Society of the Philippines, the Association of Photographic Manufacturers of Mexico, and the Health Industry Manufacturers Association of the United States.

Active in community affairs, Palermo is currently on the board of trustees of National 4-H Council and was a member of the board of directors for the 1991 Special Olympics Games.

Education Is Essential

A fundamental factor in the definition of success lies in one's own evaluation of the quality of choices one has made. Without a quality education, there are no choices. Life simply "happens" and the consequences are, at best, painfully less than they could have been, and invariably, someone else's fault.

Understanding one's own value and capability is the wonderful by-product of a quality education. Understanding and believing that one can choose alternative roads to follow often separates those whose choices have been directed by a passion for life from those whose choices have been thrust upon them solely by ignorance and fear.

Education enables you to see, to understand, and to more fully appreciate just who and what you really are. It gives you a view of yourself independent of the reflections others provide suggesting who and what they would have you be. Education gives you the gift of yourself.

TOM PARKER
Educator/School Administrator
In Memoriam (1935-1991)

Tom Parker was born to be a teacher. He spent his entire life in the field of education, after deciding when he was a student at Taft High School in Chicago, that he wanted to be a teacher.

As an undergraduate student at Northwestern University, he used summer vacations to work for foreign steamship lines serving Chicago to finance his education. He earned bachelor's and master's degrees at Northwestern.

Tom began his career as an educator as a fourth grade teacher in the Highland Park (Ill.) School District, where he was to spend 31 years as a teacher and school administrator.

In 1960, he was granted a Fulbright Award to teach in a primary school in Nottingham, England, where he also was a guest lecturer at the University of Nottingham. During that year abroad, and in future years, he travelled extensively then used his first-hand experiences and photographic journals in his curriculum as a social studies teacher.

His interest in children led to his taking a two-year leave of absence to start a program for gifted children, in Bucks County, Pennsylvania. The program was recognized by his peers to be an outstanding contribution to education.

Returning to his home district in Highland Park, he joined the staff of the new John F. Kennedy School and later became principal. He taught at Utah State University during the summer of 1967 before beginning a doctoral program at Stanford University and completed his course work in 1972.

During the next 18 years, he held numerous administrative positions including those of curriculum director and district administrator. One of his major contributions, prior to his early retirement in 1990, was his development of a resource center for his colleagues. He also created a staff development program that became a model for other Illinois school districts.

Tom Parker, age 56, died on August 22, 1991, a victim of cancer. In honor of his memory and contributions to education, the facility he started has been rededicated and is now the Tom Parker Teacher's Resource Center.

Travel and Read

If the following experienced-based suggestions benefit one young person planning his or her future, I will be grateful.

The more knowledge you acquire, the better you will be prepared to cope with the problems of our day. A college education will help you acquire that knowledge, but it is only the beginning, you must continue to study all your life, if you hope to achieve your goals.

The most rewarding personal educational experiences in my life came from my travels and in reading books. Not everyone can visit foreign lands and far-away places. But you can read about them and through your mind's eye learn to understand the life-styles and cultures of other people. In this electronic age, you can tour the world via audio-visual documentaries and travelogues, especially the quality programs found on public television stations. Nothing, however, is as rewarding as reading, whereby you use the greatest computer ever created—your mind.

The classroom, where you probably interacted with other people for the first time, is a reflection of the American society in which you will live. Everyone is different and unique. No two persons are alike. Some are gifted, some are not. What is important is that you learn to respect each individual for what he or she is. Always have a high regard for yourself and everyone you meet along life's highway.

My hobby is restoring antique furniture. It gives me an opportunity to work with my hands. I believe doing hands-on work is one of the best ways to relieve the stress we all experience in our fast-paced environment. If you select a creative activity as an avocation you will enjoy rewards that are fulfilling and relaxing, too.

Also, stay in touch with nature. Revel in the beauty of mountains, oceans, birds, animals, wildlife—and realize that "all the best things in life are free." Again, there are hundreds of books, with outstanding photography, that will take you into the world's greatest natural resources, should you not be able to visit them.

Two final suggestions, set a goal you have to stretch to reach, have high expectations that you'll be successful, then follow through with determination. But, along the way, don't take yourself too seriously. Have some fun and smell the roses. You will only pass this way one time—make sure you don't miss anything you want to do.

Thomas M. Parker

JOE PATERNO
Head Football Coach
Penn State University

Joe Paterno celebrated his Silver Anniversary as Penn State head football coach in 1991. Paterno is the figurehead of a program that shines with all the brilliance of a highly-polished precious metal.

He has guided the football program to 220 victories, 20 bowl appearances, two National Championships and a level of popularity that has produced 71 consecutive sellouts of 83,370 seat Beaver Stadium and nearly 100 appearances on television.

Paterno's stature has been enhanced by the success of his football teams, but is also a reflection of his reputation for integrity, for graduating the athletes who enter his program and for facing the tough issues fairly and honestly.

The role of teacher is one that Paterno finds most comfortable. "I would prefer to be thought of as an educator rather than a coach," he has said. Paterno's wishes notwithstanding, his reputation as a football coach is difficult to shake. He entered the 1990 season with 220 career victories (vs. 57 losses and three ties), which ranks him No. 6 on the list of lifetime major college coaching leaders. He heads all current Division 1-A coaches in total victories.

Only the legendary Bear Bryant appeared in more bowl games (29 for Bryant, 20 for Paterno) and recorded more bowl wins (15 for Bryant, 13 for Paterno). His teams have posted six undefeated regular seasons and have won two National Championships (1982 and 1986).

Paterno has received a host of honors including the National Football Fund's 1991 Distinguished American Award. The Philadelphia Sports-Writers Association recognized Penn State as "Team of the Decade" and he holds the Joseph M. Sheehan Memorial Trophy honoring him as the Eastern "Coach-of-the-Year" in Division 1-A.

(Continued on page 258)

Striving for Success

A man's reach must exceed his grasp;
or what's a heaven for?

— Robert Browning

That Browning quotation has always been a favorite of mine. If everything worthwhile is within reach, what satisfaction is there in achievement?

Genuine satisfaction results from honest effort, often in the face of immense odds. Any athlete, indeed any ordinary citizen, gets a larger thrill from earning something than having it given to them. I've always told my players there is as much passion in the *pursuit* of excellence as there is in the *achievement* of excellence.

We establish exacting standards for ourselves on the athletic field. Eleven men must function as one. A player who operates independently can frustrate the goals of the team. Because football demands players act in harmony, I think success on the gridiron is especially satisfying.

Great individual efforts often turn the tide in college football but, acting alone, one athlete seldom produces victory. A great passer needs a receiver. A great kicker needs a holder and snapper. A gifted running back needs blockers. Even a respected coach needs assistants.

Football is a great game, most of all, for the lessons it teaches. Players must learn to be disciplined. They must conform to the team concept. They must become familiar with pain and deal with the limits of their own endurance. They learn to play within the rules. They face the disappointment of failure and the sweetness of success. These are all lessons which young people in the stands also need to learn as they move through life.

I've always preached to our players to have respect for their opponents. There is no victory so sweet as one over a formidable foe, an opponent who has tested our every resource before reluctantly bowing.

Most of all, football is about reaching—to become better as an individual, as a team, as a conference. And, as Browning said, the goals should require a healthy stretch. I always challenge our Penn State players to be the very best they can be. Twice that has been to the National Championship in 1982, and 1986. Future Penn State teams may come up short of the No. 1 ranking. But, I fervently hope, no one will be able to criticize us for not reaching!

Joe Paterno

JENO F. PAULUCCI
Chairman
Paulucci Enterprises

Jeno Paulucci is best described as an "incurable entrepreneur." His rags-to-riches success is legend. A fruit stand barker who started the Chun King Corporation with a $2,500 loan, he sold the company 20 years later for $63 million dollars cash, then became the first chairman of R.J.Reynolds Foods, now Nabisco-Reynolds. That accomplished, his Jeno's Inc., achieved phenomenal growth with unique and revolutionary products, packaging and merchandising symbolic of Jeno's creativity.

His spectacular achievements in business are but part of his story, for Jeno Paulucci is a crusader for the common man, a man of dedication to the responsibilities of life in our changing America, a man who cares and a man who makes things happen. He is a champion of the American system of free enterprise, and the social and economic responsibilities of all factions operating within that system.

The Paulucci Family Foundation, which he has endowed for worthwhile civic charitable work, is noted for its many acts of philanthropy. In 1982, he arranged for a contribution by Jeno's, Inc., of nearly $500,000 in foods to needy families in areas hard-hit by recession.

He has counseled Presidents Johnson, Nixon, Ford and the Carter-Mondale administration on economic problems in the U.S.; served as liaison between the White House and Rome to arrange economic conferences; and was presidential emissary to evaluate U.S. disaster relief efforts in Italy for President Ford in 1976 and President Carter in 1980.

Among accolades and honorary degrees too numerous to mention, Jeno has been acclaimed as the nation's Outstanding Italian American three times, was accorded the National Horatio Alger Award for business success, was the guest of President Johnson on Liberty Island at the signing of the Immigration Reform Law, and has received the highest civilian honors accorded by the Republic of Italy.

Today he's leading the Paulucci family in developing Heathrow, an amazing self-sufficient "city of tomorrow" spanning ten square miles of Central Florida.

Be an Entrepreneur

You may remember a little jingle kids used to chant, mostly while skipping rope, to help decide what they would be when they grew up:

"Rich man, poor man, beggar man , thief.
Doctor, lawyer, merchant chief."

As kids, we didn't know the word "entrepreneur" existed. Yet you can be an entrepreneur in any field you choose. Just be prepared to commit everything—money, time, desire, dedication, and most of all, your personal life and all of your strength—to back your good ideas to the limit.

Whatever you plan to be, be sure to start with the right tools. Competition for the individual out there in the business jungle is intense, fierce. While corporations play monopoly to dominate their markets, the individual—you—must win his or her daily bread on your own performance, so you'd better be equipped to compete.

Take advantage of every opportunity to enrich your education. Your knowledge and especially your ability to communicate—the gifts of education—will be great assets throughout your life. Then, trust yourself. Learn to rely on your wits and instincts. When I started more than 50 years ago, I didn't have anything but a high school education, some street smarts, and damn little money. I trusted my judgement and took chances. But that, alone, won't cut it anymore. Today's business world is too sophisticated. You have to get the best education you can to survive.

Being an entrepreneur is not just long hours and hard work—it's guts. You have to go at it with sheer determination. Otherwise the pitfalls will put you off. That's why big companies have to go out and acquire smaller ones. There is a quality in starting a business that only an entrepreneur can provide.

The entrepreneur also must be like the farmer who puts back some of his harvest every year in order to deserve another harvest. Therefore, an entrepreneur must work constantly, tirelessly, stubbornly to make his area a better place to live and earn a living—for all. He must understand that making a profit is not his only responsibility.

The reward, of course, is a legacy of pride of achievement that stands as a challenge to the next generation. Be prepared when your turn comes.

WALTER PAYTON
President
Walter Payton, Inc.

Walter Payton retired from professional football in 1987 leaving behind a substantially rewritten record book. During 13 seasons with the Chicago Bears he set ten NFL records; became the all-time leading rusher with 16,726 yards; broke 25 Bears records; had ten 1,000 yard seasons; one most valuable player award and nine Pro Bowl and one Super Bowl appearances.

As owner / president of Walter Payton, Inc., he's an energetic entrepreneur operating 21 entertainment clubs nationwide, serves as a spokesman for six large corporations, promotes his own line of nutritional products and dabbles in real estate.

His consuming interest is his campaign to bring an NFL expansion franchise to St. Louis. If Payton's dream comes true, he'll be the first black owner in NFL history.

Business isn't the only outlet for his competitive juices. He has his own auto racing "Team 34" and is also into speedboat racing, likes to fly helicopters, plays drums, and is a jazz music buff.

Despite his exhausting schedule, Payton manages to make time for charitable causes. He majored in special education at Jackson State and recently formed the George Halas-Walter Payton Foundation to help fund college scholarships for underprivileged youths. He works with 14 different charities including the Special Olympics, Society for the Prevention of Child Abuse, and the American Cancer Society. Walter has received numerous awards for his charitable work including the prestigious 1990 Personality of the Year Award

Compete with Yourself

I have a secret I want to share with you. Before I tell you what it is, I want you to promise you'll put it to work in your life. If you do, you'll find it is a great game plan for successful living.

Competition is an intrinsic part of our daily lives. It encompasses schools, sports, business, even personal relationships. I have always been considered a fierce competitor. I still am in my business, motorsports and other ventures. Sure, I compete against other people, but, my main competition is MYSELF! I learned that from the Bible, when I was still in school. That's my secret.

"Do you know that those who run in the race all run, but one receives the prize? Run so that you may obtain it." That's found in 1 Corinthians 9:24, 25. Most people don't understand what it means. The race is not against other contenders, but against ourselves. The measure of success is not the margin of victory over our rivals, but how well we did compared to how well we could have done. St. Paul makes that clear when he tells us: "not to boast in another man's sphere of accomplishments."

To run life's race we need to be fit. Fitness of mind and body, over which you have a great deal of control, should be one of your lifelong top priorities. Health should always come ahead of wealth. When it does, you'll have the energy and drive to reach your goals—then financial security will follow.

Youth is a spendthrift of health and strength because there seems to be such a surplus. It isn't taken seriously nor appreciated. I want to put the thought into your head, and the urge into your heart, to be your best physically. There's no secret to good health other than just plain, good common sense. No need to be a fitness faddist—make a game of it. Eat right, exercise regularly and get plenty of rest—that's a simple regimen for good health.

Faith is the starting point for all accomplishments in life. The power of strong desire backed by faith is incredible. We conquer fear with faith. The absence of faith is a guarantee of failure. If you believe you can do it—you can!

CHARLIE PLUMB
"Top Gun" War Hero
Motivational Speaker

Charlie Plumb is a former P.O.W. and one of the most sought after achievement speakers in the United States.

Born in Gary, Indiana, he graduated from high school in Kansas and became a midshipman at the U.S. Naval Academy in Annapolis. He was graduated in 1964 with a bachelor of science degree and commission in the U.S. Navy.

From Annapolis, he went to flight training bases in Florida, Mississippi and Texas. He was one of the first in his class to receive wings of gold in the Navy jet aviation program. From flight training, he went to San Diego where he was trained to pilot the F4-B Phantom, the Navy's newest supersonic interceptor. There he helped start the "Top Gun" school before being sent to the South China Sea.

As flight officer for Fighter Squadron 114, Plumb was in charge of the air wing detachment. After 74 combat missions, he had received 3 Air Medals, 2 Navy Commendations, Combat Action, Navy Unit Citation, National Defense, Vietnam Service, Unit Citation, and Republic of Vietnam Campaign ribbons.

On May 19, 1967, he was shot down south of Hanoi while on a fighter cover mission. He was captured and taken to the Hanoi prison complex where he was tortured. He spent the next five years and nine months in captivity. During his imprisonment, he distinguished himself among his fellow prisoners as a professional in underground communication. He also served as chaplain of his prison unit for two years.

He was repatriated on February 28, 1973, underwent medical and security debriefings, and returned to Kansas City where he was awarded the Silver Star, two Purple Hearts, the Bronze Star, the Legion of Merit and the POW Medal.

A captain in the Naval Reserve, he was seen on television as an analyst during Operation Desert Storm. He lives in Santa Barbara, California, with his wife, Cathy, and their two children. Charlie is author of two books, I'm No Hero *and* The Last Domino, *as well as audio and video tapes.*

Qualities of Survival

Several years ago I found myself a long way from home in a small prison cell. I had just made the violent transition from a "Top Gun" fighter pilot to the very scum of humanity: a Prisoner of War. I had been tortured, humiliated, starved, and left to languish in squalor for the next six years.

It's important that you get a vivid mental picture of this scene, because the most value I can be on this page is to invite you into my prison cell. I would like you to try your best to smell the stench of the bucket I called my toilet, and taste the salt in the corner of your mouth from your sweat, your tears, and your blood, and feel the baking tropical heat in a tin roofed prison cell. Not that you'll ever be a P.O.W.—but if I am effective in these few moments we spend together, you'll see that the same kinds of challenges you face as a teenager, as a student, a leader, a parent, are the same basic challenges I faced in a prison cell: those of fear and loneliness, feelings of failure and breakdown of communication. More importantly, your response to those challenges, if you're going to succeed, is the same menu of responses I had to have in a prison camp just to survive.

So, once you can vicariously put aside your comfort zone and assume the painful position of a prisoner of war, I would ask: "What qualities do you have within you that would allow your survival in a prison camp?"

Please pause here, think about this question, and write in the margin of this page at least five different qualities of survival.

Do it now!

(If you've written faith, commitment, dedication, etc., you've already broken the code.)

As I worked my way through the first several months and then years of imprisonment, I found I already had a foundation of survival factors learned early in life from my parents, preachers, youth leaders, and teachers. And that life saving techniques in that prison camp had more to do with my value system, my integrity and my religious belief than anything I had learned from a textbook.

Now here's the test (you were expecting a test weren't you?): the next time you have a huge problem facing you, turn back to this page and read not my writing but your writing in the margin. You'll find that the same factors you've written here, which would serve you well in a prison camp, will serve you even better in the challenge of every day life. Thumbs up!

Charlie Plumb

MURRAY RAPHEL
Partner
Raphel Marketing

"First of all, I'm a business man," he says. Murray Raphel developed Gordon's Alley, a multi-million dollar shopping center in Atlantic City, New Jersey. He found that direct marketing was a major factor in his success and wrote about it in several books on marketing, advertising, and promotion including The Great Brain Robbery, The Do It Yourself Direct Mail Handbook, *co-authored with Ken Erdman,* Mind Your Own Business, *and* Tough Selling for Tough Times, *co-authored with Ray Considine. He has written a monthly column in "Direct Marketing" magazine for over 25 years.*

He works as a consultant for retailers, the food industry, insurance and financial service companies, and banks. He speaks internationally on how to use direct marketing to increase business for private companies, direct marketing associations, and the Montreux and Pan Pacific Symposiums.

Murray put together the first direct mail program for Australian Mutual Provident, Australia's largest insurance company. And he received the prestigious Montreux Award in Switzerland for bringing direct marketing techniques to businesses around the world.

For 15 years, Murray has produced a multi-media show on advertising, marketing and promotion for the Food Marketing Institute, the trade organization of supermarkets.

He is a partner with his wife, Ruth, and son, Neil, in Raphel Marketing.

Help Someone Else

There's no such thing as a "self-made man" or "self-made woman". The next time you hear someone say that, don't believe them. Because someone: a mother, a father, a grandparent, a friend—opened the door to their success. And, once you walk through, you assume an obligation to help someone else.

I had just lost $406,000!

It started out at an enthusiastic meeting with a group of local business-men. Casinos had just arrived in Atlantic City and we were excited about the new opportunities. Why not open a television station?

Everyone contributed $5,000 and thought it was a sure thing. It was not. Despite the initial enthusiasm, progress was slow and expensive. Soon we found ourselves signing one bank note after another promising to pay back loans that were reaching astronomical peaks. And soon, the TV station failed.

Over 25 years our family had developed a shopping center in Atlantic City. Starting with a tiny children's shop, it grew into nearly a city block in size. What I learned to do (and not to do) I put into books, columns and seminars. I was just beginning to achieve success in this new motiva-tional business, when the bill for the failed TV station came due.

With all my resources and income, I was still short $2,000 a month! Where would this money come from? I called family and friends for advice. Mentor Tom Haggai reassured me and said I had the ability and talent—that I would persevere.

Then, one day, I received a phone call from Tom. He said he wanted me to meet him in a distant city. Was I to give a speech? What was the reason for the trip? No speech. No reason. Just be there.

I met Tom and we drove to see the CEO of a major corporation. Obviously, the meeting had been arranged by Tom. The CEO talked about his plans for the future and wanted me involved to consult and do programs for the small businesses that belonged to his giant conglomer-ate. He suggested a monthly retainer for my services. "Would $2,000 a month be acceptable?" (Yes, the exact amount needed to pay back our debt to the bank.) I accepted graciously and, through the years, did programs, seminars and consulting for this great company.

After the meeting, Tom took me back to the airport and we were unable to talk, completely caught up in the emotion of the moment. He left me off at the departure gate and I quietly asked, trying to keep myself under control, "How can I ever pay you back?" He smiled, and waved goodbye.

I remember standing there, watching his car drive away, feeling the tears of gratitude and then, suddenly, his car backed up. The window

(Continued on page 265)

ORVILLE REDENBACHER
Entrepreneur

Undoubtedly one of the most successful and daring entrepreneurs of the past decade is popcorn king Orville Redenbacher. At the time he broke into the industry, there were 82 other popcorn brands competing with him. Within five years, Redenbacher, who advertised his product as "the world's most expensive popcorn," had become number one. In 1983, he came out with his microwave oven popcorn which became the top seller almost overnight.

Orville grew up in Brazil, Indiana, and as the son of a farmer he had an early interest in agriculture. He began his agricultural career by studying agronomy and genetics at Purdue University, where he earned his degree in agriculture.

Upon completing college, he taught briefly before becoming a county agricultural agent in Terre Haute. Later he managed a 12,000 acre farm which was partly owned by Tony Hulman, the late owner of the Indianapolis Motor Speedway. It was there he met Charles Bowman, manager of Purdue's Agricultural Alumni Seed Improvement Association, who became Orville's future partner.

They bought a hybrid see business and developed it into the world's biggest producer of popcorn seed. But, when Redenbacher and Bowman developed a special line of seed, they had trouble selling it because of the high price. Instead they decided to market their own gourmet brand of popcorn in 1971, with Orville's face and name on the jar. Redenbacher's great down-home believability proved a natural, especially in TV advertising. He once spent six solid months on the road promoting popcorn while emphasizing it is a health food recommended by the AMA and the American Cancer Society.

The popcorn industry has grown very rapidly in the past 15 years and Orville Redenbacher is one of the biggest reasons why. From 1976 to 1990, North American popcorn consumption has doubled. Total sales have reached 600 million pounds a year as popcorn has become a billion dollar industry.

No Magic Formula

Education is one thing in life you can never get too much of (except perhaps popcorn). At any age, the things we learn shape our lives and the lives of those around us, for education is the tool with which we build an understanding of the world.

Education is the bridge that non only connects us to the ideas of the past but also provides us with a clearer path to the future.

I set off on my path as a young boy in rural Indiana, where I first learned about business by selling popcorn grown on our family farm for extra spending money. In 1924, I enrolled at Purdue University, where pioneering research in popcorn hybridization heated up my boyhood dream of developing a popcorn kernel that would consistently pop up lighter and fluffier.

Forty years later, after cross-breeding more than 30,000 popcorn hybrids, I introduced a gourmet popping corn.

If it hadn't been for the solid foundation of knowledge I gained on the farm and later formalized at Purdue, my name wouldn't be a household word today. Armed with a college degree and a lot of perseverance, I was able to realize my ambitions. So can you.

With good job opportunities for those with only a high school diploma growing scarce, post-secondary education is becoming increasingly necessary in finding a fulfilling and financially rewarding career. So, get all the education you can, formal or otherwise.

Beyond education, I simply followed some homespun principles: Never say die. Never be satisfied. Integrity is a must. Be stubborn and persistent in seeking your goals. Anything worth having is worth striving for with all your might. Does all this sound corny? Honestly, that's all there is to becoming a success—there is no magic formula.

Orville Redenbacher

SPENCER ROBINSON, JR.
General Secretary
Rotary International

Founded in 1905, Rotary International is an international association of more than one million service-minded business and professional leaders belonging to over 25,000 clubs in 172 countries and geographic regions around the world.

In 1968, Rotary founded Rotaract which has developed into a worldwide organization of more than 100,000 young men and women, ages 18 through 29, who believe they can make a difference. They are dedicated to improving themselves, their communities, and the world by actively carrying out community service projects, providing members with leadership training and professional development opportunities, and expanding international service and understanding.

The general secretary of Rotary International, Spencer Robinson, Jr., a certified public accountant, is also the general secretary of the Rotary Foundation, which provides funding for a wide range of humanitarian and scholastic programs.

Prior to joining the staff of Rotary International, Robinson was the executive vice president and chief operating officer of the University of Alabama Health Services Foundation. From 1963-85, he worked for Deloitte & Touche (formerly Deloitte, Haskins & Sells) and served as managing partner in Tokyo, Japan and New Orleans, Louisiana.

Robinson was educated at Georgia Institute of Technology, Jacksonville University, and the University of Alabama at Birmingham from which he received degrees in industrial management, accounting and health administration.

Service above Self

One of the most important needs in the world today is to gain a new perspective concerning success and failure. It is only by superficial standards that we have come to judge greatness in terms of being served rather than of rendering service. Jobs are often judged not in terms of what is accomplished or whether they are constructive, but in terms of hours, wages and ease. Even people are judged by ability to take from life, not give to life.

It is never too early or too late to come to the realization that greatness should be measured by contribution and service. Time and eternity stretch out before us all with all their possibilities. We each have one life to live, just one life. We shall not have unlimited opportunities to make our lives count the most—we must consciously decide how to spend our time and use our energies.

How can each individual make his greatest contribution? It is a wonderful day in a person's life when one makes up one's mind to be oneself—to do one's own work—to fill one's own special niche. Each of us has certain intuitive feelings about what we are capable of doing. These feelings are based upon those happy and satisfying moments when what we are about seems right for us. Time means nothing. Energy spent means nothing. We simply lose ourselves and are consumed.

We must listen to our inner selves. We must each discover and nurture our innate abilities and freely express our identities as unique persons. We owe this self-discovery to ourselves and we owe it to others. We will contribute the most when we are expressing our true nature and using our own special gifts.

What if this self-discovery seems elusive? Statistics show that 70% of Americans have already determined their life work by the age of 15. Perhaps this reveals how little attention this decision really gets—perhaps it is even made haphazardly, according to immediate opportunities or family background. We can do better. We can each actively seek our best self. We may consult family, friends or professionals at guidance centers. We may join a group of caring, service-minded individuals who will encourage and inspire us. It will be worth the time and effort becaus achieving personal awareness will free us to share ourselves with others.

True success then, seen in this new perspective, will be measured by what we give to life, not what we get; by what we put into life, not what we take from life. We can do it. Personal fulfillment and a higher quality of life await us all!

Spencer Robinson Jr.

ROY ROGERS
King of the Cowboys

Roy Rogers, Hollywood's King of the Cowboys, is a full-blown American legend. He starred in 91 movies, singing in all of them, and also made 120 episodes of NBC's The Roy Rogers Show. Astride his palomino, Trigger, he was the hero in the white ten-gallon hat, who from 1943 to 1955, was America's leading cowboy star at the box office.

Over 2,000 Roy Rogers Fan Clubs dotted the United States and the London chapter had 50,000 members. A Life magazine survey asking children what person they would want most to be like found Roy sharing top billing with Franklin Roosevelt and Abraham Lincoln!

The legend has been kept alive by the ongoing success of his old movies and records. One of the highlights of the 1991 CMA Awards featured Roy and Clint Black, a current headliner, singing a duet on Hold on Partners, from Rogers' current album, Tribute, on which he performs with 20 top country artists, including his wife, Dale Evans, who joins him on Happy Trails, their signature song. Roy is the only person ever inducted into the Country Music Hall of Fame twice—in 1980, as a member of the Sons of the Pioneers and, in 1988, on his own.

Rogers' strong faith has helped him to withstand tragedies in his life, including the death of his first wife and three of his children. Now 80, he recovered from his second heart operation and a serious bout with pneumonia in 1991. He is now involved in numerous business ventures, including a chain of Roy Rogers Family Restaurants, owned by Hardees Corporation, real estate holdings, the Paramount-Roy Rogers Music Publishing firm and the Roy Rogers-Dale Evans Museum in Victorville, California, where he has his office.

Among the many honors he has received are Man of the Year and Father of the Year awards. He and Dale are members of the Cowboy Hall of Fame, as well as recipients of the National Film Society's Humanitarian Award, the USO Liberty Bell Award, the Kiwanis Decency Award, and citations from the Freedoms Foundation and The American Legion. Happy Trails, the story of their lives, was published in 1977.

Happy Trails

True success includes a happy and enjoyable journey along the way. I like to call that Happy Trails.

But, whatever trail you ride, there will be ambushes and rough terrain to travel along the way. For me, faith in God and having a loving family got me through the difficult times.

Surely, at best, life was not intended to be easy. But, just as surely, Jesus came to show us safe passage. I've sung a lot of songs in my time, but the most beautiful verse ever written isn't found in a songbook. It's the 23rd Psalm, "The Lord is my shepherd; I shall not want." It assures us of the only success that is meaningful—our eternal salvation.

Family, the one you are born into, or, one you may help create in the future, is the most important relationship you'll have in your entire life. It is in the family setting we most often learn the real lessons of life—love, forgiveness, self-discipline and work.

Our memories of home are usually pleasant or unpleasant in direct proportion to the amount of love we experience there. In today's materialistic society, we've built thousands of houses but it takes love to make a house a home. So, if one of your goals is to have your own dream house some day make sure it is not just a material house. Fill it with love—the strongest foundation on which it can stand.

If you set out from such a home each day you'll find that most of your travel will be along "Happy Trails."

Roy Rogers

JOHN W. ROLLINS, SR.
Chairman & CEO
Rollins Environmental Services, Inc.

If you look up the definition of "home study" you might find a picture of John Rollins. He graduated from Cohutta High School in Georgia and then completed his education through correspondence and extension courses.

Before starting his own business in 1945, Rollins worked as a laborer, boilermaker, ordinance inspector, plant manager and management consultant. While working these jobs, he took courses through International Correspondence Schools, which provided him a corporate management background.

Rollins was such a successful student that he was chosen ISC's Home Study Man of the Year and is a member of the school's Hall of Fame. His accomplishments earned him the Horatio Alger Award and today he is chairman emeritus of the Horatio Alger Association of Distinguished Americans. Acknowledging the need for student support, he funds John W. Rollins Scholars in the Fuqua School of Business, Duke University, and provides Rollins Scholarships for Jamaican students attending Reinhardt College, Waleska, Georgia.

Today, Rollins heads Rollins Environmental Services, Inc., a major hazardous waste treatment and disposal company. He is also founder / chairman of Rollins Truck Leasing Corporation; chairman of Rollins Jamaica, Ltd.; and is a director of Matlack, Systems, Inc., and RPC Energy Services, Inc., among other firms under the Rollins umbrella.

From 1953 to 1957, he served as lieutenant governor of Delaware, president of the Senate, and president of the State Pardons Board. Delaware observed John W. Rollins Day, August 24, 1981, acknowledging his achievements in business, industry, charity, family and religion.

Rollins is the recipient of the Commander Cross / Knights of Malta, Gold Plate Award from the Academy of Achievement, and SAM - Executive of

(Continued on page 259)

I Can, I Will

The most important thing in life, whether we're talking about people, horses or anything else, is the desire to succeed. You can do anything if you want it badly enough.

When I was a boy growing up on our Georgia farm, my brother and I were always taught that we could make our lives count. I feel this is true of anyone, anywhere. Young people today have the whole world in front of them, and they can succeed if they try with all their energy. I remember when I was young I once applied for a job twelve times. Each time they told me I didn't have the proper experience or the college background. But I kept applying, and eventually, on the 13th try, I was hired. This is the kind of relentless drive I am talking about, the kind that never lets you give up.

I wasn't fortunate enough to attend college full-time. I compensated for that by working and studying exceptionally hard in correspondence courses. I see this same determination in the immigrants to this country. They love this country with a new and wonderful love, and they value education above all else. They will starve to educate their children. This is the kind of employee I look for. Their dedication, loyalty, and work ethics will enable these people to succeed in whatever they attempt.

If I had one piece of advice for today's young people, it would be this: dedicate yourself to whatever you are doing, whether it be school, work, or athletics. Hard work will pay off in the long run. If nothing else, it will teach you the value of determination, which will guide you through life.

One of my proudest accomplishments is my chairmanship of the Horatio Alger Association of Distinguished Americans. I enjoy talking to young people about our scholarship program and letting them know it is possible to rise above economic circumstances and achieve great things. When my brother and I were youngsters, our mother used to read us the Horatio Alger stories, and the one lesson I still keep with me today is "I can, I will." This is the underlying principle of success in any pursuit. Those who practice it will accomplish whatever they want.

Today's young people are faced with challenges my generation never had to deal with. Drugs and violence are everywhere. Despair is common among our youth. But there is a way out for all of you. Commit yourself to self-improvement, work hard and never quit. With those guidelines, you will rise above any challenge that confronts you.

Remember: You can do it, you just have to want to do it!

KYLE ROTE, JR.
Owner
Athletic Resource Management, Inc.

• *Motivational speaker for such diverse clients as IBM, AT&T, Polaroid, Pillsbury and 3M, among many others. Has spoken at the White House for President Ford and in London for Prince Philip.*

• *In 1984, selected as one of the "Ten Outstanding Young Men in America."*

• *National television commentator on numerous occasions for CBS. Veteran "Game of the Week" announcer for USA Cable in football, track and soccer.*

• *Only American-born player to ever win a major professional soccer league scoring championship. Represented the United States in international competition from 1973-1976 and is the all-time leading scorer in Dallas Tornado history.*

• *One of only two people to win more than one of the popular, nationally televised Superstars competitions. He won three times (1974, 1976, 1977) over such greats as O.J. Simpson, Pete Rose, and hundreds of others including three Olympic Decathlon Gold Medalists.*

• *As a Christian, Kyle is dedicated to helping the youth of our nation develop their unique abilities and God-given potential In addition, he took a one year leave from pro sports in 1980 to join the efforts of Mother Teresa and others in the battle against hunger—a cause he remains committed to.*

• *Kyle currently maintains an extensive speaking and broadcasting schedule in addition to being an active owner of Athletic Resource Management, Inc., a diverse financial services company and sports agency.*

• *Author of numerous articles and two books, Simon and Schuster's* Complete Book of Soccer *and* Beyond the Goal.

• *Kyle, his wife Mary Lynne, and their four children live in Memphis, Tennessee, where they are involved in many sports and civic activities.*

Success Formula

In the last few years, we have been reminded of many sports stars who were told at some point "You Can't Do It"!

The NBA Scoring Champion Michael Jordan was told at one point in high school he wasn't good enough.

World Series MVP Orel Herschiser was told he "wasn't a pitcher" both in high school and college.

Terry Bradshaw was told he was too dumb until he quarterbacked the Pittsburgh Steelers to four Super Bowl titles.

San Francisco's Joe Montana was told he was too small until his 49ers began their big string of Super Bowl victories.

And, oh yes, a promising 16-year-old football player named Kyle Rote, Jr., was told he was too old to start playing soccer and he could never succeed in a foreigner's game until he won Pro Soccer's scoring championship at age 22.

In each case, the athletes rejected "the rejection" and persevered—so can you. Now, that's not to say your life will have similar results as these men. In fact, God doesn't promise us Cy Young awards, MVP trophies, or Super Bowl victories—but he does promise us an abundant life if we will fully give ourselves to Him.

And frankly, overcoming our desire to "be in charge" is the biggest challenge any of us will ever face whether we love sports or dislike them. Who will win the next Super Bowl is of minor temporary consequence when compared with the eternal significance of who will win the battle for control of your life—you or God.

The Bible reminds us, in one of the good ironies of life, that "if you lose your life you will save it"—and therefore be in a position to overcome anything that life throws at you!

So what is the formula for you to follow when you face problems? What is the formula so YOU CAN DO IT? It has four parts, simple to understand but very hard to do:

1. Serve the Savior

2. Reject the Rejection

3. Decide to be Dedicated

4. Go for your Goal

May God Strengthen you in these pursuits!

Kyle Rote Jr

DONALD RUMSFELD
Chairman & CEO
General Instrument Corporation

Don Rumsfeld, who has more than 20 years of public service, now heads the world's largest maker of broad-band equipment for cable television and satellite broadcasting.

Prior to his present assignment, Rumsfeld was chief at G.D.Searle & Co., where he is credited with turning around the ailing worldwide pharmaceutical company. During his business career, he continued in public service in a variety of federal posts, including service as an adviser to the U.S. Departments of State and Defense.

A native of Chicago, he attended Princeton University and holds eight honorary degrees and the nation's highest civilian award, the Presidential Medal of Freedom.

Rumsfeld started his public life as a congressman from Illinois, serving three terms. He eventually served in the Nixon, Ford, and Reagan administrations. His posts included service as ambassador to NATO in the Nixon years, as Ford's chief of staff and secretary of defense, and as Reagan's Middle East envoy.

After leaving Washington, D.C., he lectured at Princeton University's Woodrow Wilson School of International Affairs and at Northwestern University's Kellogg Graduate School of Management, prior to entering business.

Rumsfeld serves on numerous corporate boards of directors and is involved in numerous civic activities including the chairmanship of the Eisenhower Exchange Fellowships.

Don and his wife, Joyce, have two daughters, a son, and a granddaughter.

Help Make America Better

When President Dwight Eisenhower left the White House, he was asked why he had bought a small, somewhat run-down farm in Gettysburg. He responded that he "always wanted to take a small piece of America and make it better, with my own hands."

That is the opportunity and challenge for each of us.

Whatever your next challenge may be, do it well! Do it with tolerance and understanding of others. But, do it with all of the drive, enthusiasm and joy of life you have in you.

Attack it, so that when you look in the mirror you'll know, with absolute certainty, that whatever God has given you, you've done the best with it that was humanly possible.

And, from time to time, look back. Look back and see if you are leaving footprints, and more, if you like where they are going. And, see if you too, "with your own hands," can help to make a small piece of America better.

Above all, don't be blown by the winds. A world of dramatic change, as our world surely is, is still underpinned by the timeless values of faith, family, honor, and community.

CHARLES B. RUNNELS
Chancellor
Pepperdine University

Charles B. Runnels, chancellor since 1985 of Malibu-based Pepperdine University, has helped guide Pepperdine on a steady course toward academic excellence since joining its administration nearly a quarter century ago. Working closely with the University's president, he is actively involved in policy matters, strategic planning, and external activities for the 7,000 student school.

Recruited by Pepperdine in 1967, he left a senior corporate post at Houston-based Tenneco, Inc., to assist in laying the groundwork for a new campus. His service to the University includes membership on the Board of Regents and leadership of Pepperdine's 100-member University Board.

From humble beginnings in East Texas—where he picked cotton and cut wood to help with school expenses—Chancellor Runnels began his college studies at age 16 at Stephen F. Austin University, working as a bellboy and a hotel night clerk during his freshman year. He enlisted in the Navy Air Corps at 17, completed his midshipman school at Columbia University and flight training at Pensacola, Florida, and served one year with a seaplane squadron in the World War II Asia theatre. He returned to Stephen F. Austin to complete his bachelor's degree and earned a law degree at the University of Houston.

A member of the board of the Los Angeles Philanthropic League and the Americanism Educational League, Chancellor Runnels works tirelessly for higher education and Pepperdine. His dedication to young people is demonstrated in his annual leadership of the Southern California Youth Citizenship Seminar, which each year brings 250 outstanding high school students to Pepperdine to instill in them a greater understanding and enthusiasm for America and its pluralistic system.

Read the Guideposts!

My advice to anyone traveling the road of life is: read the guideposts! Certain people and events can become road signs, giving us a vision of what lies beyond the horizon.

I was raised on a farm during very difficult times, and my parents, though uneducated, were my first guideposts. They encouraged me to finish school and "dream the impossible dream." Thanks to them and others, I've succeeded in two different careers. For 15 years, I worked in industry, then I joined Pepperdine University's administration and have enjoyed integrating business and education as chancellor. I've tried to be a guidepost to youth, helping them to see that the corporate world is more interested in your work ethic, imagination, and character than with letters in sports or Phi Beta Kappa keys.

In naval flight school during World War II, my roommate was a young man named Herb Kalmbach. He convinced me that we could become whatever we wanted, if we concentrated on our goals and believed in ourselves. Norman Vincent Peale became our guidepost, and later, Dr. Peale also became our personal friend. Herb Kalmbach went on to become a personal attorney for President Richard Nixon.

A guidepost I often share with youth is: "Never greet the dawn without a map"—time management is crucial. My wife, Amy Jo, encouraged me to seek a law degree at night while working full time. I didn't think I could handle it. But my spiritual mentor, LaGard May, convinced me that not only could I work and attend classes, but I could teach a Bible class as well. He was right. In fact, teaching the class actually helped put other things into perspective.

A special guidepost for me was my own son, Raleigh. Stricken with cancer as a teenager, Raleigh refused to give in to apparent limitations. He valiantly finished school before succumbing to the disease at 17. He taught me to be conscious of time—to never postpone what can be done today.

A little lady nearing the century mark in her life has been a tremendous guidepost to me. Mrs. Frank Roger Seaver is the single greatest motivating factor in the building of Pepperdine's beautiful campus in Malibu. In fact, she has probably given more money to education in California than any other person. This outstanding woman has touched the lives of thousands, and her friendship and inspiration caused a change in my own career. Perennially young, she says, "If you want to do something for our country, do something for the youth, for they are the future of our nation."

I'll mention one other guidepost for me. George Page left school and his native Nebraska at age 15 because of difficult circumstances. He hitch-hiked to Los Angeles, arriving with nothing but change in his pocket.

(Continued on page 265)

DR. ROBERT H. SCHULLER
Founding Pastor
Crystal Cathedral Ministries

Dr. Schuller reaches millions weekly around the world with his "Hour of Power" televised ministry which was first broadcast in 1970. Today it is the highest rated religious program in the country.

In 1989, Dr. Schuller became the first non-Soviet pastor ever to be invited to speak on Soviet television. In 1990, he was asked by the Soviet government to begin a monthly televised program there called "From Heart to Heart."

Dr. Schuller came to Garden Grove, California, in 1955 to found the Reformed Church of America's congregation there. With his wife, Arvella, as organist and $500 in assets, he rented the Orange Drive-In Theatre and conducted Sunday services from the roof of the snack bar.

The congregation's growth over the years dictated the decision to build the internationally acclaimed Crystal Cathedral, which was dedicated in 1980 to "the glory of man for the greater glory of God." Today the congregation numbers about 10,000.

Born in Alton, Iowa, in 1926, Robert Harold Schuller knew all his life that he wanted to be a minister. He fulfilled that dream in 1950 when he was ordained by the Reformed Church of America after receiving his bachelor of arts degree from Hope College and a bachelor of divinity degree from Western Theological Seminary, both in Holland, Michigan. After ordination, he became minister of the Ivanhoe Reformed Church in Chicago, where he remained five years before establishing his ministry in Garden Grove.

Dr. Schuller is the author of more than 28 hard cover books, including four which appeared on the New York Times best seller list. His latest, Believe In The God Who Believes In You, *is based on the Ten Commandments. In 1970, he founded the Robert H. Schuller Institute for Successful Church Leadership, which has more than 20,000 graduates.*

He has received numerous awards and serves on various boards. He has

Believe and Succeed

Your success in life depends upon the degree of belief you have in yourself and in God.

That's a very profound statement. But, as you read the messages written to you by successful people in this book, you will find ample evidence that it is true.

I recently wrote a book called *Believe In The God Who Believes In You,* which is based on the Ten Commandments. The Lord's commandments were given to us to help us find our way through life.

I'm reminded of the story about the little girl who misquoted the first line of the 23rd Psalm saying, "The Lord is my shepherd, that's all I want!"

Talk about a blueprint for success. We should all be so firm in our decision as to where we're going, who we are following, and where we will end up.

Surely, at best, life is difficult—it was never meant to be easy. So, we've been given the commandments for our own good, our own peace and comfort.

If you will live by these God-given rules, I guarantee you'll be successful—not only spiritually, but, in an earthly sense as well. That's because God believes in you and, in His own time, will give you the hope and help you need to reach your goals.

All you need to do is Believe In The God Who Believes In You.

honorary doctorate degrees from Azusa Pacific College, Hope College, Pepperdine University, and Barrington College in Rhode Island.

Dr. Schuller and Arvella have five children. His only son, Robert A., also is an ordained minister of the Reformed Church of America, the oldest Protestant denomination in the U.S., with a continuous ministry since 1628.

CHARLES "RED" SCOTT
President & CEO
Fuqua Industries, Inc.

Red Scott became president and chief executive officer of Fuqua Industries, Inc., in February, 1991. Prior to joining Fuqua, Scott was president and chief executive officer of Intermark, Inc., a California based operating/holding company.

An Horatio Alger Award winner, he is chairman of the Horatio Alger Association of Distinguished Americans, an organization which provides scholarships and a "mentor" program for aspiring high school students. He frequently speaks to students and business leaders on his principles of success and achievement.

Scott is founding director and vice chairman of the American Business Conference, past president of the Greater San Diego Sports Association, and former chairman of the Special Feasibility Committee that staged the first Holiday Bowl game.

He has served on the boards of numerous civic, charitable and industrial organizations, and was honored in 1988 by San Diego Mayor Maureen O'Connor with the State of the City "Seahorse Award." In 1990, Scott was named by California Business as one of the "Top 25 CEOs of the Decade" in California.

In 1986, he was honored by the Boy Scouts as "Distinguished Citizen" of San Diego, was one of five honorees of the California Museum of Science and Industry in 1973, and in 1968 was a national recipient of the Sales Masters Oscar Award.

A native Texan and 1949 graduate of the University of Texas, early in his career he was selected as one of the Outstanding Young Men of Dallas. Scott and his wife, Katherine, live in Atlanta. They have two grown sons.

Six Secrets of Success

These secrets to success hold true whether you're seeking success in business, athletics, art, politics or just in your personal life. They need to be "top of mind" and referred to every day as guiding principles.

First, you must believe you are lucky. Consider the fact that there are five billion people on the face of the earth, and only 250 million, or one in 20people, are lucky enough to be Americans and to enjoy the gifts of freedom and opportunity.

Second, you have to be a dreamer, and dream bold dreams. You can do and be anything you dream. Remember, all great achievements in life are the result of someone dreaming. You too can dream and achieve, if you choose to.

Third, you must be enthusiastic. "I will" is more important in life than "IQ." You must have the energy and spirit to achieve, and when you mix enthusiasm with your dreams, you're on your way to being successful. It's like pouring lighter fluid on a fire!

Fourth, don't be afraid to fail. Remember, you fell down the first time you walked. Even the great success stories started with failures. Babe Ruth struck out 1,330 times. Thomas Edison failed 548 times before inventing the light bulb. Don't give up, and don't fear failure. It's better to try and fail than to not try at all. You can't learn without failing.

Fifth, you must believe in yourself. A high level of self-esteem is critical to personal success. Don't confuse this with egotism. To succeed you must think you can succeed and have self-confidence. Accept yourself as you are, improve where you think necessary, and make the most of your God-given talents.

Finally, believe that a supreme being loves you and believes in you, just as you believe in yourself. Remember, you never walk alone. This is not a religious issue, but an issue of success versus failure. I've made a life's work of studying success and I have never yet met a successful person who didn't accept the love of a higher being. It was from that basic belief that they drew their strength, their courage and wisdom.

Cecil R. Scott

WILLIAM S. SESSIONS
Director
Federal Bureau of Investigation

William S. Sessions was born May 27, 1930, in Fort Smith, Arkansas. He graduated from Northeast High School in Kansas City, Missouri, in 1948. He enlisted in the United States Air Force in 1951, received his wings and commission, then served two years active duty. In 1956, he was awarded a Bachelor of Arts degree from Baylor University, and in 1958 received his LL.B degree from Baylor University School of Law.

Sessions was a private practitioner of law in Waco, Texas, from 1958 until 1969, when he left his firm, Hale, Fulbright, Winniford, Sessions and Bice, to join the Department of Justice, in Washington, D.C., as chief of the Government Operations Section, Criminal Division. In 1971, he served on the board of Federal Judicial Center in Washington, D.C., and on committees of the State Bar of Texas and Judicial Conference of the United States.

On November 1, 1987, Sessions resigned his position as United States District Judge to become director of the Federal Bureau of Investigation.

Sessions has received the Baylor University Distinguished Alumni Award and has been awarded honorary degrees from John C. Marshall Law School, St. Mary's University School of Law, and the Dickinson School of Law. In 1988, he was honored as Baylor Law School's "Lawyer of the Year," was named "Father of the Year" for public service by the National Fathers' Day Committee, and received the Golden Plate Award from the American Academy of Achievement. In 1989, he received the Law Enforcement Leadership Award from the Association of Federal Investigators.

Repay What You've Been Given

(Adapted from remarks by William S. Sessions, Director, Federal Bureau of Investigation, before the American Academy of Achievement, Nashville, Tennessee.)

I want you to know that when I was asked to come here it caused me to reflect back over the years and go over briefly those things that were going through my head when I had reached the ripe old age of eighteen.

I was born in 1930, and as the older folks here remember, we were in the midst of the Great Depression. So, I was a child who understood that things were very dear and times were very tough. As I began to grow, I began to worry about those things that were happening all around me over which I seemed to have no control. It was very personal to me, because I truly, at that time, did not have any idea at all what would happen to me.

When I was sixteen I had polio. Suddenly my world was shattered because I had thought I would probably be the world's greatest 6'1" basketball player, yet I realized that my dream was not going to work for me. And I realized that life did not necessarily deal with you fairly. I learned that, in life, you did not necessarily succeed at what you originally wanted to do.

I have talked to so many of you and I find that you have some very definite goals. Yet, all of you seem to be searching; all of you seem to be looking. I want to talk about some of those things which helped me in my search.

The thought that gave me the determination to enter public service was the realization that we have so much to give and so much to repay. All of us here are privileged—we are privileged to have education; we are privileged to have people who care about us deeply, love us sincerely, and want us to succeed. So, we are compelled to try to pay back, to try and see the truth for what it is, and to try to express it and be a part of it.

I believe you have an absolute obligation to repay what has been given to you. The fact that you are 16, 17, or 18 does not take away from that at all. And, if you forget your obligation, then God help you, because it is yours whether you want it or not.

My father had a great effect on me and upon my spirit. He told me years ago, and he repeated it a number of times, that he was not concerned about what I was going to do. He was concerned about what I was going to be! That is our concern for you, the kind of men and women you are going to be, the kind of character you will portray, the strength you will have, the kind of determination you will display. We're deeply concerned about your willingness to serve this country and to give back part of what was given to you. I foresee great days ahead for America because of what you are and will be.

(Continued on page 266)

JOHN SILBER
President
Boston University

John Silber was born in San Antonio in 1926. He took his B.A. summa cum laude in philosophy at Trinity University and his Ph.D. at Yale. After teaching at Yale he returned to Texas, where he joined the department of philosophy at the University of Texas at Austin. After serving as chairman of his department he became dean of the College of Arts and Sciences. He was the first chairman of the Texas Society to Abolish Capital Punishment and a leader in the integration of the University of Texas. He was also instrumental in founding Operation Head Start.

In January, 1971, John Silber became the seventh president of Boston University. At Boston University President Silber has emphasized the attainment of financial stability and academic excellence. Under his leadership the University has balanced its budget every year since 1972, sponsored research has quintupled, its net worth has sextupled, and its endowment has increased tenfold. Going against a national trend of declining SAT scores, Boston University's increased steadily. Boston University's standards for appointment and tenure of faculty were, in Silber's words, raised to an easily understood standard: the highest.

President Silber's innovative program under which Boston University has contracted to operate the schools of Chelsea, Massachusetts, has attracted international attention.

Silber has written widely on philosophy (especially on Immanuel Kant, on whom he is a leading authority), education, and social and foreign policy. His work has appeared in the philosophical journals, the Atlantic, Harper's, New Republic, New York Times, Wall Street Journal *and elsewhere. His book* Straight Shooting *was published by Harpers in 1989. A German edition,* Ist Amerika zu retten?, *will be published this spring by Verlag Ullstein.*

In 1983, President Reagan appointed Silber to the national bipartisan commission on Central America. President Silber has been decorated by the governments of France, Germany, and Israel.

John and Kathryn Silber are parents of seven children.

Be a Great Boy!

When I was growing up in San Antonio, Texas, there was a sign posted on the wall of the YMCA: "Don't wait to be a great man; be a great boy!" I think back to that sign as I try to put myself in the place and point of view of a young person today thinking about the future.

Being young is different for every person. I wish we were all born healthy and loved. We aren't. I wish we had all the time we need to fulfill our dreams and be with the people we love. We don't. I'm not the first one to tell you these things, and I think you know more about life and death than many grown-ups give you credit for.

Recently I watched a television program about a house in Portland, Oregon, where children who have lost relatives and friends—often violently—come and talk with each other about their loss. I was deeply moved and impressed by the maturity and courage with which these children faced devastating loss and helped each other to face it. Many of them could have taught adults how to deal with tragedy and grief.

This program was an example of television at its best. Television at its worst is another challenge imposed on young people today. I want to give you credit for trying to get your bearings amid the relentless flow of stimulation and false expectations that comes out of the television set. That is a challenge that children in my generation didn't have to face. Before television, we were forced to find ways to pass the time, ways that challenged our abilities to create rather than to consume. I think we were lucky in that.

When I think back to the injunction "Be a great boy!" I wish for you the kind of freedom that was provided to me as a child—not the freedom to do as I pleased or freedom from the consequences of my actions, but freedom from the cares and expectations of adulthood.

The protection my family gave me allowed me the freedom to develop my awareness of myself and the world. Now we seem less and less able to nurture the young in safety. But "Be a great boy!" remains an important message for me because it taught me that hard work and achievement shouldn't be put off to the future. They are possible right now. Not that easy rewards are there for the taking, but the search for fulfillment can begin at any time, and the rewards of the search are great.

I took many steps as a young man that might now be seen as wrong turns: I studied art, music, law, and theology before I settled into the study of philosophy. I did not see these studies as side trips or failures, but as means to discover who I really am. When I found that I lacked the

(Continued on page 266)

DEAN SMITH
Head Basketball Coach
University of North Carolina

Dean Smith is a man who has accomplished almost everything imaginable in his sport. In 30 seasons, as North Carolina's head coach, he has won 717 games at Chapel Hill and lost only 209. That's a winning percentage of .774, the fourth best in history by anyone who has coached at least 20 seasons. Only the legendary Clair Bee, Adolph Rupp, and John Wooden are ahead of him.

Teams coached by Smith have won an NCAA championship, a National Invitation Tournament title, and an Olympic Gold Medal. His NCAA crown came in 1982 with a 63-62 victory over Georgetown. His 1971 team won the NIT, and he guided the United States to a sweep of the 1976 Summer Olympic Games.

In the last 25 years Smith's Tar Heels have been the most dominant in the college game. Carolina has posted a 651-165 record in that stretch, a percentage of .798, despite playing in the rugged Atlantic Coast Conference. He has now had 21 straight 20-win seasons, the longest streak in history. Smith has also had 18 seasons in which his teams have won at least 25 games, more than any other college coach in history.

Smith passed Wooden in 1992 for the most NCAA Tournament victories with 49. His nine trips to the Final Four are topped only by Wooden's 12. It's no wonder that in a 1986 poll of college head coaches by the Dallas Morning News, Smith received 49 votes as the nation's best coach. No other coach was named on more than 35 ballots.

A native of Emporia, Kansas, Smith attended the University of Kansas on an academic scholarship. He was a member of Jayhawk basketball teams which won the NCAA title in 1952 and finished second in 1953. Smith, who played for Phog Allen, is one of only two men to play on an NCAA championship team and then coach one.

In 1977, Smith was named National Coach of the Year by the National Association of Basketball Coaches. He won that same honor in 1979 from

Success in Perspective

Each basketball season colleges from across the nation begin a quest to win the NCAA championship. Being the national champion means your team is number one. That is a worthwhile goal.

It is also a harbinger of failure because 63 entries in the 64-team tournament fall short. Some will lose early in the tournament, some will lose late. But, 63 of the 64 will eventually lose one game and not be declared champion. Are they failures? Of course not.

To help our players understand that genuine success is not just climbing to the top and staying there, each year I have them read an article, "How To Be A Failure." It was written by Dr. Ernest A. Fitzgerald, a North Carolina Methodist bishop and a regular contributor to the old Piedmont Airline magazine, *Pace.*

As Dr. Fitzgerald sees it, and I agree, "Success is doing what you can, with what you have, where you are." I suggest you write that down and read it every day. It will help you keep things in perspective.

A contemporary of mine, former UCLA Coach John Wooden, expressed the same philosophy another way: "Things turn out best for those who make the best out of the way things turn out."

Failure can often be the beginning of success. Let me share a personal experience with you. After a 1965 loss at Wake Forest, one of our biggest rivals at the time, our team returned to campus to find some disgruntled fans had hung me in effigy. That might be considered first-class failure. In reality, it motivated the players and myself to do better.

In basketball, as in life, everyone will not and cannot make it to the top. Each of us has unfulfilled dreams, incompleted plans, and unrealized hopes. For some this spells failure, while others see opportunities. Throughout this book you will read about people who turned failure into success. These are people who realized that adversity was a circumstance which enabled them to make their greatest leap forward.

The Special Olympians, to whom this book is dedicated, are great examples of Dr. Fitzgerald's beliefs. Who better than they do what they can, with what they have, where they are?

Dean S. Smith

---

the U.S. Basketball Writers Association and Basketball Weekly *and in 1982 from Medalist.*

Smith was inducted into the Naismith Basketball Hall of Fame in 1983. He is also a member of the state of North Carolina's Sports Hall of Fame.

Smith has five children. Two of his daughters, Sandy and Mrs. Sharon Kepley, and his son, Scott, are Carolina graduates. He also has two young daughters, Kristen Caroline and Kelly Marie. Smith's wife, Linnea, is a physician.

RAY R. SODEN
Past Commander-in-Chief
Veterans of Foreign Wars

Ray Soden's dedication to serving the nation's veterans resulted from his service in the Navy during World War II. He served aboard the USS Claxon in the European and Pacific theatres. After surviving the North Africa, Okinawa, Leyte Gulf, Guadacanal and Iwo Jima invasions, he pledged himself to serving his fellow-man upon his return home. He holds European and Asiatic theatre ribbons with seven battle stars and shared in two Presidential Unit citations.

Following the war, he joined Illinois Bell Telephone Company which enabled him to become active in a variety of community service and philanthropic programs in which the company was involved. Concurrently he began a progressive personal program in the Veterans of Foreign Wars. From commander of his home Post 2149, in Bensenville, Illinois, he worked his way through the ranks to become Commander-in-Chief of the national organization in 1973.

During his tenure, he became a tireless champion of veterans' rights and has been working on their behalf ever since. His VFW activities include service on a score of committees. He served as chairman of the National Voice of Democracy Committee which today directs a program serving 700,000 young Americans.

Soden served as chairman of the Illinois Veterans Commission and was the first president of the National Combined Veterans Association. He received the Freedom Foundation's Americanism Award in 1961.

Upon retiring from Illinois Bell, he was elected a commissioner on the DuPage County Board and the Forest Preserve Commission. He presently is president of the DuPage County Forest Preserve District.

As a youngster, Soden gained fame as a singer on the National Barn Dance, a network radio program. He worked with future greats George

Treasure Freedom

Freedom did not come to America on a silver platter. Over 1,000,000 men and women have died to gain and preserve the freedoms we enjoy today. I don't know that I gave much thought to that as a youngster. So, I doubt that today's youth does either—except in a time of crisis like Operation Desert Storm.

The greatest freedom we enjoy is not freedom from want. It is the freedom to choose, to try, to compete, even the freedom to fail. But, most of all, we have the freedom to succeed and go as far as our initiative and talent will take us.

You are living in a fabulous age, in the greatest country in the world, filled with opportunities, where you can accomplish any carefully planned objective.

Each human being is unique; there will never be a carbon-copy of you. Discover what is unique about yourself. Then seek employment which will make best use of those talents uniquely your own. That's a sure road to success and happiness. Keep in mind that happiness comes not from having much to live on, but much to live for.

When you become a success, as you will if you make an all-out effort and sacrifices, don't forget to give something back. Practice good citizenship through service to your family, church, school, community and country.

Volunteerism has always played a role in American progress. Working together, helping one another and getting involved is the only way we can overcome the mounting human and social problems which beset our nation.

Make your life meaningful and productive. You're never too young, so start here and now! Make today the stepping stone to tomorrow. There is no challenge that you cannot meet—You Can Do It!

Gobel, Homer and Jethro, Red Foley, Bob Atcher and the Williams Brothers, a singing act which featured a youngster named Andy Williams.

Soden resides in Wood Dale, Illinois, with his wife, Shirley. They have three grown children and six grandchildren.

BART STARR
Football Great
Business Executive

Bart Starr was born in 1934 in Montgomery, Alabama, where he was to begin his athletic achievements.

Bart was an All American high school football player before becoming a four-letterman at the University of Alabama. He was named to the Dean's List for academic excellence in his junior and senior years, before graduating in 1956 with a B.S. degree in education.

Drafted by the Green Bay Packers, he played 17 years with the legendary National Football League team. He was the NFL's Most Valuable Player in 1966 and MVP in the 1967 and 1968 Super Bowls. NFL Man of the Year in 1969, he is a member of the Pro Football Hall of Fame and the Green Bay Packer Hall of Fame. The Columbus Touchdown Club named him Professional Player of the Decade in 1970.

After retiring as a player, Starr served as coach of the Green Bay team from 1974 to 1983. He also was a game analyst for CBS.

Recognized not only for his athletic achievements, he was the first recipient of the Byron White Award (NFL honor for citizenship and exemplary conduct as a professional athlete); named as one of the Jaycees' 10 Outstanding Young Men in America in 1968; member of the President's Council on Physical Fitness and President's Advisory Committee for Environmental Protection, just to name a few of his honors.

Besides his chairman duties with Starr Sanders Properties, he's a general partner in RAL Asset Management Group, and director of Sentry Insurance Company and Barry, Huey, Bullock & Cook.

Make the Effort

"For when the One Great Scorer comes to mark against your name. He writes—not that you won or lost—but how you played the game."

That maxim, written by the late, great sportswriter Grantland Rice, could be a blueprint for living. It is applicable not only to sports, but to business and every aspect of life as well.

Winning is not the most important statistic, but making the effort is. Therefore, whatever the task, at work or play, always seek to excel, but do so honestly and within the rules. In the real world, everyone seeks to gain a competitive edge. There's nothing wrong with that, as long as you do so with integrity.

There will be tough times along the way. All of us suffer failures of some kind. Vince Lombardi, whom I had the privilege of playing for with the Green Bay Packers, had this to say: "Failure isn't getting knocked down. Failure is not getting up after you've been knocked down."

The one common denominator in the lives of successful men and women is a superb attitude—they got up when they were knocked down!

Bart Starr

JERRE STEAD
President
AT&T Business Communications
Systems

In August, 1991, Jerre (pronounced like Jerry) Stead was named president of Business Communications Systems at AT&T, Bridgewater, New Jersey. He accepted the post because he wanted the challenge of turning around a troubled business of one of the world's premier companies.

It was a challenge to make a difference that had brought him to Square D Company in Palatine, Illinois, in 1987. He was appointed president and chief operating officer just a week short of his 44th birthday. Stead went on to become chairman, president, and chief executive officer as he directed the company to world leadership in industrial control and electrical distribution products, achieving record sales and earnings.

Stead graduated from the University of Iowa with a BA in business administration in 1965. He participated in the Harvard University Advanced Management Program in Switzerland in 1982. Prior to joining Square D, he had 21 years of management experience in international and domestic marketing, sales, production, finance, and general management with Honeywell, Inc.

Jerre was born and reared in the small town of Maquoketa (population 6,500) in Northeastern Iowa, where his parents still live. He was an outstanding athlete, captaining the football, baseball and basketball teams at Maquoketa High School. He was also elected president of the Student Council and of his senior class. Stead was brought up in a Christian heritage with a strong positive, upbeat influence from his father, Victor (an independent insurance agent), his mother, Anna, and his grandparents.

Jerre is a member of the boards of directors of Square D Company, Ameritech, USG Corporation, and Eljer Industries. He is a member of the board of visitors of the University of Iowa, the board of trustees of Coe College, and the advisory board of the Kellogg Graduate School of Management of Northwestern University.

People Power

All my life, from my youngest days, thanks to my parents and grandparents, I've believed in "You Can Do It"—that you have the power to make the decisions to do what needs to be done to reach your life goals and objectives—that you can do whatever you set out to do if you have the right positive mental attitude.

That was basically the philosophy of Don Scholfeldt, our high school basketball coach. Don had only one arm (he lost his lower left arm in an accident while a freshman in high school) yet he always said, "No matter how far down you are, you can do it!"

In business, "You Can Do It" translates into "People Power"— the power of people to make decisions, to take educated risks, even to make mistakes in pursuit of ways to do a job better and more efficiently.

Take educated risks? Make mistakes? Yes, indeed. I've always believed that the best work culture rewards risk taking. It's a culture in which people have the right to be wrong and it's okay to make a mistake. But when you make a mistake, make sure you can identify it to someone else, talk to them about it, and put the appropriate resources into correcting it. Secondly, learn from your experience and don't make the same mistake again.

I believe in rewarding and recognizing people who meet or exceed their own increasingly stringent job requirements—and our work environment is designed for people to have fun striving for new levels of excellence.

This same self-managing "people power" ability applies to achieving personal life objectives. Set forth what you want to accomplish. Don't be afraid to set goals that appear unreachable, that even may appear risky. Determine the best ways to reach your goals. Follow through on every detail that needs to be done. Keep moving forward. Always think positively.

You'll find that no matter what you want to accomplish, with good planning and the right positive mental attitude and determination, You CAN do it—You CAN make it happen!

MICHAEL LEO STEFANOS
President
Dove International

Mike Stefanos was born October 3, 1951, in Chicago, Illinois. He attended Northern Illinois University, received a B.S. degree in business administration, and was licensed as a certified public accountant in Illinois in 1973. While attending the University of Chicago in pursuit of a master's degree, in 1977, his father passed away and he became head of the family's candy and ice cream business.

Inspired by his father's passion for his most famous creation, the DoveBar, Mike upheld family tradition while expanding the business. When he took over, the ice cream treat was only sold in local speciality stores and chains. In 1984, he decided it was time to go national with the popular product, which had become a regional favorite.

He formed a new company, Dove International, built a new processing plant, and put a sophisticated marketing team in place. Since then, production has increased from 300,000 to several million annually.

In keeping with his father's tradition, each DoveBar is still produced under stringent quality control. As a result, Leo Stefanos' creation has become the standard of the industry—but his greatest achievement may be the passion he passed along to his son.

In 1986, Mike sold the company to Mars, Incorporated, where he now serves as president of Dove International, its ice cream division.

Feel the Passion

My dad knew the secret. He never wrote about it or talked about it—he simply lived it. The secret of success is to have a passion. You lock on to that passion as a goal and you focus and channel every drop of energy to it, and lo and behold success comes along as a consequence. The motivational books all say it—don't do it for the money. The problem is that the message only comes out to those who have already attained success. The people who read the books are rarely in a position to listen to the message. Let's take a look at my dad's life and see that passion come alive.

My dad grew up in a small farming village in the poor rugged mountain country of Messenia, Greece. His father had passed away when he was only four and his very existence drew from the support of a strong loving mother and family. In 1936, he left that village and travelled to join his brothers in the land of opportunity. To this day, when I find life's problems a little tough to take, I put myself in my father's shoes on Ellis Island, 32 years old, without language, without clothing, without money, and I realize how cruel this opportune land must have seemed.

My father made his way to Chicago and began working first in a restaurant as a dishwasher, then in a confectionery store where he learned the fine art of candy making. Within three years he owned his own store, named after the dove of peace! Hard work, perseverance, and unrelenting devotion to quality served him well as the business grew and thrived. Clerks, customers, and vendors helped him with the need of wax paper and festive ribbon, but he, and he alone, controlled the quality of the hand-made boxed chocolates.

By 1956, the store was relocated to a bigger location and my dad had a family of two sons and a daughter. As refrigeration became prevalent, he added ice cream with sit down service featuring ice cream sodas and banana splits. In summer, fate came to my dad's door in the form of a traditional ice cream truck. My brother and I took off after the truck, not only hurting my father's pride but raising his concern for our safety. This is where the passion took hold and out of love for his family he created the DoveBar! He drew on everything he learned through years of experience to create an ice cream bar that was so good that it would keep his sons in the store. He was acting on love! After a week of family consumption, he made them available to the public in a small freezer in the front of the store.

My father passed away in 1977, and I found myself driven by a passion to tell the world how much I loved and respected my dad. My desire to get his product out was only to show the world what a tremendous man he

(Continued on page 266)

JUDITH M. SWEET
President
National Collegiate Athletic Association

Judy Sweet was elected president of the NCAA in January, 1991. She was secretary-treasurer from 1989 to 1991, becoming the first woman to serve in each of these positions.

Judy has been director of athletics at the University of California, San Diego, since 1975, when she became one of the first women in the nation selected to direct a combined men's and women's intercollegiate athletics program. The UCSD athletics program involves 23 varsity teams, with an even distribution of men's and women's teams. Prior to her faculty appointment at UCSD in 1973, she taught at the University of Arizona, Tucson, and Tulane University.

A native of Milwaukee, Judy is a graduate of the University of Wisconsin, Madison, where she majored in physical education and mathematics. She earned a master's of science degree from the University of Arizona, Tucson, and a master's of business administration degree from National University, San Diego.

Judy's presidential duties for the NCAA include presiding over the NCAA administrative committee, council, and executive committee, as well as the NCAA convention. She also serves on numerous other committees.

She has served on various local, state, and national committees including the board of trustees of the United States Sports Academy, the board of directors of the Council of Collegiate Women Athletic Administrators, and the board of directors of the National Association of College Directors of Athletics.

In 1984, Judy was selected as an Outstanding Young Woman of America and, in 1990, the Los Angeles Times selected her as the Top College Sports Executive of the '80s.

Academics and Athletics

Education is both the primary challenge and the primary opportunity facing American youth today. It is essential that students learn to read and write in the early grades. The computer age has greatly accelerated the learning time-frame and the need for early development of basic learning skills. Colleges and universities are institutions of higher learning, yet in many cases these schools have had to provide remedial reading and math programs for a number of incoming students. It has been reported that some college athletes have earned a college degree without the ability to even read what appears on their diploma.

One of my responsibilities as president of the NCAA is to help enforce the rules governing collegiate athletics. As a teacher and administrator at a major university, I must also abide by those rules. I have a sincere appreciation of how important it is to play by the rules. Part of playing by the rules means that an athlete must perform well academically. A "student-athlete" must be a student first and foremost. Student-athletes must put the same energy into being successful in the classroom as goes into pumping iron, shooting baskets, or spiking a volleyball.

As a teacher and athletics administrator, it is my obligation to see that our athletes are held as accountable in the classroom as every other student on campus. Some of the lessons learned on the playing field need to be brought into the classroom also. Discipline, the desire to learn, an aggressive pursuit of classroom studies, the commitment to do one's best, and the realization of the value of proper academic training are most important to a successful future.

Academics and athletics provide excellent preparation for the future. Achievements in athletics may be important in your career plans, but academic tools are essential to a productive career. Very few athletes have the opportunity to become college and/or professional athletes, and even those who do need to be well skilled in other areas in anticipation of when their playing days have ended. It is not enough to just be a successful athlete. The best combination is a healthy mind and a healthy body.

I urge you to maximize your educational opportunities. Academics are the tools for life.

Judith M. Sweet

RICK TELANDER
Senior Writer
Sports Illustrated

Rick Telander was born and raised in Peoria, Illinois, where he spent his time playing sports, reading books, running in the woods and cornfields around his home, all the while trying to figure out what he was going to do with his life. In a manner of speaking, Telander, now 42 and a senior writer for Sports Illustrated, who lives in Chicago with his wife and four children, is still trying to answer that question.

He was an All Big 10 football player at Northwestern and a two-time Academic All Big 10 selection, but, his concern over the meaning and integrity of the college game led him to write a book called The Hundred Yard Lie, *revealing the corruption he saw spreading from high level entertainment-driven collegiate sport to the educational system itself. The book, published in 1990, won him few friends among college football coaches, athletic directors, and some college presidents, but it thrust Telander into the limelight as a crusader for fairness and integrity in the ivy towers as well as on the gridiron.*

Telander has written two other books, one of which, Heaven is a Playground, *about inner-city kids playing basketball, was recently made into a feature movie. He has taught English and journalism at Northwestern University. In 1987, he was awarded the Arch Ward-Warren Brown Award for Excellence in Sports Journalism by the Notre Dame Club of Chicago.*

His love of play, generally, and his ability to continue playing at the things he loved as a kid—and write about those things to make his living—has led him to believe it is possible to never quite grow up. It also has made him aware that the things a child intuitively knows often far outstrip the knowledge of experts and adults.

Hang in There

Giving someone advice on how to be successful always has the ring of fraud to it, if you ask me. There is smugness rooted in the message, whether the giver means it or not. Hey, kid, the advice-giver is saying, I'm the big shot and you're not; that's why I'm up here polishing my apple and you're down there looking for an errant seed or stem.

Okay, that's a cynical way of looking at the passing on of knowledge, but I think you all know what I mean.

I'll never forget a coach I had during my ever-so-brief career with the Kansas City Chiefs. "Men," he told us players, "you've got to be winners in everything you do. I surround myself with winners. All the people I associate with are winners. Whether it's a doctor or a businessman, he's successful. He's made it to the top. I don't want anyone but winners around me."

I thought of my own friends, mostly guys like me, just out of college. What a crew. None of them had any power or money. A lot of them didn't know what they wanted to be. Waiters, cab-drivers, one guy who volunteered for psych experiments to pick up extra cash, one guy who sold firewood. Jeez, I was surrounded by losers. I felt terrible. I'd never be a winner like the coach.

Then a few years later, long after I'd been released from the NFL, the coach himself was fired. The winner had lost. I didn't feel good about that, but I did come to a realization: winning is a relative thing.

Nobody wins all the time. Indeed, nobody SHOULD win all the time. That's not the way life works. A lot of apparent success is simply the result of good fortune, whimsy, or good timing. A lot of successful people are in positions of power because they're just older then the people under them. In time, the younger people will replace them. My vagabond friends are now getting into positions of power, because, well, because they've hung in there.

And that might be the truest lesson any successful person can give someone eager for direction. Hang in there. You must try hard, and it's nice—sometimes essential—that you have talent. But if you don't hang in there, you'll never be in position to capitalize on such things as whimsy, timing, or the inexorable march of time when they affect your own life.

You also have to be realistic. For me to hang in there at football would have been pretty dumb. A cornerback with a 4.6 40 time is like a birdwatcher with bad eyes. You're just setting yourself up for trouble.

So try a lot of things. Don't be terrified of quitting when you know you're in too deep. But never let quitting be the easy way out. It should always

(Continued on page 267)

WILLIAM G. THEBUS
President
Logan House, Ltd.

Bill Thebus and his late associate, John Hurst, founded Logan House to work together in the fields of literacy, language, and basic employability skills. Each had spent nearly 30 years as an educator and trainer in those areas. They chose to pool their resources for the benefit of the American work force, many members of which now find themselves unable to compete in an increasingly technological society.

Thebus began his career as a writer, editor, and journalist in San Antonio, Texas. He joined the Navy to see the world, but never was assigned outside of the Pentagon in Washington. After his military service he became an English language teacher and worked in Syria, Turkey, Thailand, and Iran over a period of 15 years, and finally satisfied his desire for international travel and intercultural experiences.

His language teaching career expanded into other areas of education and training, and he spent more than ten years as a designer and developer of language, basic skills, and technical training programs, both in the U.S. and abroad. This work has taken him throughout the U.S., Europe, the Middle East, and Southeast Asia, to countries as diverse as Saudi Arabia, the United Arab Emirates, Egypt, Indonesia, Brunei, Taiwan, and the Peoples' Republic of China.

Thebus is now settled in Evanston, Illinois, where he continues the operation of Logan House, specializing in promoting literacy training for American workers, developing basic level technical training curricula, and advising on the readability and usability of such material.

He was educated at St. Mary's University in San Antonio and the University of Southern California. He holds a B.A. degree in English and an M.S. in education.

"I Have Made It!"

I know that "you can do it." I know that you can be a success. I know because for many years my partner, John Hurst, and I worked with people who did it—people who moved from "hopeless" to "successful." These were people who, for a variety of reasons, were unemployable in our society. No job meant no money. No money meant no future. They appeared to be headed for hopeless lives.

But we've seen hundreds of such people reach "success." You don't read about them in the newspaper, or see them on television. They're not rich and famous. Then how are they successful? After all, Webster says that success is "the gaining of wealth, fame rank, etc." But, Webster also has another definition: "A favorable or satisfactory outcome or result." That's what these people achieved. They set a modest goal, and they reached it.

Like some breakfast cereals, success comes in bite-size portions. John and I could tell you of many people who bit off only a very small piece of success—but enough to change their lives. A favorite example is a story that John told me many times, the story of Cleveland Davis.

As a young man, Davis had a job as a stock clerk in a warehouse. He also had a problem—he couldn't read. It's a problem not uncommon in this country today. He got by, though. He worked by memory and other tricks. He hid his problem. Then his company got bigger, and the number of parts he had to memorize grew too large. His mental computer finally crashed. His illiteracy was exposed and he was fired.

Davis couldn't find another job. He had a wife, a growing family, and an apparently hopeless future. But life offered him one small chance. He found and joined a program to teach employability skills. He approached it with not only a "can do" but with a "must do" attitude. His family's life depended on it.

Davis worked at it. John was proud to be able to say that he was there to help Davis when he needed it. John found him in class one day with his infant child on his lap, almost hidden beneath the work table. "Kind of young for a trainee, Cleveland," John said. Davis scowled a bit, and said: "I couldn't get anybody to stay with her." After a pause, he added, "And I *had* to come to class."

Davis' ambition, his vision of success, was to be an auto mechanic. He felt if he could be a good mechanic he could make a meaningful life for himself. He didn't aspire to wealth or fame or rank. He had a modest goal,

(Continued on page 267)

R. DAVID THOMAS
Senior Chairman/Founder
Wendy's International, Inc.

R. David Thomas was born on July 2, 1932, in Atlantic City, New Jersey. Adopted at six weeks, he never knew his birth parents. His adoptive mother died when he was five. His early years included moving from state to state as his adoptive father sought work.

As they traveled, Thomas was fascinated with the restaurant business. When he was 12, he lied about his age and landed a job at the lunch counter at Regas Restaurant in Knoxville, Tennessee.

At 15, in Fort Wayne, Indiana, he made the decision to remain in town with his restaurant job rather than continue traveling with his family. Later, while in the Army and trained in the cook and baker school, Thomas became one of the youngest soldiers ever to manage an enlisted men's club.

It was back in Fort Wayne, in 1954, he met and began to work with a Kentucky entrepreneur named Harland Sanders. In 1962, Thomas took over four failing Kentucky Fried Chicken carryouts in Columbus, made them successful, and built four more outlets. The deal he had made in making the franchise profitable and the cash sale of the restaurants back to KFC in 1968 made him a millionaire at age 35.

But Thomas was always drawn back to one of his favorite foods— hamburgers. Using fresh beef and making hamburgers to order, he opened the first Wendy's Old Fashioned Hamburger Restaurant in November, 1969, in Columbus.

Wendy's and its franchisees operate about 3,800 restaurants throughout the U.S. and in 23 countries worldwide, providing employment for 130,000 people.

Citing his commitment to "return something to the communities" which make Wendy's prosper, Thomas favorite charities include St. Jude Research Hospital in Memphis, Children's Hospital in Columbus, Recreation Unlimited, the Ohio State University Cancer Research Institute, and the Children's Home Society of Florida.

Opportunity Doesn't Knock

There's an old saying that opportunity only knocks once.

That's not true. Opportunities don't knock at all. They don't have to, they're already all around us. It's up to us to see where they are and take advantage of them.

A lot of times when the news media interview me, they want to know about my early years. Things like the fact I had my first job when I was 12, and was pretty much on my own when I was 15. Some writers have even called my life a rags-to-riches story. It never seemed that way to me.

It's true I didn't have a lot of material things when growing up, but I was fortunate to realize there were opportunities all around me. It created a drive in me, but it wasn't just to make money. There also was the pride of accomplishment, of doing the best I could even on the smallest jobs.

This is a wonderful country filled with opportunities, but you have to be ready to take advantage of them. You have to work and learn all the time.

Effort brings success. Whatever career you choose, your best efforts to gain knowledge and experience will give you an advantage that others will lack. The simple truth is success is earned.

Doing a job right—no matter what it is, no matter how small it seems—is education that isn't going to be forgotten.

There always will be leaders and followers, but leaders don't start at the top, they learn and work their way there. They see opportunities, do their jobs, and are rewarded with promotions.

That's important to remember: Leadership is learned. It begins by doing small jobs well, so that the individual is ready for the next step—to learn a new job, to take on more responsibilities, to be promoted, and to grow as a person.

When I started Wendy's, I saw the opportunity of having a few restaurants. When they were built, we saw other possibilities, and the company grew, and still more opportunities opened up.

None of them knocked, but they were all around us.

Look, and you'll see them, too.

Dave Thomas

Thomas is a national spokesman for the White House adoption initiative called "Adoption Works—For Everyone." Profits from his autobiography, Dave's Way, *will go to the cause of adoption.*

BRIAN TRACY
President
Brian Tracy Learning Systems

Brian Tracy is one of America's foremost authorities on the development of human potential. He is the author / narrator of many best-selling audio and video programs on success, sales, business, and personal achievement. His programs have been translated into 14 languages, and are used in 26 countries. He speaks to thousands of people each year throughout the U.S. and other countries.

Brian has an M.A. and C.P.A.E. and is president of Brian Tracy Learning Systems, Inc., a human resource company based in San Diego, California. As a consultant, he has trained key executives of more than 1,000 corporations in the U.S., Canada, Mexico, the Far East, Australia, and Europe.

Role Models Help

Its been said that great men and women spend their formative years studying the lives and stories of great men and women who have gone before them. Many of today's most successful people have patterned their lives after just one famous person, Napoleon or Churchill, Schweitzer or Mother Teresa.

Great men and women then spend their working years striving to emulate the characteristics and qualities of those they admire. We all have a tendency to identify with and emulate people we read about, our heroes and heroines from history or literature. The more we immerse ourselves in their lives, the more we internalize and demonstrate the qualities that made them great!

A famous book, a runaway best seller many years ago, told of a town in which everyone agreed to ask the simple question, "What would Jesus do?", prior to every decision. The story told how dramatically the lives of every person in town improved as the example of Jesus became the guiding principle for each person.

I worked with Dr. Albert Schweitzer in Lambarene, Africa, before his death, and quite honestly, I've never been the same person. From that day to this, I still strive to practice his "reverence for life" and his gentle practical approach to living the spiritual life. Many people have had similar experiences as a result of being exposed to Mother Teresa, or to some other positive and uplifting person.

Finally, great men and women spend their later years helping and guiding others up the rungs of the ladder of life, and helping them ascertain that the ladder is leaning against the right building.

The wonderful help that comes from studying biographies and autobiographies is the realization we have that it is mostly ordinary people who do extraordinary things. And what they have done, we can also aspire to.

You can do it! Choose great role models and pattern your life after them. Decide right now to become a great man or woman, a person of courage and character and deep, abiding faith. Select your heroes and heroines with care and commit yourself to being as admirable as they were, or are.

Remember, you were born for personal greatness, and anything anyone else has done, you can do too, if you really want to, long enough and hard enough. You CAN do it!

JIM TUNNEY
President
Jim Tunney Associates

Jim Tunney is a recognized professional speaker and corporate consultant, specializing in leadership, team building and peak performance. He has received the National Speaker's Association's highest award, the CPAE (Council of Peers Award of Excellence).

Tunney gained national recognition during his 31 years as an official for the National Football League. Regarded by many as the "Dean of Referees," Tunney distinguished himself by officiating three Super Bowl games and ten Championship games, along with many divisional and Pro Bowl games.

As an educator, Tunney served 27 years as a teacher, coach, high school principal and superintendent of schools in southern California. During this time, he earned his doctorate in education from the University of Southern California. His undergraduate degree is from Occidental College.

Tunney devotes time to a number of community and professional organizations, serving on the boards of the California State Special Olympics, the Los Angeles Boys and Girls Club, and the National Football Foundation and Hall of Fame.

Tunney has appeared on numerous network and cable television and radio shows, including "CBS This Morning," "Sports Talk" with Roy Firestone, and "The Larry King Show." He is a member of the Screen Actors Guild and AFTRA.

His book Impartial Judgement *(Franklin Watts, 1988) expands on the ways that athletic discipline is beneficial in everyday life: Goal-setting, commitment, and preparation to develop the winner in you.*

Making the Cuts

Yes, you can do it, but what is "it?"

Without a goal, confidence, energy, and the willingness to strive won't get "it" done. You have no route, no destination.

General uncertainty gets the blame for much of this type of indecision. Chaos is a hot new buzzword, but making uncertainty trendy and using it as an easy cop-out doesn't speed you toward accomplishment. It makes no sense to wait for all the quandaries to get solved, or, for uncertainty to disappear from daily life.

So, what is "it?" Recently a poll gave us the news, startling to some, that more than 60% of the undergraduates at a major university said they "didn't know themselves" well enough to decide what they wanted to do after graduation.

I wasn't surprised. Twenty-seven years in public education taught me something about the difficulties encountered in acquiring self-understanding. These undergraduates join psychologists, humanists and virtually everyone in search for a sure path to self-understanding. Still, we've learned more about what doesn't work than what does. There is no set formula. Gaining self-understanding is an individual progression, developed ultimately by one person seeking an authentic, distinct identity.

The idea of being a "winner" persists on everyone's mind, even if you haven't named "it" yet. To help, consider the word W-I-N. It contains a clue on how to make the necessary distinctions—What's Important Now?

The process of lining up your options, putting the most important at the top, the less important at the bottom, appears to be an intimidating task for the undergraduates who were polled just as it is for many.

Here's where being a good coach to yourself comes in. Not everyone who shows up to play makes the team. You have to make the cuts. You have to be straight with yourself. You have to declare what's important to you.

When you learn to cull the options (which requires naming what's important to you), commitment and focus result. Your confidence, energy, and willingness to strive then have a destination.

Once "it" is known, the goal is set. The next step is reassuringly inevitable: Do it yourself, and do it now.

JACK TWYMAN
Chairman & CEO
Super Food Services, Inc.

Jack Twyman, former basketball star, has made the transition from sports to the corporate executive suite as smoothly as he raced up and down the court enroute to the NBA Hall of Fame. But his contribution as a humanitarian outshines his other successes.

While playing with the Cincinnati Royals, his teammate Maurice Stokes was critically injured in a game. From then on Stokes could only communicate with eye signals. In those days, there was no insurance, no hospitalization, as the fledgling league tried to establish itself. Stokes' savings were wiped out in one year.

Twyman organized an annual benefit game to help defray medical costs for Stokes, for whom he eventually was appointed guardian.

Over the next 12 years, until Stokes death, Twyman raised over $1 million to pay his hospital bills and set up a foundation in his name that today still dispenses grants to help former NBA players and their families with medical problems and personal tragedies. The story of the incredible relationship between the two basketball players is depicted in the film "Maurie."

After his basketball career, Twyman went into the insurance business. He also worked NBA Game of the Week telecasts for ABC. One of his clients was Super Food, which elected him to its board of directors. He was asked to take over when the chairman and CEO died in 1972.

Today, Super Food Services, Inc., is one of the nation's largest corporations, a $1.7 billion in sales food wholesaler based in Dayton, Ohio.

Jack Twyman has received a host of awards and honorary degrees as befits a man of his stature.

Try, Try, Try

As I look back on my life, thinking about the experiences I have been privileged to enjoy during my 57 years, and the people from whom I have learned, one overriding experience comes to mind. It occurred when I was a senior in high school and proved to be the foundation for every endeavor that I have embarked upon during my adult life.

To begin the story, I must go back to my freshman year at Central Catholic High School in Pittsburgh, where I was born. As a "hot shot" grade school basketball player, I came to Central and set my sights on making the high school basketball team. I prepared very hard during the summer and tried out that fall with all the confidence and enthusiasm a youngster could muster. I was very disappointed when I was cut from the team early in the tryout process. Being very stubborn and very upset, I dedicated myself to focusing on making the team my sophomore year.

After an equal amount of sacrifice and hard work, I once again tried out. The result was the same and again I was cut. Not being willing to recognize the obvious, I redoubled my efforts in my junior year and was cut for the third time.

Again, not accepting what the popular belief was, and still believing in myself, I tried out in my senior year and made it. We went to the finals of the State Championship. I was able to go to college on a basketball scholarship and after 11 years in the NBA was pleased to conclude that aspect of my athletic career with my induction into the Hall of Fame.

The point in sharing this experience with you is that, at a very early age, I proved to myself that if I worked hard enough, wanted it bad enough, and was willing to pay any price to accomplish it, I could have it.

This philosophy has served me well during my business career and it continues to be the prime motivation to any challenge that presents itself. I proved early on that with the proper commitment I could do it and I'm suggesting that You, too, can do it!

Jack Twyman

R.J. VENTRES
Chairman
Borden, Inc.

R.J. Ventres was the first of his Italian immigrant parents' six children to be born in the United States, and the first to attend college. His father was a blue collar worker who often worked two jobs to make ends meet.

Ventres grew up in Worcester, Massachusetts, and worked his way through Worcester Polytechnic Institute, earning a bachelor's degree in chemical engineering in 1948. He served in the Navy in World War II.

After graduation, he became an oil-industry engineer for Atlantic Refining (now ARCO), then spent two years in the Middle East training Iraqis to operate oil refineries. He joined Borden in 1957 as assistant chief engineer at the company's PVC operation in Leominster, Massachusetts.

He rose steadily through management ranks, becoming a vice president of the Borden chemical division in 1968, and group vice president four years later. He became president of the chemical division and an executive vice president in 1983.

In 1985, Ventres was elected Borden's president and chief operating officer, and a director of the company. He became chief executive officer in 1986, and chairman in 1987.

Ventres led a transformation of the 134-year-old company, moving Borden out of commodity chemicals and focusing it on six business areas, and used selective acquisitions to grow these businesses rapidly.

Ventres is a director of Banc One Corporation, Marsh & McLennan Companies, Inc., and Schering-Plough Corporation, and a trustee of St. Clare's Hospital and Health Center, New York.

Success Is Open to Anyone

The most important life lesson I can share with others is this: *Success is open to anyone—if you really want it, you can have it.*

Success and achievement are two different things.

Achievement depends on more than your own individual talents and preparedness. It also depends heavily on timing and opportunity.

For opportunity we have to rely on *others* to give us a chance to work on ever-bigger canvases in our chosen fields.

Throughout my life, the Lord has taken care of the timing—and other people have been generous in giving me the opportunities.

Success on the other hand is entirely under your own control.

Successful people have a purpose in life and hunger to live a meaningful life.

Successful people are able to distinguish the difference between what they have and what they are.

I've met successful people at every level of achievement, from the humblest occupations to positions of power and importance.

Their success was the product of how they lived: doing the very best with what life presented them, working hard, always learning, never losing faith or integrity.

Each successful person glowed with the courage, confidence and inner peace that follow when you do your best with what you're given.

A wise man said: "Some men and women make the world better *just by being the kind of people they are.*"

To me, *that's* success—the *only* success that really counts. It is open to every one of us.

E. DEAN WERRIES
Chairman & CEO
Fleming Companies, Inc.

Dean Werries' work in the grocery business began in an uncle's retail store at a very early age. After completion of college and service in the U.S. Army in Korea, he pursued a career at Fleming Companies, Inc. in wholesale food distribution. His retail experience proved to be helpful as he advanced through various responsibilities at Fleming. In the first ten years, he served in numerous functions including advertising, procurement, merchandising and sales. He became division manager in Topeka, Kansas, in 1957, and a short time later moved to the same position in the company's facility in Houston, Texas.

In 1972, he returned to Topeka as vice president/division operations. Later, he directed the company's Eastern Region based at Fleming's location in Philadelphia, before moving to the Oklahoma City corporate office and assuming responsibility for all wholesale food operations. He was elected executive vice president and director in 1979, became president and chief executive officer in 1988, and was elected chairman of the board in 1989.

Mr. Werries is immediate past chairman and a member of the board of directors of the Food Marketing Institute, the largest trade association representing supermarket retailers throughout the world. He is a director of the Independent Grocers Alliance (IGA), National-American Wholesale Grocers Association, and Sonic Industries, Inc. He also serves as a director of the Oklahoma State Chamber of Commerce. He is a member of the board of advisors for the University of Oklahoma's College of Business Administration and a member of the board of governors of the Oklahoma Christian University of Science and Arts.

A graduate of the Business School of the University of Kansas, he has also completed the Program for Management Development at the Harvard Graduate School of Business.

The Power of One, Multiplied

During my many years in the food industry, I have learned a great deal about the world, other people and, especially, about myself. I was first introduced to this great industry at age 11, sweeping floors and stocking shelves in my uncle's IGA store in Kansas.

Years have passed since those days of serving customers in a small community. Today, I am privileged to be chairman of the board and CEO of the Fleming Companies, the country's largest wholesale food distributor, and we continue to serve many outstanding IGA retailers, just as Fleming supplied my uncle's store years ago.

Along the way, I've learned many important lessons. For example, if you never challenge yourself, you'll never achieve important goals. As strong as you are as one person, interacting with others has a multiplying effect. While individual effort is required for success, *one* can only go so far, and often you need more than your individual strengths to achieve your goals. For me, this has been one of life's most constant lessons.

Great leaders recognize that their success depends, in large part, on their ability to multiply their strength by the strength of those around them. Be the best person you can, but, never at the expense of others. Always remember the value of helping others achieve their goals and that others have helped you reach yours.

The only real limit to the power of *one* is by how many others it is multiplied.

Dean Werries

TED C. WETTERAU
Chairman & CEO
Wetterau Incorporated

Ted Wetterau can best be characterized as a dual leader—a civic leader in his hometown of St. Louis, Missouri, and an industry leader in the nation's food industry. He is noted for his many contributions to both his community and to his profession, and has been honored as an outstanding example of the modern, civic-minded business executive.

Ted is past chairman of the board of the National-American Wholesale Grocers' Association (NAWGA). During his tenure, he was instrumental in planning and implementing the reorganization and move into a NAWGA-owned national headquarters in Washington, D.C. In 1990, he received the highest award in the wholesale food industry, the Herbert Hoover Award. In addition, he is a director of the Food Marketing Institute, the country's largest retail association, an ex-officio trustee of the Food Industry Crusade Against Hunger, and served as honorary chairman of its 1988 fall campaign.

He is an acknowledged and respected leader in the nation's food industry. He demonstrated his innovation and creativity more than 20 years ago when he received international acclaim for his concepts for the design of a series of modularized supermarkets. During his 40-year career with Wetterau Incorporated, Ted has led the company to unparalleled growth— from $200 million at that time to nearly $6 billion in sales today.

In addition to his business leadership, Wetterau has devoted a great deal of his time to various community and charitable organizations. He is a director of the United Way of Greater St. Louis and recently served as the general chairman of the 1991 campaign, which successfully raised $50 million; a former director of the Salvation Army and past chairman of its "Tree of Lights" fund-raising drive; a former director of Operation Food Search, Inc., the largest distributor of food for the needy in the Midwest.

(Continued on page 259)

Determination Pays Off

When I was a young man I was blessed to grow up in a close-knit, loving and successful family. The family had been in the wholesale grocery business for nearly 80 years at that time. The company was founded by my grandfather and a partner back in 1869. In addition to my parents, I had uncles, aunts, and some cousins, who were involved in the business in one way or another.

The company's original location was in St. Louis, on a spot which is now very close to the south leg of the famous Gateway Arch. This location, on the west bank of the Mississippi, was very important because most of the supplies that it distributed came in by steamboat. In those days, the company sold provisions to pioneers and miners heading west. In that way it made a contribution to building our country. A very proud family heritage and tradition ran deep in the management.

This heritage was so deeply endowed that when I became a young man with new and radical ideas about the future of the company, my suggestions were ignored. And, even though I lobbied for my concepts, a deaf ear was turned my way and I was reminded of my lack of experience.

I had been trying to explain that independent grocery retailers needed more than just grocery distribution. I felt they needed the kind of support that chain stores were getting from their headquarters, such as accounting, design and construction, printing, and other fundamental business services. Management disagreed, and I eventually became so frustrated that I left the company.

I then opened my own IGA supermarket, a 15,000 square-foot store, which was one of the largest grocery stores in the St. Louis area at the time. Using my marketing ideas, the store became a great success. While gaining first-hand experience, I kept pressing my family to try my ideas in other IGA stores. Eventually, my family welcomed me back into the business and gave me the green light to implement my proven methods. That was the beginning of internal developments and acquisitions that continue today as the hallmark of Wetterau Incorporated.

At the time I rejoined the company, it was the 15th largest food wholesaler in St. Louis. Now, Wetterau is the fourth largest food distributor in the United States.

My experience has proven that sometimes you should not take no for an answer, when you believe in your ideas. Determination and persistence does pay off.

Ted C. Wetterau

ROGER WILLIAMS
Entertainer

A child prodigy from Des Moines, Iowa, Roger Williams played 13 different instruments by the time he was eight years old. He was his church's organist at age 12.

His schooling was interrupted when he left Drake University to join the U.S. Navy. Despite his accomplishments in the field of music, to this day Williams claims his proudest achievement was being voted "Man of Warsmen" by the men of his entire company at the end of military training. His hitch included being a boxing champ, imperiling the hands which have since made him a piano virtuoso and an electrifying performer. Billboard calls him the largest selling pop pianist in history.

At his home in Encino, California, in addition to 18 gold albums and presidential mementos, the walls are lined with keys to cities, citations for humanitarian acts, honorary doctorates, and memories of a career that began when he was three years old. At that age, he literally walked up to the piano and started to play!

Called the "pianist of the presidents," Williams has played for Truman, Eisenhower, Kennedy, Johnson, Nixon, Ford, and Reagan. Shortly after Kennedy's death, they found Roger's recording of "Yellow Bird" on the turntable of JFK's portable record player. It was the last music the president ever heard.

Today, still touring the globe nine months a year, he may be on his way to Japan, to a concert date in Hollywood, a symphony performance in New York, or headlining in Las Vegas. Annually he kicks off the summer season at Disney World's EPCOT Center as pianist-conductor of the All-American College Orchestra, a Disney talent search for the brightest young musicians in America.

His hobby is mountain climbing! Just show him a high hill or rugged terrain and he's off to see if he can get up—or down, as the case may be. His wife, Louise, is his inspiration and, coupled with his music, his fountain of youth, which he says "may keep me young forever."

How to Be a Winner

Winners do things that losers don't like to do. Read that sentence again because it is sage advice.

Like most young people, I found things that I did not like to do—and still don't particularly enjoy doing to this day—but I do them. The five things I've made myself do have each contributed to my success.

First, I hated to practice. Practicing exercises on the piano for hours is a tedious, tiresome task. But it pays off. Whenever I get a standing ovation I remember those practice sessions. By the way, I still practice up to eight hours a day. Practice may not make perfect, but it comes as close as we'll ever get.

To be mentally alert you must be physically fit. Exercise is essential to maintaining good health. I still jog three miles a day, five days a week. I hate every step of it—except the last one! I've travelled as much as 30,000 miles in one month, and been on stage 24 out of 30 days. That's when my exercise regimen proves its worth.

Vegetables have always been distasteful to me. But, I realize that a balanced diet, including vegetables, is necessary for me with my grueling schedule. So, each morning I toss a mixture of produce into my blender, hold my nose, and down my vegetable cocktail—then I don't worry about salads for the rest of the day.

Worrying and agonizing over decisions is something most people don't like to do. It's tough to sit and hope you get an idea. I remember my first recording. I was asked to come up with a special arrangement and given just three days to do it. I sat up two nights searching for the right sound. I was ready on the third day and recorded Autumn Leaves, my first recording which became a big hit. When you've got something important to consider, give yourself some quiet time. It will prove worthwhile.

Cooperation was not always one of my strong suits. In fact, there was a time when I was a loner. I liked to conceive an idea, then carry it out from start to finish, taking all the credit or blame as the case might be. I've since learned the importance of listening to and working with others. I have the privilege of conducting some of the major symphonies from time to time. Symphony means sounding together. It epitomizes what team-work is all about—together we can make beautiful music.

You'll find that life's not always fair, but, if you will do the things that loser's don't like to do—you'll be a winner, too!

BOB WOOLF
President
Bob Woolf Associates

Ever since former Red Sox pitcher Earl Wilson chose Bob Woolf to represent him in 1964, more than 500 other athletes have followed suit, thus establishing Woolf as both the first and the top sports attorney in the country.

He has been nationally and internationally recognized for negotiating over 2,000 contracts in the fields of sports and entertainment in a manner respected by players, owners, and fans. Author of two widely acclaimed books about his experiences, Behind Closed Doors *and* Friendly Persuasion. *Woolf has been lauded by the media for his expertise and philosophy of fair play, as well as his reputation for honesty and integrity.*

Carl Yastrzemski, Joe Montana, Doug Flutie, Larry Bird, Al and Florence Joyner are just a few of the sports figures he has represented, while entertainment clients have included Larry King, Gene Shalit, and New Kids on the Block.

A native of Maine, Woolf attended Boston College on an athletic scholarship prior to receiving his LL.B degree from the Boston University School of Law, where he was president of the senior class. He established a successful criminal law practice in Boston prior to pioneering the field of sports law that is now being taught at law schools throughout the United States.

Woolf has been selected as one of the 100 Most Powerful People in Sports. Massachusetts Governor Michael A. Dukakis proclaimed December 28, 1990, Bob Woolf Day in State House ceremonies.

Widely recognized in his field, Woolf has appeared frequently on the Today Show, Johnny Carson's Tonight Show, Good Morning America, Lifestyles of the Rich and Famous, CBS' Sports Illustrated, and has been interviewed in a wide variety of newspapers and periodicals, including Time, People, and Fortune.

World's Most Important Rule

You can do it, and do it well, whatever you set out to do. by trying harder and by following a simple philosophy of friendly persuasion.

One of the oldest and most revered guidelines to treating people fairly is the Golden Rule. Philosophers of all persuasions have preached it over the millennium. Zoroaster taught it to his followers in Persia 2,500 years ago. Confuscius preached it in China 24 centuries ago. Lao-Tzu, the founder of Taoism, taught it to his disciples in the Valley of the Han. Buddha preached on the banks of the Holy Ganges 500 years before Christ. Jesus taught it in Judea 19 centuries ago. He summed it up in one thought—probably the most important rule in the world—"Do unto others as you would have others do unto you."

In reviewing my experiences over the years, I've followed a three-part philosophy for dealing with people from all walks of life. It's been a constant through every one of my negotiations, professionally and personally:

Number one: You don't have to be disagreeable to disagree.

Number two: The Golden Rule, which is timeless.

Number three: Be true to your convictions.

Stick to what you believe in: your convictions, values and standards. For your own self-esteem and for the respect you hope to earn from others, you can't change your beliefs to fit each new situation and fashion.

Following this philosophy makes things easier and produces successful results. Taken together, the philosophy adds up to a method of treating people with fairness and respect.

You CAN do unto others as you would have others do unto you.

Bob Woolf

MICHAEL W. WRIGHT
Chairman/CEO/President
Super Valu Stores, Inc.

Mike Wright practiced law for 13 years with the firm of Dorsey and Whitney, Minneapolis, before joining Super Valu as a senior vice president in 1977. He was elected president and chief operating officer of Super Valu in 1978 and became chief executive officer in June, 1981. He assumed the additional responsibilities of chairman of the board in October, 1982.

A native Minnesotan, Mike graduated from the University of Minnesota College of Liberal Arts, and graduated with honors from the University of Minnesota Law School in 1963. While attending the University of Minnesota, Mike was captain of the varsity football team. Later he played professionally at Winnipeg, Canada, under former Minnesota Viking coach, Bud Grant.

In addition to his position on the board of directors of Super Valu, he serves on the board of Norwest Corporation, Honeywell, Inc., ShopKo Stores, Inc., and Musicland Stores Corporation. He is also immediate past chairman of the Federal Reserve Bank of Minneapolis and the Minnesota Business Partnership. He is vice chairman of the Food Marketing Institute (FMI) and a member of the board of directors of the International Association of Chain Stores (CIES) and the National American Wholesale Grocers Association (NAWGA).

Parental Examples

I've been trying to think of advice to give to young people. I guess I came to the conclusion that maybe the best thing I could do was to outline what I feel was the reason I was able to achieve some success in my lifetime.

It was not something that I did, it was what my parents did. They really programmed me to be successful, and if I wasn't, it was my fault. Let me explain.

My parents had very basic values that they set for their children. First, education. Neither of my parents went beyond high school, in fact, my father left school to work after the eighth grade to help support his family. But they wanted each of their children to get as much schooling as possible. Because of their urging and desire for education I went on to obtain a law degree. It is interesting to me to remember that at my graduation from law school my father urged me to continue in school and get a graduate degree in business, which I gracefully declined because of lack of funds.

Second, integrity. There was never any doubt in my mind that my parents were absolutely, totally forthright and honest in their dealings. They didn't have to talk about it. They just merely set that example in everything they did. It is clear to me now that everyone learns more from example than from lectures.

Third, fairness. They were always fair in what they did with other people and made sure that people—regardless of who they were—were treated with dignity.

Fourth, always work to the fullest extent of your abilities. So often times the urgings were "nice going, but I know you can do better" and, you know, I could—because they *believed* I could.

Fifth, attitude. How you approach your job, how you approach your life, is critically important to your success. A negative attitude usually results in failure, a positive attitude usually results in success. They clearly demonstrated that positive attitude all the time. It is really quite remarkable what the power of positive thinking can do.

Sixth, don't be afraid to assume responsibility. My parents, again primarily through their example, showed me that leaders believe in themselves and leaders assume responsibility, and once the responsibility is assumed, they do their very best to accomplish the mission.

I think at the time they were "molding" me I didn't know what was happening, probably because so much of it seemed so simple and right. Luckily for me their teaching got through my thick skull and it became a natural way to respond to different situations. It was because of *their example and their teachings* that I've been asked to contribute to this

(Continued on page 267)

KAY YOW
Women's Basketball Coach
North Carolina State University

Kay Yow is a winner on and off the basketball court. She rates as one of the all-time great women coaches with an overall record (high school and college) of 532 wins, 182 losses (.754 winning percentage).

In 17 years at North Carolina State, she has posted a 386-136 record, including four Atlantic Coast Conference Championships. Her teams have won five ACC regular season championships. Equally impressive, she has achieved a graduation rate of over 97 percent among four year players.

Her athletic achievements are what legends are made of and the honors she has received too numerous to list. Highlights include leading the USA women to the gold medal in the 1988 Olympics. She was head coach of the USA National Squad which won gold medals at the 1986 FIBA World Championships and Goodwill Games, beating the Soviet Union in the finals of both events in Moscow, marking the first time in 29 years that an American women's team had beaten the Russians in major tournament competition.

Kay is a member of the Women's Sport Hall of Fame and the fifth woman ever inducted into the North Carolina Sport Hall of Fame. In 1990, she was named Converse/WBCA Coach of the Year and District III Coach of the Year. The Fellowship of Christian Athletes named her Coach of the Year in 1989.

Off the court, she is involved in numerous associations. She's been a tireless cancer crusader since undergoing a mastectomy and is the recipient of the Outstanding Volunteer Award from the Lineburger Cancer Research Center.

She hold a bachelor's degree in English from East Carolina University, and a master's degree in physical education from the University of North Carolina at Greensboro.

Attitude Quotient

"We can't change the direction of the wind, but we can adjust our sails." Attitude is the key to success. Though there are many things in life which we have little or no control over, we have 100 percent control over the way we will decide to respond to our situations or circumstances. One hundred percent control—it is our choice! Thus, in essence we *choose* to succeed or fail.

To enjoy success we *must* have the ability to overcome obstacles and adversity. It is our choice to be negative or to be positive! We choose whether to make the circumstance one in which we learn or one in which we complain. We become a better person or a bitter person depending on the way we choose to respond to our situation. "When life kicks you, let it kick you forward!"

We are always faced with circumstance control versus attitude control. Do our circumstances control our attitude or does our attitude control our circumstances. Herein lies the difference between winners and losers— between ChAmps and chumps. The A (Attitude) is the key!

Be a winner. Winning is choosing to have a positive attitude no matter what the circumstance. A positive response will transform each setback into a step forward. Winning as a person is most important! Choose the response that will help you to find the winning way in any circumstance. When you are a winner as a person, you will have your best shot at being a winner in sport or any other area. A positive attitude enables you to give your best and be determined in your effort.

I have always believed that AQ (attitude quotient) is much more important than IQ (intelligence quotient). Always remember that attitude will determine your altitude!

Kay Yow

E.R. ZUMWALT, Jr.
Admiral, U.S. Navy (Ret.)

Admiral Elmo Russell Zumwalt, Jr., was Chief of Naval Operations and a member of the Joint Chiefs of Staff from 1970 to 1974. He is currently president of Admiral Zumwalt and Consultants, Inc., a consulting firm in the fields of management, energy, health care, overseas business operations, foreign and defense policy, and strategic planning.

A cum laude graduate of the United States Naval Academy, at age 44 he became the youngest officer ever promoted to rear admiral. At 49, he became the youngest four-star admiral in U.S. history. He was promoted over 35 senior admirals to become the youngest man ever to serve as Chief of Naval Operations.

Admiral Zumwalt initiated wide-ranging reforms and is credited with revitalizing the Navy and making service careers much more attractive. As the Navy's senior officer, he increased the fighting capabilities of the dwindling United States fleet by outfitting remaining ships with more sophisticated and efficient weapons.

Admiral Zumwalt was commander of the United States Naval Forces in Vietnam from 1968 to 1970.

Currently he is co-author of "Zumwalt's Report," a weekly column on vital current issues published in newspapers around the country. He has also authored two books. On Watch *recounts his naval career and warns Americans about the Soviet naval threat.* My Father, My Son, *which he wrote with his late son, Elmo Russell Zumwalt III, is an account of their Vietnam experiences.*

Admiral Zumwalt has received honorary degrees from Villanova University, the University of North Carolina, United States International University, National University, Central Michigan University, and Michigan Technological University. He has been a visiting professor and guest lecturer at Stanford University, the University of Pennsylvania, Vanderbilt University, the University of Nebraska, and Whittier College.

Keep Trying

As the grandfather of a 14-year-old boy who has participated in the Special Olympics, I am writing to commend all of you who participate in this great event—as well as those who support it.

The essence of what I have learned in 70 years of life and adventure is that perseverance and drive are far more important than one's physical or mental capabilities when it comes to both happiness and success in life.

To me, the most important model with which to guide one's life is "if at first you don't succeed, try, try, again."

He serves as a director on numerous corporate boards, as well as charitable organizations and not-for-profit foundations.

Admiral Zumwalt is married to the former Mouza Coutelais-du-Roche of Harbin, Manchuria, and has one son and two daughters.

Henry (Hank) Ketcham (from p. 128)

in Monterey, California, brings enjoyment to children in the area all year round and has served as a model for similar parks across the country.

With a constant flow of new projects and the demands of a daily newspaper panel, Ketcham arrives at his Pebble Beach, California studio every morning at 8:30. He puts in eight-hour days on the panel, working at least 10 weeks in advance of the publication schedule. Today he is aided by a secretary and two artists who work on the panel.

Ketcham's autobiography, The Merchant of Dennis *(1990) provided a look back over the invention of his slingshot-toting tyke.* Dennis the Menace: His First 40 Years *is a paperback compilation of cartoon strips tracing the evolution of the five-year old mighty mite.*

Joe Paterno (from p. 186)

Fifty of his players earned first team All-American rankings and he has sent more than 100 players to the National Football League. Two of his products, linebacker Jack Ham and fullback Franco Harris, have been elected to the Pro Football Hall of Fame.

Born in Brooklyn, N.Y. on Dec. 21, 1926, Paterno attended Brooklyn Prep and Brown University. The late sportswriter Stanley Woodward, described him as an athlete who "can't run and can't pass. All he can do is think and win." He's still doing it today.

John W. Rollins, Sr. (from p. 202)

the Year Award from the American Management Association. Goldey Beacom College presented him an honorary doctorate degree in business administration; he received an associate in humanities degree from Reinhardt College, and a doctor of law degree from Cumberland College.

The Montego Bay Chamber of Commerce recognized his 25 years as investor/developer and major contributor to advancement of tourism in Montego Bay. In addition to his scholarship programs, Rollins' philanthropic efforts include sponsorship of the Rollins Wing at Beebe Hospital, Lewes, Delaware.

Ted C. Wetterau (from p. 246)

In 1986, he successfully chaired Goodwill Industries' $3.5 million "Growing With Concern" capital fund-raising campaign.

Ted Wetterau is an ardent supporter of the community's cultural and artistic activities. He serves as a director of the St. Louis Symphony Society, the St. Louis Zoo Commission, the Metropolitan Zoological Park and Museum district, and the Municipal Theatre Association. He is a former member of the President's Council of the St. Louis Conservatory and Schools for the Arts.

You Must Have Goals: Marva Collins (from p. 55)

have the unique ability to make my students whatever I would like them to be. I believe that when my students fail, that I, too, have failed. I, in other words, am selfish in my teaching.

I consistently create the kind of student that I would like to have as my surgeon in a life-threatening situation, the kind of attorney that I would like to have if my life depended upon it, the kind of neighbor that I would like to have if my very safety depended on it, and the kind of citizen I would like to have if my freedom depended upon it. With this kind of attitude, there is no room for failure, and there is no room for mediocrity and excuses.

We tell our students that not to reach your goal is no sin, but to have no goal to reach is a sin. We tell our students when they give us a mediocre paper that if they could not give that paper to God, or, drop the paper anywhere in the world and be proud to say that it is their paper, that we, too, will not accept mediocre work.

Marva N. Collins

Use Your Ability to Reason: Michael W. Copps (from p. 63)

combined with poor performance the complaint will never be listened to. Poor performance will over-shadow everything. He/she will not be promoted because of the fear that the poor performance will be repeated.

Do yourself a favor, perform well.

Michael W. Copps

Have a Role Model: William E. C. Dearden (from p. 69)

girls, ages 4 through 18, and has over 6,500 graduates. It is still privately funded through the original trust.

What's the point of the story?

1. If Milton Hershey would have listened to his detractors in 1886 and abandoned his dream there would not be a story of success to relate.

2. He had the courage of his convictions, and believed in himself when everyone else gave up on him.

3. Early on in his business success he decided to share his wealth so that others could get a better start in life than he had.

4. Only in America under our competitive free enterprise system can success stories like this happen then and now.

Have a plan for your life—a dream—which you will not compromise, even when the going gets tough. Then, work hard to make it happen! It works!

Principles for Productive Living: Arthur DeKruyter (from p. 73)

is in keeping with your best instincts. If you succeed, you will be contributing something to make this world a better place in which to live.

Finally, I want to share a very rudimentary bit of philosophy. When I was young, I learned from my older brother one very simple bit of wisdom. He would often say to me, "If something is not going to matter two months from now, it isn't worth worrying about." I thought about that often. It helped me set priorities in my life. I learned to make moral judgements and to form work habits. I learned to discipline myself.

Ask yourself the question, "Will it matter two months from now?" If not, dismiss it. It is not worth your time, and it certainly should not soak up your energies for thought and for worry.

These five things I offer to you as simple principles for productive living. They will help you in life and give you a hold on some of the essentials which will make you a productive and happy person.

Something Greater than Self: Fred Grandy (from p. 93)

year-old youth who thanked me for coming. He explained his father was fearful of losing his farm and if that happened his own ambition to someday be a farmer wouldn't happen. "It means something to us that you gave up what you were doing to come and get involved in our problem," he said, "I just wanted to say thanks."

That young man, whoever he was, taught me a lesson that night and I resolved to stay in the race regardless of what seemed like impossible odds.

My epiphany, my discovery, was that I knew I had to serve something greater than myself. Each of us, at some point in our lives, will have a similar epiphany—somehow, some way, you will be called to serve something greater than yourself. It may be your church, your community, or your country. But when you decide that you want to measure your life, not by what you've gotten but by what you can give, I hope you will work to leave this world a better place than you found it.

Lovers and Leaders: John Haggai (from p. 101)

And yet who, more than He, has achieved goals of beneficial permanence and fulfilled humanity's real needs? No one. And two thousand years after His death and resurrection, He has a far larger following than any mere political leader. So when He says, "Greater love has no one than this, to lay down his life for his friends," I, for one, take Him seriously.

Never Stop Learning: T. Marshall Hahn, Jr. (from p. 103)

leaders are the ones who never stop learning. The people who succeed will be the ones who keep challenging themselves, exploring the world and their role in it. Education is a life-long process.

You can do it. Learn to question conventional wisdom, trust your own intellect, and recognize and appreciate the abilities of others.

Helping Others: Patricia Harrison (from p. 109)

another were exchanging addresses, demonstrating products, talking and creating support groups to foster new businesses.

One woman, who traveled to Budapest from the country, raised her hand at the end of the conference, came up to the microphone and said, "I want to thank all of you for coming here and encouraging us. Please forgive us if we have not been able to match your smiling faces. For a long time we have had nothing to smile about. I think now, we can begin to hope and take a chance on smiling."

The best feeling second to discovering you can do it, is helping others to understand they have the same power you do and they can do it too!

Patricia Harrison

Let the World Come to Your Life: W. Daniel A. Lamey (from p. 139)

another person's point of view, can prove invaluable in daily life. The same is true in learning and appreciating the customs and traditions of people from other countries, with whom you may one day do business or with whom you may simply "do lunch".

It is a surprise for some to learn that many Japanese young people feel that they are not that "international" in their outlook and knowledge. They don't mean "international" in terms of naming world capitals or calculating the time half way around the world; what they mean is understanding what makes an American, Canadian, or French business person tick or react in a particular way. How do they approach a problem? How would they go about finding a solution?

To you, the world may be important only as a headline that flashes by on CNN or as a vacation destination featured in a travel brochure; but it is much more important than that. You may think that travel by itself will make you knowledgeable of the world. Without the right attitude, however, you might just as well stay home; with it, you may not even need to leave home.

What I urge you to find is the state of mind in which you will be open to the world outside; that you anticipate how it will affect your life; that you learn from the people from other countries whom you may meet from day to day; and that you will be ready to act on the opportunities which come to you as the world comes to your life.

W. Daniel A. Lamey

Ten Commandments for Failure: Bonnie McElveen-Hunter
(from p. 119)

once asked about the secret of his success. The secret, he said, was a fast outfield. Give others credit, no one succeeds alone. I've had a superbly fast outfield!

Commandment 7: Thou Shalt Not Be Accountable. Accountability often stands between success and failure. The ability to stand up when you are wrong, admit it, and accept responsibility marks you a winner, and distinguishes you from the people who fail.

Commandment 8: Thou Shalt Have No Sense of Humor. Many business situations in which I have been involved have been successfully resolved by the inclusion of some levity. We need more laughter in our lives. Learn to laugh, especially at yourself!

Commandment 9: Thou Shalt Give Nothing Back. Companies and individuals who focus on nothing but material and bottom-line success reap only those rewards and miss the reality that ultimately in life all we keep is what we give away.

Commandment 10: Thou Shalt Believe that Failure Is Final. Failure is never final. Failure is an opportunity for success in disguise. How we respond to failure determines what is final.

Daily we have opportunities through our choices to succeed or fail. What commandments will govern your life? What standards will you adhere to? What principles will you embrace? What values will you instill?

Ernest Fitzgerald, a Methodist bishop, asked these questions in an article written for Pace Magazine several years ago, in which he reminded us that we will all stand in a higher court than one where we are judged by our fellow man. It's a splendid thing to hear the shouts of acclamation coming from the grandstand, but it's even greater to feel the applause from within. The person who feels this inner applause, even if he has failed, provided he has given his all and played his very best, is a winner. Winners are not necessarily those at the top, but those who have come the farthest over the roughest road. Your personal victory may never make headlines, but you know it and that's what counts. This book is dedicated to the Special Olympics and, more important, the Special Olympians—they are the *real* winners.

Bonnie McElveen-Hunter

I Dare You: Robert S. MacArthur (from p. 153)

accomplishments, each of us can do better to achieve our best. And each of us can do more to make a positive difference in the lives of others.

I dare you, reader, to seek the best that is in you and never be satisfied with less than your best. I dare you, reader, to burn with a vision for a better world, and to become a spark for others. I dare you to become "my own self, at my very best, all the time." You Can Do It!

Help Someone Else: Murray Raphel (from p. 195)

rolled down. Tom looked at me and said, "I just thought how you can pay me back."

"How?" I asked. "Anything. Name it."

He looked at me and said, "Help someone else..." and he drove away.

In the years that followed, the loan was paid off and my speaking and consulting business grew. There is no doubt in my mind, success came my way because of "the door that was opened" at the airport. From that day forward I have opened doors for others. When they say "thanks", I simply remind them they now have an obligation to "help someone else."

Read the Guideposts!: Charles B. Runnels (from p. 209)

Working night and day, he finally saved enough to start the first gift fruit shipping company on the West Coast. He later sold his famous Mission Pak Company and went on to invest in other opportunities. Today his name appears on buildings at Children's Hospital, the George Page Museum, Pepperdine University, and other important facilities. He has invested his life in others and has been an inspiring mentor to me. He advises youth, "You'll be the same person five years from now as you are today, except for the people that you meet and the books that you read."

So read the guideposts along the way. You are but one person, but you can make a difference. You Can Do It!

Repay What You've Been Given: William Sessions (from p. 215)

You'll recall that Winston Churchill was a man whose hour came during the great Battle of Britain. He was a man who knew more about defeat than victory; who had been out more than he had been in; who had been down more than he'd been up; who had been accepted only on an occasional basis; who was picked for his character to lead that great nation from the depths of despair to victory.

The following quote from Churchill exemplifies part of what I believe about character traits that you must have and you must continue to stress: "Never give in; never give in; never, never, never—in nothing great or small, large or petty—never give in except to convictions of honor and good sense." These are things of which great Americans are made.

So, conscience, determination and a strong sense of responsibility are things I think should guide your life. I have tried to let them guide mine. You will be called upon to undertake unusual endeavors. You will be called upon to do things that you do not want to do, but feel compelled to do. Yield to those compulsions. Decide where you will walk and decide that you will do so with honor and that your conscience will always be your guide.

William F. Sessions

Be a Great Boy!: John Silber (from p. 217)

talent to be a professional musician, I learned the hard lesson of when to let go of one dream and search for another.

The search for true fulfillment is tiring and difficult, and it is rarely down the road that leads to pleasure. But the search does follow the road that leads to happiness. If you listen to those whom you most admire and love, and try always to hear the voice of your best self, your contributions to the world will give meaning to the lives of others and thereby to your own.

John Silber

Feel the Passion: Michael Leo Stefanos (from p. 227)

was. It was on this passion that the company grew from a single store to an international corporation.

Remember, it is said that they beat a path to the man's door because he built a better mousetrap; what is not said is that he built the trap acting on a passion to rid his house of mice.

Feel the passion and act on it. Live by respect with instinct from your heart and success will find you!

Michael Leo Stefanos

Hang in There: Rick Telander (from p. 231)

hurt—quitting. Still, quitting under the right condition can be the smartest thing a person can do.

But hanging in there might really be the key. Through thick and thin. And when your time does come, grab everything you can. I don't mean money and power. I mean happiness. Happiness is the only success there is.

Rick Telander

I Have Made It!: William G. Thebus (from p. 233)

and he took advantage of an opportunity that, with his own hard work and conviction, got him to his goal.

John's last contact with Davis was through an audio tape, sent by Davis as a Christmas greeting. John played the tape for me several times. On the tape, Davis told about his success. He was able to read, was employed, and looked forward to a better future. He prefaced his story with a personal greeting, one that embodies all the pride and glorious sense of achievement that bubbles over in those who have conquered hopelessness: "Merry Christmas, Mr. Hurst. This is Cleveland Davis, and *I have made it!*"

Wm. G. Thebus

Parental Examples: Michael W. Wright (from p. 253)

book. I consider myself very, very lucky to have had such great parents. I just followed their lead and it was really quite easy.

I think there's nothing stated above that any person with the will and the desire would have a hard time accomplishing.

Mike Wright

ABOUT THE AUTHOR

Bob Budler is an author, former reporter, editor and nationally syndicated newspaper columnist. For more than 35 years, he headed corporate communications for some of the nation's leading companies.

His first book, *Patient: Heal Thyself!,* written while he was recovering from heart surgery, has helped thousands of patients and their families deal with the same traumatic experience.

Now retired, he's a "grandpa-preneur" pursuing a free-lance writing career embodying his "You Can Do It!" philosophy. Again using personal experiences, he is now researching a book to aid families of Alzheimer's victims. He will include methods he's found useful in helping his wife, Rita, cope with the illness.

HOW TO ORDER

Individual books @ $20.00 each; bulk orders (25 or more books) @ $15.00 each.

Postal orders:	You Can Do It! P.O. Box 257 Bensenville, IL 60106-0257
Sales tax:	Please add 7% for books shipped to addresses in Illinois.
Shipping:	Book rate: $1.75 (surface shipping may take three weeks). First class: $3.00
Inquiries:	(708) 766-8144

NOTE: All purchases must be prepaid. Please include your check with your order, and consider your canceled check your receipt.

DON'T DELAY — ORDER TODAY

(See page 271)

JOIN NATIONWIDE CAMPAIGN

We are conducting a nationwide campaign to place *You Can Do It!* in schools and libraries throughout the country.

We invite individuals, corporations, and other organizations to join us in this educational effort. To participate, simply send in your check (see order form on page 269) and inform us where you want the book(s) sent in your name.

As a special service, we'll complete the presentation form in the front of the book. Then we'll send the books to your designated recipients. We will, of course, send the books directly to you for personal presentation, if you so desire.

We look forward to hearing from you. Thanks for your consideration.